This Is a Book About Healing

. . . And with a fresh, innovative approach to monogamy: that it's possible, desirable, and fulfilling. Drs. Barbach and Geisinger show how, with a willingness to change the rigid and defensive behaviors that often defeat our attempts at happiness, we can find suitable partners and build loving, erotic, and stable relationships. From early "commitment phobias" and vulnerabilities to later "relationship fatigue," these experienced therapists provide guidelines for coping, healing, and moving on—together.

LONNIE BARBACH, Ph.D., and DAVID L. GEISINGER, Ph.D., are both on the clinical faculty in the Department of Psychiatry at the University of California Medical School in San Francisco. They are practicing psychotherapists, treating individuals and couples. Dr. Barbach is author of the acclaimed bestsellers *For Yourself* and *For Each Other*, and Dr. Geisinger is the author of the notable *Kicking It*. They live in Mill Valley, California, with their six-year-old daughter.

ALSO BY LONNIE BARBACH
For Yourself: The Fulfillment of Female Sexuality
Women Discover Orgasm: A Therapist's Guide to a New
    Treatment Approach
For Each Other: Sharing Sexual Intimacy
Pleasures: Women Write Erotica
Erotic Interludes: Tales Told by Women

BY LONNIE BARBACH AND LINDA LEVINE
Shared Intimacies: Women's Sexual Experiences
The Intimate Male: Candid Discussion About Women, Sex,
    and Relationships

VIDEOTAPES BY LONNIE BARBACH
Falling in Love Again
Sex After 50: A Guide to Lifelong Sexual Pleasure

AUDIO TAPES BY LONNIE BARBACH AND BERNIE ZILBERGELD
An Ounce of Prevention: How to talk to a Partner about
    Smart Sex
American Health: Sex in the 80's

ALSO BY DAVID L. GEISINGER
Kicking It: The New Way to Stop Smoking Permanently

Going the Distance

Lonnie Barbach
AND
David L. Geisinger

GOING THE

A PLUME BOOK

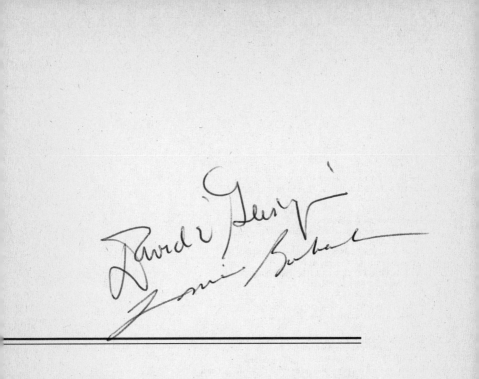

DISTANCE

Finding and Keeping
Lifelong Love

PLUME
Published by the Penguin Group
Penguin Books USA Inc., 375 Hudson Street,
New York, New York 10014, U.S.A.
Penguin Books Ltd, 27 Wrights Lane,
London W8 5TZ, England
Penguin Books Australia Ltd, Ringwood,
Victoria, Australia
Penguin Books Canada Ltd, 10 Alcorn Avenue,
Toronto, Ontario, Canada M4V 3B2
Penguin Books (N.Z.) Ltd, 182–190 Wairau Road,
Auckland 10, New Zealand

Penguin Books Ltd, Registered Offices:
Harmondsworth, Middlesex, England

Published by Plume, an imprint of New American Library,
a division of Penguin Books USA Inc.
Reprinted by arrangement with Doubleday,
a division of Bantam Doubleday Dell Publishing Group, Inc.

First Plume Printing, February, 1993

10 9 8 7 6 5 4 3 2 1

Ⓟ REGISTERED TRADEMARK—MARCA REGISTRADA

LIBRARY OF CONGRESS CATALOGING-IN-PUBLICATION DATA
Barbach, Lonnie Garfield, 1946–
    Going the distance : finding and keeping lifelong love / Lonnie
Barbach and David L. Geisinger.
        p.   cm.
    Includes index.
    ISBN 0-452-26948-2
    1. Marriage—United States.   2. Interpersonal relations.
3. Intimacy (Psychology)   I. Geisinger, David L.   II. Title.
[HQ734.B236   1993]
306.84'22—dc20   92–34806
                                                 CIP

Printed in the United States of America

FOR TESS
Light of Our Lives

This attitude—that nothing is easier than to love—has continued to be the prevalent idea about love in spite of the overwhelming evidence to the contrary. There is hardly any activity, any enterprise, which is started with such tremendous hopes and expectations, and yet, which fails so regularly as love.

—ERICH FROMM,
The Art of Loving

Acknowledgments

The three years it took us to complete this book only confirms the idea that if you just wait long enough, everything changes —yet, despite the changes, one can still find a way to go the distance.

Due to a changing of the guard at Doubleday, we have a number of people to thank: first, Nancy Evans and Loretta Barrett for believing in the value of our idea for the book well before we had written a word of it; next, Susan Moldow for taking over midway and guiding it through the second half; and last, Casey Fuetsch for seeing the process through to its launching.

Rhoda Weyr, our marvelous agent and friend, changed only her address during this time. We are grateful for this, but we are most grateful to her for being such a staunch ally—always there with guidance, support, strength and clarity.

During the course of our writing, the book went through more changes than we care to remember: visions and revisions, and revisions of revisions. Throughout all of this, Daniela Johnston did a great job: typing endless drafts, deciphering handwritten comments with each of our different editing conventions, maintaining order out of what could have easily been chaos, and never once losing her equanimity. We thank her. Carolyn Rice gets our thanks for typing the transcripts of the interviews and filling in when we needed her, often at a moment's notice, so that we could meet our deadlines.

Our sincere gratitude to our friends and colleagues Robert Cantor, Brandy Engel, Lewis Engel, Jeri Marlowe, and Deborah Shames, all of whom gave us valuable feedback on the first draft.

We are grateful for the support of Piedad Zarceno and her assistance in taking care of Tess. Without Pia we might never have had more than ten minutes at a time to work together.

We owe a profound debt to all our clients over the years who helped us to discover and understand the ways that couples can go astray, and who showed us that with hope, commitment, and serious work, they could find their way again.

Finally, we extend our thanks to the many couples in vital and satisfying relationships who so generously let us into their lives, sharing with us the details of their successful journey to intimacy.

Contents

Introduction

To commit or not to commit, that is the question.

Is it lust or is it love? Is this the "right" relationship or simply another tragic mistake? Should we jump in with two feet or retreat early, before suffering the heartache of yet another breakup?

As we stand at this critical juncture in life, poised on the brink of commitment, ready to enter the ring or perhaps sprint quickly in the opposite direction, many of us are filled with fear . . . and generally with good reason. We are about to enter into a relationship fraught with endless unknowns and no guarantees, in an attempt to create a fulfilling lifelong bond —the deepest, most complex relationship of our lives.

How many times have we been burned in previous relationships? How devastated were we by the last one? How long did it take us to get back on our feet again once it was over? The risks of commitment are clearly enormous. Potentially, however, the positive payoff is even greater, and in *Going the Dis-*

tance we make explicit our ideas for creating a healthy, vital relationship from its inception.

As psychologists we have spent a total of more than thirty-five years doing extensive therapy with couples, seeing the results of our work in the repair of seriously disintegrating relationships, assisting in the resolution of conflicts that were eroding intimacy, and in some cases helping couples whose relationship had passed the point of no return or who were mismatched from the beginning, to part amicably. Many of these couples could have been saved much trauma and heartache if only they had had some practical information to guide them in the early stages of their relationship—before they had gotten into trouble, or at least before small problems had developed into serious ones.

This is just the kind of information that we wish we ourselves had had, as over the years we each wandered through a number of relationships in an attempt to find mates of our own, despairing at ever succeeding. Like many people, eventually we tried to convince ourselves that being single, independent, and self-sufficient was probably the best way to go—at least it was the best we could reasonably hope for . . . that is, until we found each other.

Despite the realistic difficulties in finding the right partner and negotiating the complexities of an intimate relationship in these confusing and confused times, we remain convinced that the pursuit of such a relationship is a worthwhile endeavor. And there is reason for optimism, for believing that it is quite possible to be lovingly mated for life, ultimately to reach death having known the kind of deep sharing and closeness that a fulfilling, committed relationship brings. While it may be that only a relatively small percentage of couples have attained the depth of intimacy we are writing about, we firmly believe that it is available to nearly everyone. Furthermore, we're certain that you do not have to squeeze yourself into some preconceived model, losing your own identity in the process, in order to attain this intimacy. In fact, quite the opposite is true: the richest relationships result when two well-articulated individuals unite. And you do not have to be married to attain this degree of intimacy. More and more couples are living together enduringly, and raising children, without the sanction of marriage. The pact between two people who love each other and choose to live life with one another must exist in their hearts and minds. Whether they have a license or not, their relationship will be only as good as they make it.

There is no one "right way" to have a relationship. This has become abundantly clear as we have worked with couples over the years, and in the numerous interviews we conducted with people who have been in flourishing, committed relationships of ten or more years' duration. The lengths of their courtships; their socioeconomic backgrounds; the presence, absence, or number of children; and a myriad of other personality and situational factors differed markedly, but certain other underlying principles appeared to be quite basic to successful relationships in general. It is our thesis that many of these underlying principles which differentiate happy relationships from unhappy ones can be identified and, more important, can be conveyed as skills and attitudes that can be taught.

The earlier in the relationship these skills are learned, the better chance the relationship has not only to survive but to thrive. Unless we were fortunate enough to grow up with the enviable model of two parents who achieved a loving and lively relationship, most of us, in fact, have been left to our own devices, to invent the process of working out a relationship by trial and error as we go along. Sometimes it works, but often it doesn't—or it doesn't work as well as it could. Research has shown that fewer than one-third of those who first married during the 1970s were still happily married by the mid-1980s.[1] In fact, many of the couples we interviewed who considered their relationships to be particularly gratifying had gone through an extremely difficult period during which they con-

1. Norval D. Glenn. "Duration of Marriage, Family Composition, and Marital Happiness." *National Journal of Sociology*, Spring 1989.

sidered splitting up. A few had even separated briefly. While every relationship goes through its ups and its downs, a startling number of marriages end in divorce and far too many others succumb to a form of apathy or dull but tolerable coexistence: a kind of death-in-life.

We are disturbed that mating—this central part of the human experience, which holds such enormous potential for fulfillment and happiness as well as for danger and even tragedy—has virtually been relegated to chance. If and when we do get into trouble, there are few places we can turn to for advice and guidance. Consequently, *Going the Distance* focuses principally on *prevention*. In relationships in particular, the proverbial ounce of prevention is worth one hundred pounds of cure. Therefore, we wanted to explore in detail the necessary skills for analyzing and resolving difficulties right from the beginning, before either member of the couple has emotionally bailed out. For these reasons, we begin with an investigation of the initial phase of the relationship: courtship.

Too often courtship consists of a series of unexamined episodes of excitement and fantasy punctuated by occasions of anger and confusion. But courtship is a critically important and instrumental time, a time during which we can gradually discover the often hidden dimensions of our potential partner as well as the ways in which our interactions might become problematic.

We have explored the difficulties that commonly arise as a result of differences in personality styles, individual areas of sensitivity or vulnerability, and the first open conflicts. We have detailed the kinds of testing that should be a part of courtship and have spelled out better ways to evaluate how well you and your partner are suited to each other, so that you are more likely to choose one another for the "right" reasons, reasons that are associated with healthy, lasting relationships.

Since healthy relationships come in a variety of different forms, we have presented a number of alternatives for handling the potentially problematic situations that can arise during their course. We also thoroughly examine the influence of attitudes and points of view on both the causes of problems and their solutions. In doing this, we have attempted to provide a general, practical, and philosophical approach to potential trouble spots rather than merely describing a series of slick and artificial exercises or other simpleminded answers to what are often knotty problems.

Finally, once the decision to commit has been made, we have provided a road map of dangers that typically arise along the path of most relationships, such as those caused by the stresses of work or finances, the flagging of sexual interest, or the propensity to devalue and neglect the relationship after a number of years, a process that can lead to a dangerously stultifying boredom. When rocky terrain is unavoidable, as with the birth of a child or after both partners have retired, we have presented some practical and effective ways to bridge the transition period.

When intimate relationships go awry, they produce painful wounds which can create long-lasting areas of sensitivity and vulnerability. It then becomes even more difficult to learn how to reverse the negative patterns and defenses that eventually alienate us from each other. Instead, some of us may be inclined to change partners when problems become too severe or too prolonged, and if we enter the next relationship having felt betrayed in the previous one, we are likely to be even less trusting, less able to be vulnerable and open, less likely to grow and develop.

Our view is that a good relationship is a place of *healing*. In such a relationship people can express and reveal themselves without fear so that issues can safely be grappled with and resolved. This, of course, does not mean that all areas of conflict disappear. Times of turbulence occur in the lives of nearly every couple, but in a healing relationship areas of conflict change and become less intense as the partners grow more accepting and loving. Children of these couples then have the best role models to help guide them in their own future romantic liaisons.

Since most contemporary couples don't operate in accordance with the more clearly defined role scripts of the past, many issues need to be worked out anew, in individual and unique ways. With both people busier than ever, time management has become one of the major contemporary dilemmas: how to manage a job or career, attend to personal interests, while still devoting sufficient time and energy to nurturing the primary relationship (and possibly children as well) in the precious few waking hours available. The ways of managing the family finances are also up for grabs as two-career couples grapple with various systems for dividing income into combinations of yours, mine, and ours.

Relationships need to become more flexible in order to deal with these changes, and the ability of the partners to negotiate creatively has become more critical than ever. Some of these negotiations may require a good deal of practice before they become a natural part of a relationship's repertoire.

With good intentions and conscientious attention, these complex skills *can* be acquired and a healing relationship that is vital and healthy can be attained, even for people who have had self-defeating behaviors ingrained for many years.

Surely, progress will not be perfect and backsliding will occur now and then, particularly during stressful periods. But the information contained in *Going the Distance* will enable you to become aware of the negative patterns that are not working and will provide you with constructive alternatives.

We believe that the deepest, most rewarding intimacy can develop in a monogamous relationship, a relationship that can flourish because of the trust and security that only monogamy can provide. By monogamy we do not mean to refer solely to the aspect of sexual fidelity within a relationship, but to the entire panoply of dimensions involved in mateship: a bonding that includes sexual fidelity, a profound spiritual connectedness, a rich and relaxed companionship, and an enduring commitment to a life lived with one another in a uniquely intimate association.

A surprised scientific community (including us) has recently learned that absolute *sexual* fidelity, is relatively rare—only about three percent to ten percent of all mammals appear to mate monogamously for life.

Whether or not it is biologically natural to us, as humans, to be sexually monogamous, we know that millions upon millions of couples *are* sexually faithful. We have a singular capacity to further the goals of an intimate relationship by choosing to control our instincts rather than to reflexively express them. This is one of the most important ways in which we differ from other mammals. And if we do choose to "travel" this way, to be fully monogamous, there is all the more reason to learn how to do it well, in all ways. That is what this book is about.

We hope that the guidance provided here will shed a useful light, illuminating the long path of your own relationship as it proceeds on its way to an ever deepening and more rewarding intimacy.

I

The Influence
of the Past

1

The Healing Arena

Intimacy and Healing

. . . as there are as many minds as there are heads, so there are as many kinds of love as there are hearts.

—TOLSTOY,
Anna Karenina

We are all the walking wounded.

Virtually none of us manage to come to adulthood unscathed by injuries from those we have loved or tried to love. We have been involved in innumerable conflicts, misunderstandings and painful dramas with parents, lovers, spouses, and others, and too often these have led to the destruction of those relationships. We have suffered heartaches and heartbreaks—most of us more than once—and we all carry the baggage of our histories.

For some of us, these psychological injuries are deeper and more extensive, particularly when they occurred during the most sensitive, formative years of our lives. It has been said that no one had the parents they deserved. It seems that no matter how hard parents try, they inevitably fall short somewhere along the way.

Some of our parents were so beset with their own problems that they ignored us or visited their problems upon us. They may have been absent when we most needed them or invasive when we needed our privacy. Inadvertently, they may have said hurtful things that damaged our fragile egos, or punished us when we needed understanding. They may have disappointed us by ignoring our successes while scolding us or making us feel guilty for our failures. Such examples are commonplace, and to a certain extent, they occur in even the healthiest families.

But there are parents, unfortunately, who fell *very* short in providing what we needed to grow up healthily. Far too many of us grew up in seriously troubled environments: in broken homes, or with parents who often quarreled, who drank and behaved irrationally, who frightened us, or who were abusive to us physically and emotionally.

The psychic wounds we sustain are not limited to those occurring in childhood, however, nor are they exclusively the by-products of our interactions with our parents. We may have been deeply injured by teachers, friends, and, as we grew older, by employers, employees, and especially by our lovers. There is hardly anyone who has not been spurned by a lover—at least once. Particularly keen are the pains caused by opening our hearts and then being rejected, by betrayals of our trust, or by a partner's oppressive attempts to control us and limit our freedom to be ourselves.

Particularly during the last twenty years or so changes in the culture at large have contributed to promoting relationship wounds. As commitment was on its way out and a wave of sexual freedom took its place, we saw numerous brief sexual affairs or perhaps a series of slightly more prolonged relationships—serial monogamy—becoming the order of the day.

The throwaway culture was upon us: razors, cigarette lighters, clothing made of paper, cheap ballpoint pens, and dozens of other products were made to be used a short while and then discarded. When difficulties in a relationship arose, they were often treated like other short-lived commodities. Finding another partner seemed often to be the simplest and most attractive alternative. Partners, however temporary, were relatively easy to find. Yet the heartbreak, even when we *chose* to end a relationship, was taking its toll.

Like a contagious disease, we were besieged by an epidemic of divorce. Within a decade, the incidence of divorce escalated until it reached fifty percent of the marriage rate. As one man said, "We amicably divided up the records and the property and did all the things that modern couples did in the seventies. It was almost too easy. Everybody was divorcing and as I look back on it, we were caught up in it as well."

The window of sexual adventurism and superficial relationships that was so breezily flung open during the past few decades seems to have begun to close. Many of us have grown disillusioned with one-night stands and multiple short-term relationships: brief flashes of excitement that soon faded away into nothing, like mouthfuls of cotton candy. We have become weary with the tedium of waking up next to someone we hardly know, awkwardly seeking delicate excuses to extricate ourselves from the situation. And we are becoming exhausted by the repetitiveness of endless "getting-to-know-you" conversations: so many introductions without the follow-up, like constantly walking out of the theater before the beginning of the second act.

Vincent and Tracy were in their late thirties when they met. Both had good jobs and were well educated, and both had suffered a divorce; in fact, Tracy had been divorced twice. Neither had expected to find themselves, at this stage in their lives, single and childless. Yet by the time they met, they were each quite skeptical that they would ever find a love that would last. They were both operating under the assumption that they would remain single. Their friendship, which had become sexual, was just a small comfort, a way to get from day to day without the complexities of a serious, romantic relationship.

They were simply friends, intimate friends. Then, after four months, a surprising thing happened. Vincent went to Tracy's house as usual to pick her up for a movie, but this time he brought flowers. He seemed more enthusiastic, more animated, and this made Tracy feel rather shy and awkward. Something had begun to change.

As Vincent moved forward, expressing his growing affection, Tracy pulled back. Vincent began to realize that he was falling in love. This surprised him and terrified Tracy. She had been hurt too many times to feel safe opening her heart to love once again.

Like Tracy, many of us have grown quite cynical about finding lifelong love. We may also feel frightened, angry, distrustful, and wary. We may even have give up hope: "Sure, there must be some healthy relationships out there, but they're few and far between . . . It's not in the cards for me . . . I just don't seem to have what it takes."

After enough frustrated attempts at finding Mr. or Ms. Right, we begin to deal with our hopelessness and our exhaustion by repeating trite sayings from the book of rationalizations: "All the good ones are already taken, or else they're gay" (unless we ourselves are gay, in which case the good ones are straight). "Those who aren't already taken are probably not interested in a serious, long-term relationship; even if they were, I'm too happily set in my ways to make the concessions marriage would require. I'm better off being single and avoiding the heartbreak."

Not only do we have our own disappointing track records to contend with, but our pessimism is increased as we become painfully aware of the devastation caused by the marital dissolution of our parents and friends. Most experts consider divorce or its equivalent to be one of the most severe emotional shocks a person can experience in a lifetime, and the effect on our children can be even more disastrous. If the current rate of divorce prevails, almost half our nation's children will be living with a single parent by age sixteen.[1]

Besides, being single is not all that bad. If you can't be happy *in* a relationship, the next best thing is certainly being happy outside of one. In fact, even being unhappily single is far superior to being unhappily married, as many of us who have been divorced can attest. And although we feel great anguish when we witness a couple splitting up, the pain of being around couples who are miserable but still together can be worse. If they are not openly conflict-ridden or subtly undermining each other, they may seem passionless, tired, tense, emotionally flat, unsexy: two ships passing in the night, divorced from each other emotionally and spiritually if not legally—a good argument for staying single. And, in fact, it probably is easier to be single now than ever before in the past, with apartment complexes, health clubs, vacation resorts, and gourmet frozen dinners designed for the single person.

Yet, even though more people are single today than ever before, "intimacy hunger" is becoming increasingly pervasive in this society. The number of dating services catering to every section of the singles community has proliferated to the point where computers are currently matching people on hundreds of personal characteristics: you can even select your prospective date/mate in advance by viewing them on video. Many newspapers and magazines aimed at every conceivable interest —book lovers, music lovers, sailors, skiers, seniors, handicapped—have columns of advertisements written by people looking for life partners, for ways out of their loneliness, for someone with whom to plan a future.

Most of us are now searching for something deeper, not just more sexual partners, more material possessions, or more rungs

1. *San Francisco Chronicle*, July 21, 1988.

on the corporate ladder. Partly as a reaction to the spiritual emptiness of the 1970s and early '80s that emphasized self-centered individualism and materialism, and partly in response to the dramatic rise in sexually transmitted diseases, we are once again seeking meaningful commitments and intimacy. We want to be able to relax our guard with someone else, to feel known and cared about, warts and all, without having to be afraid of rejection. We are seeking a sense of security and comfort that comes from knowing that we have a loving partner who will be there for us when the going gets tough.

We are hoping to find someone with whom to share life's experiences: the joys, the sorrows, adventures of all kinds; someone with whom we can dream and make plans for the future; someone we can give to from our heart; someone who will help assuage our loneliness, and with whom we can grow old. As a forty-five-year-old woman who recently married after living with her partner for ten years said: "Marriage is a place where I can feel safe; where I can feel relaxed because I'm accepted. Even when we disagree I feel connected. I feel secure that we can work out any problems that arise. I don't feel the alienation; it's very intangible, but I feel a oneness with my husband. It's really an incredible comfort."

When Tracy and Vincent met, Tracy had been divorced for two years from her second husband; it was a marriage she had been convinced would last forever, but, believing that her love and sense of commitment were sufficient to make it work, she had dismissed important problems. When her husband finally asked for a separation, Tracy was shocked and devastated. At the time she met Vincent she was still raw from the divorce and had no faith that she would not be abandoned yet a third time.

Vincent had been divorced nearly ten years. He had grown accustomed to being single, to being with a woman only when he wanted her there. Although Vincent missed having an intimate and commited relationship, he told himself that he valued his freedom more.

As Tracy backpedaled, Vincent moved slowly forward and in this way they gradually got to know more about each other. They handled each other with care and respect for their different sensitivities, the way they had each always hoped a partner would treat them.

Vincent was reliable; when he gave his word he followed through. Tracy started to relax and began to open up more. Because she was independent and had a well-developed life and career of her own, Vincent realized that he did not feel asphyxiated in the way he had so many times before. He was more comfortable receiving from her and less worried that he would have to behave exclusively as a "donor," as he had in his previous romantic relationships.

Each of them then began to feel more comfortable exposing their damaged places, their weaknesses. Tracy talked about her fears of never having a child, of never experiencing an aspect of life that had always been sacred to her. Vincent talked of his financial fears, of his chronic anxiety of ending up where he had started—in the slums of Chicago, with barely enough money to pay the rent.

In this way, they each began to feel understood. They started to feel safe with each other, and as their trust deepened, they dared to reveal more of themselves. Most of the time these revelations were met with acceptance and concern, but, of course, there were occasions when misunderstandings occurred and hurt feelings and anger resulted. By and large, however, the need to protect their hurt places gradually lessened and they were able to relax their defenses and come out of the hiding places within themselves. They married almost one year later. Vincent and Tracy had begun the process of healing one another as they developed a loving, intimate relationship: the ultimate healing arena.

Like Vincent and Tracy, most of us are looking for a way to risk becoming vulnerable again, because it is only when we open our feelings, share our insecurities, rely on the support of another, that we are in the optimum position to change and to grow, and it is in an enduring, meaningful relationship with a loved one that we grow best. If we reduce our vulnerability and our willingness to risk, we reduce our possibilities as well —the possibilities of discovering love and, at long last, of healing the wounds we have sustained along the way. For the birth-place of healing is on the bed of risk.

It is difficult if not impossible to heal our psychic wounds once we close ourselves off to others, because intimacy is both the cause and the effect of healing. As we grow closer and more comfortable with a loved one we take more risks with them, gradually letting down our guard, exposing all the sensitivities, distortions, defensive exaggerations, and other signs of distrust that have developed as a result of our past experience. If our loved one is there for us without blame or judgment when we express these defensive behaviors and attitudes, and treats us with understanding and forgiveness, we then feel safer and begin to mend. As we mend, we move forward to the next level of intimacy where further healing can take place.

As we heal and peel back the layers of protective armor that we have developed over the years, our guardedness falls away and we can relax and express our true selves. When both people in a relationship feel safe to reveal themselves in this way the intimacy between them is enriched immeasurably. It is a process that can continue to deepen over a lifetime—the path to intimacy is virtually infinite in the healing arena of a loving relationship.

As a woman we interviewed said, "Safety creates the context for intimacy. If we don't feel safe with one another, it's like a logjam—nobody goes anywhere and the relationship never really moves forward."

2

Dangerous Liaisons

Mismatches
and Misguided Alliances

What we are aiming at when we fall in love is a very strange paradox. The paradox consists of the fact that when we fall in love we are seeking to re-find all or some of the people to whom we were attached as children. On the other hand, we ask our beloved to correct all of the wrongs that these early parents or siblings inflicted upon us. So that love contains in it the contradiction, the attempt to return to the past and the attempt to undo the past.

—WOODY ALLEN
(Professor Louis Levy in *Crimes and Misdemeanors*)

Hilary seemed to move in and out of relationships about as often as she changed apartments when she was a hippie in the 1960s. True, she always went for the guy with the pretty face, even when it meant overlooking some of his other characteristics. "Even dreamboats get married," she told herself each time she began a new romance. But for reasons she couldn't fathom, the dreamboats in her life always sailed off to other ports.

Most of her relationships opened the same way, with a consuming and passionate intensity. In short order, both Hilary and her new partner were convinced that this was the big one, the one that would go the distance. Unfortunately, the only distance that seemed to develop was the emotional distance that grew between the two of them, until eventually, after a few months, another relationship had bitten the dust.

Sometimes Hilary felt as though she were stuck in a revolving door, and with each revolution she became increasingly confused, disheartened, wary, and cynical.

For the first few years she blamed this frustratingly repetitive drama on men in general and on their notorious "fear of commitment." She refused to believe that she had much to do with it, since she absolutely *knew* that what she wanted more than anything was a committed relationship that included marriage and a family.

However, after more failed relationships than she cared to count, all of which followed the same general pattern, she began to suspect that *she* might have a lot more to do with her dilemma than she originally thought. Yet her exact contribution remained a mystery to her. She entered therapy in order to see if she could find some answers to the puzzle.

REPETITION COMPULSION: THE ETERNAL DRAMA

Many of us, without knowing it, repeat destructive patterns again and again and can't seem to figure out how to avoid them. The complex psychological pattern known as *repetition compulsion* refers to the tendency to repeat, compulsively, ways of feeling, thinking, and behaving that were experienced earlier in life, usually in the formative years from childhood through adolescence. These compulsions are driven by our unconscious needs and exert a great effect not only on the initial selection of a mate, but on the way we interact with them as well.

To a greater or lesser extent it is probably true that most of us have a compelling, and mostly unconscious, desire to seek out a partner with whom we can replay parts of our childhood emotional drama. We seem to be particularly attached to those dramas that were injurious, were not fully worked through, and, for better or worse, those that are simply most familiar to us.

We are not usually drawn into such familiar dramas because we have some peculiar masochistic need to reinjure ourselves: we are driven to repeat such self-defeating patterns by an unconscious desire to bring the drama to a *different*, more rewarding, conclusion. For we are always seeking a way to heal our wounds and come to wholeness, to rework our life's experience and arrive at a greater equilibrium and harmony. We seek to complete what is incomplete, and our hope is that the next time around we can give our drama a happier ending and fulfill that which was unfulfilled.

REPEAT PERFORMANCES: THE INFLUENCE OF THE PAST

The most important influences in our lives, shaping our ways of reacting and of structuring our view of reality, were, of course, our parents, since we spent our formative years with them, years when we were most impressionable, learning at a breakneck pace from what they said, what they did, how they related to us and others. If our relationship to one or both of our parents was a particularly difficult or imbalanced one, a similarly imbalanced pattern is often repeated with our life mate, particularly if the stressed relationship was predominantly with our opposite-sexed parent. The repetitive relationship pattern can take many forms. In Hilary's case, it appeared in a form we call the Ultimate Challenge.

The Ultimate Challenge

Hilary seemed to be drawn to men who were truly unavailable for long-term relationships, trying her best to transform them into "marriage material." These men continued to exert a strange, almost magnetic attraction for her despite the fact that she was left feeling resentful and unlovable when they inevitably moved out of her life.

Doug, Raymond, and Jordan had been Hilary's three most important boyfriends. To all outward appearances they were very dissimilar. Doug and Jordan were each over six feet tall; Doug wore glasses and was dark-skinned, Jordan was fair-skinned and a redhead. Raymond was shorter and stockier than the other two. Doug was a businessman, like her father; Raymond was a lawyer and Jordan was a graphic designer. All of them were fairly outgoing, but their preferences in recreational activities were quite different and so were their politics.

The one area, however, in which they were unmistakably the same was that none of them was genuinely interested in a long-term relationship. None of them would have admitted to this, however; in fact, each professed his seriousness about wanting a mate for life. Yet in each case, actions soon spoke louder than words.

Doug was separated from his wife and often talked of divorce, but the final papers were never quite completed and it was always his wife who got the blame for dragging things out. Jordan had been divorced for two years. It had been a particularly bitter parting, a long legal conflict that left him with large alimony payments and the loss of his child in a custody battle. On some level he seemed to be guarding himself against a possible repeat performance.

Raymond, on the other hand, was almost forty-four and had never had a relationship survive the two-year mark. He still brought his laundry to his mother every weekend, and Hilary couldn't dispel a vague feeling that she was in some strange competition with "Mama," a contest she couldn't possibly win.

Exactly why Hilary picked such unavailable men when she consciously desired the opposite continued to perplex her. As therapy progressed, however, she gradually began to discover that in some way she was repeating a pattern that had started well before she had even begun dating.

Divorced from her mother, her father always professed his love for Hilary, yet he rarely seemed to have time available to see her. They would make numerous plans to get together, but somehow other obligations always seemed to crop up for him at the last minute. Endless apologies followed, along with promises that he would make it up to her the next time, but the next time rarely occurred. He bought her gifts instead, and then couldn't understand why she didn't appreciate them.

Later, when he remarried, he rarely saw her at all. Apparently his new wife was jealous and quite possessive of his time —at least that was the explanation he gave. Hilary was sullen and rude when he called, and this put a further damper on their already seriously strained relationship.

At first Hilary had difficulty believing that there could be any relevant connections between her earlier history and her later life; it all seemed too pat, like something out of a Freudian textbook. Yet she could not deny that she was caught up in the repetitive scenario of trying to forge intimate relationships with unavailable men and that the motif was essentially the same one she had developed with her father.

There are many variations on the Ultimate Challenge. One involves people who only become interested when they are actively in pursuit of their partners: a compulsion that might be termed "the hunter and the quarry." When the tables are turned and they are the ones being wooed, they become very uncomfortable, even panicky, and they flee.

A second variation on this same theme occurs when we choose a partner who is fundamentally quite different from the person we really have in mind for ourselves and then proceed to try to change that person into our soulmate: a prescription for failure, *par excellence.*

Stan, for example, was a music lover. One night at Le Bek's he met Casey, the lead singer in the jazz group playing there. At first he was mesmerized by her voice, and after a few dates he was convinced that he had fallen in love with her.

Stan's mother had disappeared when he was seven years old, leaving him with a belief, on some deep level, that all women were untrustworthy abandoners. He tried with all his might to get Casey to stay home and not travel so much but, as one might predict, the more he tugged at her to settle down and find work locally, the more time she spent on the road.

Stan was, in fact, trying to work out his incomplete relationship with his mother by picking a woman whose profession required her to be on the road a good deal of the time. Leaving, after all, was in the very nature of her work. Unconsciously, Stan was attempting to bring the painful scenario of his childhood to a new and happier ending, one that finally fulfilled his need for stability and constancy, and quieted his insecurities.

The Rescuer

Daniel was an only child, the offspring of an artistically gifted father who could never seem to earn a decent living, and a mother who, despite being physically handicapped, worked double time in order to support the family.

Daniel's mother was always nagging his father, watching over him to make sure that he was out there looking for employment, not just staying home and sketching or playing his guitar.

Daniel's father, who was truly rather childlike and irresponsible in many ways, felt resentful at being pressured by his wife to become someone so different from the person he really was, though he never expressed these feelings directly. On the other hand, Daniel's mother had her own resentments since she worked inordinately hard caring for everyone but herself. Sensing her need, Daniel tried to assume some of the roles and responsibilities that his father had abdicated, but his mother would never accept his help.

As an adult Daniel repetitively chose women who needed to be rescued from one unfortunate circumstance or another, thereby trying to complete the rescue of his mother, a task at which he never succeeded during his childhood. Finding himself ensconced in a girlfriend's life, energetically attempting to take care of her every need, he would slowly come to feel resentful and irritated by what he saw as the unfair imbalance in the relationship. He would then end the relationship, relieved to be free of the awesome responsibilities. Then, after a few months, he would begin rescue operations again with another young woman. He never became aware of his role in encouraging his partners to rely upon him to such a degree that he ended up feeling oppressed.

Daniel exemplifies a person trapped in a complex Rescue Compulsion. The predominant way he related to his partners bore an extraordinary resemblance to the way in which he attempted to rescue his mother. Eventually, he himself came to feel as his father had, resentful, restricted, unable to pursue his own interests, and convinced, additionally, of the notion that a woman's needs could never be satisfied. But, like his mother, he felt overburdened. In this way he replicated both his early relationship to his mother as well as that of his parents' marital interplay. The complexities of Daniel's life provide us with an excellent example of just how difficult it can be to ferret out the precise historical dynamics that go into making up a compulsively repetitive relationship pattern.

The source of the compulsive need to repeat certain aspects of our earlier relationships does not always originate in our relationship to our parents. Other significant people during our formative years, a brother or sister, for example, can be key figures in this drama. Chelsea was also a rescuer, but it was the relationship with her sister, Edith, that set this dynamic in motion. Three years her junior, Edith was intellectually disabled, and Chelsea received a tremendous amount of acknowledgment and appreciation from her parents for taking her sister off their hands for periods of time. The caretaking role was one she knew very well, and one she derived significant self-worth from: caring for her sister and caring for her parents by caring for her sister.

Chelsea tended to pick men who were not quite able to make it in the real world. All too easily she allowed herself to support them financially, find them jobs, and solve any number of their practical problems. Her partners, unlike the members of her family, however, were neither grateful nor indebted to her. Instead, feeling undermined to some degree as a result of Chelsea's unsolicited assistance, they often covered up their own feelings of inadequacy by demeaning her contributions. Predictably, she was left with strange feelings of emptiness and dissatisfaction, embittered at being taken for granted after all she had done for them.

The Fatal Flaw

A thirty-two-year-old woman named Denise compulsively repeated a pattern that had its origin in her relationship with her brother, a pattern we call the Fatal Flaw.

Denise realized that her two exes had macho streaks much like her older brother's. "I never knew my older brother very well—we were nine years apart—but I always admired him and wanted to be close to him," she said. "He really didn't want me around, though. I just seemed to get in his way. At best he simply tolerated me, as if I were a petty annoyance he had to put up with."

In time her brother became a successful plastic surgeon, married, and had two children. To Denise, it seemed an ideal life. He and Denise never grew much closer, though he remained the standard of "perfection" against whom she unconsciously rated the men in her life. Of course, none of those men could really measure up to the idealized image she had of her brother since she never had much opportunity to experience his mortal flaws and foibles. The men she dated were mere humans with noticeable imperfections, and she became remarkably adept at finding these "fatal flaws" in her lovers and then having them become insurmountable obstacles to a developing relationship.

Hilary's boyfriend Raymond, whose "heart belonged to Mama," was searching for a fantasy as well. His mother's investment in Raymond had led to a similar set of problems. She doted on him, marveled at his intelligence, was engaged by his wit, waited on him hand and foot, and rarely had a critical word for him. To her, he could do no wrong. Needless to say, his girlfriends never measured up to these standards. No matter how much they loved him, they never seemed to adore him quite enough.

Both Denise and Raymond tended to fall madly in love, initially idealizing their lovers and the perfect future that lay ahead of them. But soon enough, reality would creep in. Denise might find herself dwelling on the fact that her lover was uncomfortable or awkward around children, that he was a terrible joke teller who insisted on telling jokes anyway, or that his taste in art was appalling. Raymond complained that one of his girlfriends never wanted to learn about football or watch it on TV, another would have been perfect, but her breasts weren't large enough, and Hilary couldn't cook worth a damn.

Any of these shortcomings can be sufficient grounds for rejection for those of us caught up in the Fatal Flaw compulsion. We can always imagine a new, more perfect partner on the horizon, but the new person's inevitable flaws will become magnified as we move in for a closer look. Ultimately they provide sufficient reason to continue with the endless search for the flawless "god" or "goddess."

Themes and Variations

Unfortunately, the most painful of our early experiences, ostensibly the ones we would try most assiduously to avoid, are often the ones that get reenacted. It is now well known, for example, that most wife beaters were themselves battered children, that children of alcoholics frequently tend to become alcoholics themselves or marry alcoholics. It is not simply the violence or substance abuse that gets repeated, but the basic emotional patterns of interaction as well. Consequently, even when a person consciously picks a partner who abstains from alcohol and drugs or who is anything but violent, it is still possible, unwittingly, *to recreate* the same *underlying psychological patterns*, but without the abuse or addiction.

For example, Vivian grew up in a family where her father would drink and then become verbally abusive and, on occasion, physically abusive as well. Since he earned a very modest salary, his wife needed to supplement the family income. Vivian's father could never acknowledge his wife's accomplishments because to him they only emphasized his own failures. Consequently, when funds were low and he was feeling particularly inadequate, he would begin drinking and lose control of his temper.

Vivian, who had always been petrified of her father, deliberately looked for his opposite when seeking a mate. She met James, a teetotaler whose quiet and calm outward appearance she found very appealing. He was just starting out in his own business, worked very hard, and earned a decent living. Since Vivian was a lawyer, James' income, while adequate, was considerably less than her own. This difference in their earnings seemed to have an exaggerated effect upon Vivian. She was chronically dissatisfied with James, perpetually carping about one thing or another. She derogated his choice of career and could be quite sarcastic and taunting about his alleged inadequacies, especially his failure to "measure up" financially. Finally her provocative insults pushed James to the breaking point, and after a quarrel that had gone on for quite a while, he lost control, hurled a burst of verbal invectives at her, and walked out.

On an overt level it seemed as though Vivian was trying to create a relationship that was quite the opposite of her parents'. Yet, even though she picked a partner who did not drink, she herself had unconsciously *created* a dynamic that was peculiarly similar to her parents' in a fundamental way. Of course, Vivian was quite unaware of being the author of this disturbing drama. She felt quite justified in behaving the way she did, and the demise of this relationship only confirmed her prejudicial beliefs about men in general.

Like many people, Vivian found herself ensconced in a self-defeating process partly because of its familiarity. Despite its serious drawbacks, these deceptive feelings of comfort can be very seductive. At least we can predict what tomorrow will bring.

The provocative and relentless "testing" of our partner is another way in which we may unintentionally orchestrate the very results we most fear. Leonard also seemed to push away the very women with whom he so desperately wanted to connect. He had grown up with a mother who, while a caring person, clearly considered her work to be her most important priority. Often, when they *did* have some time together and Leonard was starting to feel relaxed and close to her, she suddenly would be called away on a business trip and he would be left with a babysitter or brought to his cousin's house for several days. Later in life, Leonard found it ironic and puzzling to discover that he became anxious in his love relationships just when they seemed to be going best, when they had begun to deepen and grow more secure. He would behave quite erratically at these times, more grasping and in desperate need of reassurance: "Are you sure you love me? Are you sure you're not going to leave me?" Yet no amount of reassurance could quiet him for very long and he would soon be raising the same questions again.

Understandably, his lovers would begin to feel overwhelmed, swallowed up by his seemingly insatiable need, asphyxiated by his insecurities, and they would end the relationship. Leonard's anxiety over losing them actually chased them away. In relationship after relationship, even with women who were vastly different from one another, Leonard managed to engineer the same dreaded result. Each time this occurred it only confirmed his belief that when you get close to someone, they abandon you, leaving you with emptiness and a broken heart.

By excessively interrogating, questioning, and pushing our partner's limits, like Leonard, we may actually force our partner to engage in the very behavior that we dread. If this happens and one of us withdraws or terminates the relationship, we can rationalize that we tried our best, while continuing to avoid confronting the risks inherent in intimacy and growth.

Even when we are careful to avoid interactions typical of our family of origin by seeking, for example, their mirror opposite, we may still get into trouble. This *overcompensation* can create problems of its own.

Bob grew up in a religious-fundamentalist family where any expression of feelings was so stifled that what he remembered most about his childhood was a feeling of being dead inside. When Bob met Rebecca he felt as though he had come to life for the first time. Their lovemaking was tremendously compelling and intense. The relationship was always operating at one extreme or another: one minute they would be doing battle, and the next they would be making mad passionate love as a way of making up. For Rebecca, this was a pattern of relating with which she had long been familiar. Rebecca's parents had had a tumultuous marriage. They had physically separated on three different occasions; on one of these they actually divorced, only to remarry less than a year later.

Finally, Bob became exhausted by the emotional roller

coaster of breaking up and reconnecting. So much mutual distrust had accrued that the relationship ultimately ended. After a number of relationships of this kind, Bob came to realize that passion alone did not create emotional closeness. He learned that he had been drawn to tumultuous relationships not because they provided the intimacy he sought, but because he associated them with feeling alive and vital, a marked contrast to the way he had felt while growing up.

Lydia and Gilbert's relationship was dramatically different from Rebecca and Bob's despite many similarities in their dynamics. They had created a "safe" relationship.

Lydia's parents were exacting and controlling. Every question had either a right or a wrong answer; unwritten rules seemed to determine every move. Finally, after dating a number of men and repeatedly meeting with her parents' disapproval, Lydia met Gilbert, exactly the kind of man that her parents had in mind for her. The relationship persevered.

Like Lydia, Gilbert too had picked a "safe" partner, but he was drawn to her because she seemed to be almost the *opposite* kind of person he knew from his childhood experience: his mother was an alcoholic. At times he would come home from school to find her passed out on the living room sofa, and frequently he was the terrified witness to his parents' venomous fights. Life at home was frighteningly unpredictable. Lydia appealed to Gilbert because she was extremely conventional, consistent, and self-effacing. She was "safe."

In actuality, neither Lydia nor Gilbert ever felt much passion for each other, not even in the beginning. Soon enough, both Lydia and Gilbert became bored. Their relationship offered few growth-producing challenges, and the trade-off for having fulfilled their safety needs proved to be a stale and humdrum life. Their disrespect and disregard for each other turned out to be a terrible price to pay for safety, after all.

Incest survivors and those who have been sexually or physically abused are often inclined toward relationships dominated by exaggerated safety needs. Such people have usually been so traumatized as children that they may feel compelled to seek partners whom they can control. They also frequently choose partners who do not turn them on sexually, as they attempt to guard against intolerable feelings of vulnerability and the reawakening of traumatic memories.

THE RISKS OF REPETITION

We have seen how historic influences can exert pervasive effects on both our choice of mates and the course and conduct of our relationships. Clearly, the repetitive and compulsive patterns we have been discussing here—and we have only touched on several of the more common and troublesome themes—are a tricky business. Understanding the dimensions of the pattern that we are repeating can be a complex task since they are often different with each partner. The dynamics can be subtle and elusive. They may be difficult to identify and understand, and they can take considerable time to resolve.

If we engage in such rigidified relationship patterns in our attempts to address and heal the wounds we have sustained along life's path, the repetitions of these old dramas can create painful and tiresome dilemmas of their own. With each intimate relationship that fails, we grow more wary and suspicious, and we develop a network of protective mechanisms, automatic defenses designed to reduce the chances of becoming emotionally injured yet again. This is part of our most fundamental instinct: self-preservation. Yet, these very same protective mechanisms can also interfere with, or even prevent, genuine intimacy from developing, because we cannot achieve intimacy without becoming emotionally vulnerable within our primary relationship.

If our capacity to trust others has been so diminished, and our need for safety has made it too difficult to open ourselves anew to the next relationship, we may dig ourselves a well of loneliness, becoming more hopeless and cynical about the chance of ever finding our way to love. Here at last, we may feel less vulnerable to the jabs of dashed hopes and fractured expectations.

There is a tendency among some of us to panic and bail out when confronting roadblocks in the course of a relationship, dodging, rather than dealing with, the issues at hand. At these difficult junctures we may seek another, allegedly more compatible partner, justifying our decision by convincing ourselves that it was really our partner who was responsible for the problems we experienced.

The fictions that we can use to justify this form of escapism are innumerable: if only we could find a partner who didn't spend money so frivolously, or was more carefree, or more responsible, or less rejecting, or more competent around the house, or . . . , our problems would be over; our relationship would be easy and conflict free.

But there is no way around it: if our own issues are not resolved they will reappear in the next relationship and the next, although perhaps in a slightly altered form. The more firmly entrenched and repetitive the pattern, the greater is the likelihood that we have not analyzed and worked-through our own part in the process.

Unfortunately, as long as we see ourselves as innocent (at least mostly innocent) victims, we create a framework that encourages us to repeat those tiresome and painful patterns. In order to achieve intimacy, we must be able to see and accept our own contribution and responsibility for creating the outcomes of our relationships. We need to identify our destructive patterns so that we may then alter them and, in so doing, create new opportunities for healing our wounds.

While analyzing our *own* contributions to the relationship difficulties is the necessary first step toward creating a truly intimate relationship, this can be an unexpectedly difficult task. Our uncanny tendency to repeat our patterns can easily thwart common sense and obscure self-knowledge. We seem to have an unlimited capacity to pull the wool over our own eyes.

Lucy, for example, through the help of therapy, came to realize that her relationships mirrored her parents' marriage. Lucy's mother was considerably more competent than her father in many ways and Lucy had fallen in love with a long string of men who were considerably less competent and less secure than she was. Almost without exception Lucy was the more socially polished of the two of them, had firmer decision-making powers, usually earned a better living, expressed herself more clearly and forcefully, and frequently was more energetic and imaginative. Eventually these imbalances would lead to predictable resentments on the part of both Lucy and her partner, and the relationship would fall apart.

In an attempt to correct the situation Lucy made a vow not to enter another relationship unless, among other things, the man was more powerful and accomplished than her previous lovers had been. When she began dating Rob she was convinced that at last she had broken the pattern that had been responsible for so much frustration and unhappiness in her life.

Although Rob had had a fairly checkered career history with numerous ups and downs, when Lucy met him he was selling multimillion-dollar contracts in the bond and stock option markets. While only on paper at the time, he claimed that the commissions on his sales were in the hundreds of thousands of dollars. He seemed so sure of himself, so dynamic and outgoing. Lucy was captivated by his charm and by the trappings of the glamorous life they were leading: fine restaurants, expensive gifts, plans for vacations in faraway places.

And then, quite suddenly, things changed. The economy went into one of its downward cycles and Rob's business went into a tailspin. A number of major deals failed to materialize and as they crumbled so did his apparent self-confidence. He rapidly became emotionally deflated and dependent, endlessly and irritatingly complaining about his bad luck. Though Lucy tried to be supportive and encouraging, he could not be soothed; he seemed to have no emotional reserves behind his once powerful veneer, and their time together took on an unremittingly dreary cast, one that Lucy found to be unpleasantly familiar. Soon their intense, frequent quarrels led to the demise of the relationship.

Lucy's unconscious psychological antennae had actually influenced her decision once again—she had found a man who was, despite all his seductively attractive superficial characteristics to the contrary, basically very insecure.

A DIFFERENT DRAMA

Liberating ourselves from the "merry"-go-round of compulsively repetitive relationships usually requires a good deal of patience as well as the courage to take a long hard look at our relationship history, distant as well as recent.

The task, of course, is to be able to see things as they really are, rather than as we would like them to be; to free ourselves from our projections and to avoid falling into the old traps that stifled our growth in the first place. The less we transfer childhood-based feelings and needs onto our partner, the more likely the relationship is to succeed.

Begin by exploring the emotional or situational similarities that provoked difficulties in your previous relationships. Perhaps you often felt intellectually one down, or uncomfortably overindulged, or sexually rejected, or as if you had to assume far too much of the responsibility for the survival of the relationship. Whatever the pattern may be, once you have delineated it, examine it to see if you can discover a similar process that occurred with people who were close to you in your early years, particularly in the relationship that you had with your parents, or they had with each other.

Take time to reflect deeply on these similarities and consistencies even though it may make you uncomfortable to do so. While not always immediately apparent, connections from past to present will usually carry a surprising ring of truth about them once they have come to light.

Label these patterns in a way that draws attention to them: use epithets that describe the most essential characteristics of your own role in your repetitive relationship dramas, such as the Rescuer or Daddy's Little Girl or Stifled but Safe.

In your desire to grow and change you may be tempted to avoid certain issues in an effort to escape discomfort and move ahead more quickly. If you can keep these tendencies in mind and strive to confront and explore the uncomfortable feelings, you will be better able to finally resolve the distressing relationship patterns and lay them to rest.

A Different Cast

Once you become aware of your own proclivities and the harmful patterns they dictate, you will increase the likelihood of selecting a partner who can interact with you in a more constructive way.

Maureen realized that she had a tendency to become attracted to men who appeared to be quite passive but were actually sitting on a good deal of pent-up anger. She herself had a father who was usually meek and exaggeratedly self-effacing, yet who could suddenly turn cold and rejecting.

"In a relationship," said Maureen, "I would pick these wishy-washy men who were virtually seething beneath the surface and then I would 'train' them to become more assertive. Inevitably, they'd turn and behave really shitty with me—at times they were even violent. That clearly didn't work. Then Drake and I started going together. He's pretty easygoing and mild mannered, and I get to encourage him to be more expressive, but he's not a volcano waiting for an excuse to erupt like my previous partners were. He doesn't fight in the same way, and I enjoy his quietness, his well-developed feminine side. It was the underlying anger that was a problem in the past, and I finally found a man who is really different."

As you investigate your own psychology, remember to focus on the *underlying* dynamics of your relationships. We are not concerned here with such superficialities as to whether you prefer people who are dark or fair, "jocks" or "bookworms." We are talking about personalities and the way they function with an intimate partner. You can find partners who look very different from one another on the surface, who have different occupations, lifestyles, physical appearances, yet they have certain personality characteristics in common, and as you spend more time with them you'll notice that you begin to feel and interact in ways that seem strangely familiar.

A Different Scenario

Relationships are systems within which individuals function interdependently: one individual's behavior can be fully understood only in relationship to the other. One person, therefore, may create and maintain a particular dynamic or mode of interaction only as long as the other person plays their part as well. This suggests that there are basically two ways to correct negative relationship patterns. The first, as we have mentioned, consists of choosing someone who is decisively different from the partners with whom you have been involved in the past. The second is to change the dynamics of the relationship system itself by focusing assiduously on the ways in which *you respond to your partner* that create the unhealthy interaction. This means that even if you are involved with someone who fits your old choice pattern, effective options are still available that can transform the relationship.

Within a relationship system, both partners can change their own behavior. A change on either partner's part will "force" the system itself to change as the other partner accommodates to the altered behavior. For example, in the Rescue Relationship if the person playing the role of "rescuer" steadfastly refuses to assist the "victim" as he or she creates crisis after crisis, there will be no payoff for the "victim" to continue in that role. Eventually that partner will have to find other solutions to existing problems, hopefully more constructive ones.

By the same token, if the "victim" refuses to be rescued any longer, the "rescuer" will be out of a job, and the relationship will move to a new footing.

A common example of the rescuer/victim relationship occurs when one of the partners is an alcoholic and is cared for and protected by the other partner, who mops up all the messes the alcoholic creates. The unhealthy collusion between such partners actually *sustains* the alcoholism, although the sober partner usually expresses hurt, dismay, and even anger when the alcoholic doesn't stop drinking. The payoff to the sober partner—the one playing the role of rescuer—is the ego gratification of feeling deeply needed, of self-pitying martyrdom, and of having the ready opportunity to have someone to blame when things go wrong. The alcoholic, in turn, has a supportive rescuer at hand, as well as an occasional punching bag. In the parlance of the day, such a partnership is *codependent:* the system is one in which each partner fulfills and perpetuates the other partner's self-injurious needs.

Melinda and Hank had been high school sweethearts and got married when he was in his sophomore year of college and she was graduating from high school. Melinda's father was a physician who abused drugs.

Hank had begun to drink heavily in college and had never really stopped. He had lost a number of his accounting jobs because of his drinking and the family was forced to relocate several times as he sought new employment.

Although Melinda claimed to be miserable in her marriage, she was extremely dependent upon Hank for financial support and for negotiating the countless complexities of modern life. Indeed, she believed that she couldn't possibly survive on her own, since she had few occupational skills, a limited education, and two small children.

For many years she received a good deal of encouragement and advice from both her best friend and her sister, to leave the marriage and return to school. However, she felt too insecure and frightened to take the risks of making such a drastic change.

Finally, after twelve years of marriage, the children had become more independent, and Melinda entered vocational school to begin training as a respiratory therapist. Regardless of what Hank did, she was determined to take care of herself. However, at about the same time Hank decided to join Alcoholics Anonymous. With the help of AA and marriage counseling, their relationship took a decisive turn for the better; and before long, both of them were enjoying their marriage in ways that neither of them would have thought possible.

It is not always the case that when one partner changes, the other partner willingly accommodates. In fact, most often the other partner will, at least initially, resist the alteration in the relationship or unconsciously attempt to sabotage it in order to maintain the original dynamic.

Harry and Sue had a traditional relationship for many years, but when Sue, bored with her role as homemaker and mother, decided to look for a job, Harry felt threatened. To his surprise, he felt inadequate and somewhat superfluous when Sue brought home her first paychecks. Sue was irked and disappointed with him; she thought he would feel proud of her new accomplishment and happy for the additional income it provided. Instead, Harry tried to talk her out of working full-time and into having another child. At first, he dug in his heels and refused to do more around the house. Sue began to feel increasingly resentful at having to do double duty, but she persevered, and encouraging changes soon began to occur. Harry began to discover new talents as a barbecue chef and by year's end he had also signed up for a course in Italian cooking. Before long he was growing his own herbs and a few vegetables in their small garden rather than working overtime in order to make ends meet. Today Harry looks back and cannot imagine why he resisted the shifts that ultimately proved to be so beneficial and stimulating.

It is important to note that this same scenario could have

worked out in a number of other ways, not all of them quite so favorable. Sue might have yielded to Harry's original resistance, had another child, and become embittered and depressed; or perhaps if her need for a career was strong enough and Harry remained rigidly opposed to her desires, she might have left him. Or Harry might not have been willing to accommodate to a change in the status quo of their relationship and might have entered into an affair as a way of expressing his anger, thereby seriously undermining and jeopardizing the marriage.

When a relationship has become so rigidified and entrenched in ways that have outlived their usefulness, and transformation is too threatening to be permitted, then the healing process that is at the core of a successful relationship becomes thwarted, and the relationship begins a downhill slide to tedium and, all too often, divorce.

Most commonly, however, people *do* change; but they do it gradually and usually with some hesitation. This is not unreasonable: most of us become uncomfortable when life requires giving up habitual modes of behavior. Trying something new and different often produces considerable trepidation. The unknown, after all, seems less safe, and is certainly less predictable; in the face of it we are inclined to cling to our old, tried-and-true ways of relating—even when these are no longer working very well.

Growth and change, however, are absolute necessities if a healthy relationship is to endure. Every relationship that thrives over time must accommodate numerous significant changes in its fabric.

THE HEALING BEGINS

Even with a number of unsuccessful relationships and failed marriages under our belt, most of us will, nonetheless, continue to look for a loved one with whom we can heal and grow. If this cannot take place significantly enough in any one relationship because our injuries are too deep or the power struggles too great or the defenses too numerous, then some partial healing within each of a series of relationships can occur: a form of sequential resolution of our historical wounds in which one relationship begins, more or less, where the previous one left off.

Certain relationships are noteworthy because they provide arenas in which one or both of the partners learn much and ultimately change significantly, but at the cost of the relationship itself. We call these "penultimate" relationships because the person subsequently moves on to the next, and ultimately lasting, love affair—the one that goes the distance—having benefited substantially from the experiences garnered in the previous, penultimate, one.

Penultimate relationships are usually characterized by inordinate conflict. Often the tension-ridden atmosphere of these relationships promotes defensiveness and resistance to change, and when change does occur, it is commonly the result of threat and coercion. As one might suspect, coerced change is usually accompanied by an accrual of distrust, anger, and damage to the very core of the relationship.

Once the penultimate relationship is concluded, defenses are lowered and there is an opportunity to reflect more thoughtfully on the underlying issues as well as upon the meaning and relevance of the repetitive complaints that were registered by the previous partner. In this way, a person may discover, accept, and integrate important self-revelations and truths which can then be applied constructively in the following relationship.

Pamela and Aaron's relationship illustrates this dynamic. Aaron regularly put in sixty-hour workweeks at his business. Pamela was understanding and supportive of his long hours in the beginning, when the business was getting off the ground. But at last the business was running profitably, and a competent staff had been hired who could handle much of the work that originally could be done only by Aaron. Yet Aaron's behavior remained unchanged.

Pamela complained about missed vacations, meals eaten alone, and a life interrupted by frequent business demands. While Aaron was sympathetic to her plight and promised that things would soon change, his job continued to take precedence and the changes never occurred.

When asked, Aaron would insist that he wanted to spend more time with Pamela, but he couldn't seem to reconcile her demands with the demands of his career. His father, a detective, had a similar relationship with his mother, who ultimately had resigned herself to the unhappy circumstances. It wasn't until Pamela had packed her bags and moved out that Aaron fully realized the gravity of the situation, but by then it was too late. Only after the relationship failed did he become aware of how important Pamela had been to him and how serious her complaints really were.

A few years later Aaron fell in love with Johanna. This time he deliberately paid careful attention to her needs and kept his work in check. Pamela felt hurt and angry because she believed that Johanna was the fortunate beneficiary of her own suffering and sacrifice. And, in fact, Aaron's relationship with Johanna was on much more solid ground as the result of his previous relationship with Pamela. He had discovered the ways he had been sabotaging real intimacy and began committing his time and energies to his partner as he had never done before.

As Aaron's story illustrates, frequently our knowledge of how to establish a successful intimate relationship is not consciously acquired. A good deal of the most important learning takes place indirectly, subtly; at times we seem to incorporate information almost by osmosis. Certainly we are molded and influenced most importantly by the hard knocks of personal experience.

However, regardless of how we go about it, understanding the ways in which our personal histories influence our behaviors, feelings, attitudes, and thoughts about our mates can be of significant benefit in resolving any self-generated roadblocks on the path to intimacy, and of invaluable help in creating the soul-satisfying union for which we are searching.

II

Courtship

3

Possibility and Promise

The Role of Courtship

> *It is ridiculous*
> *what airs we put on*
> *to seem profound*
> *while our hearts*
> *gasp dying*
> *for want of love*

> —W. C. WILLIAMS,
> From *Asphodel, That Greeny Flower*

Most of us arrive at a time in our lives when we feel ready and eager to enter a new kind of relationship, one that involves the long future, not merely the immediate present. Once we have reached that distinct state of readiness and desire to be with that special someone with whom we believe we can build a life, we enter the realm of courtship. Courtship involves a prolonged experiment with a singularly serious purpose and attitude.

Courtship is about *mating,* not dating. It is entirely possible for two people to date for months or even years without courting, and two people do not always enter courtship at the same time. One partner may have a more casual attitude about the relationship while the other has a greater desire to deepen and advance its purpose.

At one time, not very long ago, the courtship process was carried out more formally as well as more protractedly than it is today. A couple would first get to know each other's family and friends, and the development of physical intimacy would proceed more slowly, in closer accord with the process of getting to know their partners in other ways. But as the pace of life continues to speed up, so has the pace of relationship formation, and this has been accompanied by a tendency toward shorter and less formalized courtships.

Clearly, courtship serves an essential purpose: it can and should provide us with a microcosm of the future relationship. Its duration permits real life to have its proper impact on the romanticized, getting-to-know-you stage. Within this period we are given the invaluable opportunity to assess our future life mates more thoroughly, to learn more about whether we work well as a team, whether our values are congruent, whether we negotiate our differences well, whether we are sexually compatible, whether we enjoy each other's company and whether we can agree on life plans. We are able to "sample" the various dimensions of our partners: to see them under stress, to see how they handle relationships with their friends and family, to discover conflicting interests and possible personality clashes. Most importantly, perhaps, we can find out whether mutual trust, the pivot point of all good relationships, is able to grow and develop.

In short, courtship is a critical testing ground for future compatibility. When the courtship period and its important purpose becomes abbreviated, the opportunity to get to know our prospective mates in greater depth is compromised, and the results can be most unfortunate.

Of course, a courtship can also go on for too long without ever moving forward. In fact, one woman, married thirty-three years, told us that she was flabbergasted when her husband informed her the first time they went out that he planned to date for "at least two years" before deciding whether or not he and his prospective mate were compatible. "What if I didn't pass the test?" she had wondered. "What then? I would have already given him two years of my life."

Interestingly, this couple came upon a few major problems that took them over a year to resolve. When they were finally ready to marry, one and one half years later, the time seemed right for both of them.

Since the creation of an intimate relationship is without doubt among the most satisfying, complex, demanding and crucial components of a life well lived, it makes no sense whatsoever to compromise the potential contribution that a solid courtship can make to the ultimate success of such a relationship. A conscious courtship can reduce the likelihood that we will encounter painful surprises later on, after having made a commitment to our chosen one. As the adage warns us, "Decide in haste, repent at leisure." Despite the time pressures that make contemporary life so different from that of previous generations, we can still learn to use the information we receive during the courtship period more thoughtfully so that its benefits are not denied us.

THE ROMANTIC RUSH

Relationships begin with a variety of openings. Most of us, however, seem to await the moment when someone we meet "knocks our socks off." These intense feelings then become the basis for pursuing a deeper relationship.

Joshua describes a quintessential first meeting of this sort: "I was new in San Francisco," he reported. "I had just gotten back from Asia and was going to be returning to my home in Philadelphia in a few days. Anyway, I had been invited to the home of a friend of my family's for Easter morning breakfast. I walked in the door and there was this beautiful, blond-haired, tanned epitome of a "California girl" standing in front of me. I absolutely fell in love the moment I laid eyes on her. I couldn't stop looking at her. Everything I had dreamed of was right there. It totally blew me over even before I spoke to her."

Buried somewhere in our unconscious, perhaps, is the notion that this kind of dizzyingly powerful experience identifies "the real thing." Unfortunately, this scenario is far more typical of relationships that burn out after a few months than those that last a lifetime. To be sure, there are those couples who "fall in love at first sight," marry within a few weeks, and are still happily married fifty years later, but they are clearly in the minority. Why is it then that so many of us look at the romantic rush that Joshua described as being a reliable indicator of true love?

The truth is that *we love to be in love.* Being in love catapults us into a scintillatingly alive plane of existence far away from our mundane daily lives, a deliciously captivating high that is better than that induced by any drug. So when we "fall in love," we are most often falling in love with the intensity of our own feelings rather than with the other person. The desire to be enraptured by these feelings can drive our convictions and easily capture our imagination: without knowing it, we can "fall in love" with an image based mostly on a fantasy of the kind of person we'd always imagined ourselves being with, and then project this fantasy image onto our new acquaintance. The intensity of these sweeping feelings can easily obscure the actual characteristics of our alleged loved one.

Since, at the outset we actually know very little about the real person, we can't truly love them in any meaningful sense of the word. When we fall "head over heels" for someone, we are usually aware only of relatively superficial elements about them, characteristics that have powerfully impressed us during the short time we've spent together. We are easily inclined to make more of these than they ultimately may be worth, and it is quite common to be surprised and even shocked when we later discover that what we assumed about the person turned out not to be true at all. Alas, some people never seem to stop falling in love with love, and their romantic relationships follow the same repetitive and tragically unfulfilling pattern as a result.

Janet recalled that when she first met Otis she was struck by his polished manners, and how handsome and beautifully dressed he was. The fact that he was president of his own company impressed her a great deal more than she let on, even to herself, and when he laughed at her jokes or looked deeply into her eyes, she felt overcome by a rush of excitement.

Otis called Janet the very next day, and the day after. On each of the first three dates he brought a gift—flowers, wine, a sweet card. He was attentive to her in a way she had never before experienced. She delighted in the feeling of being pursued. By the third date they became lovers, and Otis vowed his undying affection: it was a whirlwind affair and Janet had fallen hopelessly for him.

It was not long, however, before Otis began making excuses as to why he couldn't see Janet on particular weekends. Most of the time he claimed to be traveling on business, and since he was so sweet and reassuring when he did see her, she accepted his words at face value. Then one day when Otis was supposed to be out of town, Janet noticed his car parked outside a local restaurant. She watched from her own car as he emerged with his arm lovingly entwined around another woman. This was the beginning of the long, drawn-out demise of a heart-wrenching love affair, one that is all too familiar to millions of us, male and female alike.

While first impressions may be important, they rarely tell the complete story. Neither Joshua nor Janet knew much about the person they were intoxicated with. They knew virtually nothing about all the most salient dimensions that make for a lasting, intimate relationship.

THE FUNCTION OF COURTSHIP

As dating progresses and evolves into courtship, the very nature of the relationship changes; partners reasonably come to expect more from one another and to scrutinize each other more closely. It can be said that the fundamental purpose of courtship is to "tease out" the real person from the fantasized image we projected onto her or him. This deeper knowledge is the by-product of time spent together in a wide array of situations. When a date is broken, for instance, does it begin to signify the lack of importance our partner places on the relationship? Does it indicate a tendency to be rather irresponsible? Or, is it simply an innocent and insignificant lapse?

It is all too easy to brush aside some of the most salient information—our feelings, intuitions, perceptions—because of our wish to believe the best about our partner so we can go forward without impediment. Sometimes our own desperation (because we have been lonely; because we are growing older) encourages us to gloss over relevant details, but we are taking foolish chances with a very important life decision when we do so. The more we know, the wiser our decision will be, and the wiser our decision the more likely we are to have happiness instead of hurt as its outcome.

Brian was a physician who was almost forty-five, already divorced, and longing for children. While he was somewhat concerned about Connie's age (she was only twenty-six), he fell in love with her vivacity, beauty, and intelligence. The fact that he was a good friend of her older brother only seemed to make him more certain of his choice. But he was disturbed by the fact that Connie smoked marijuana and used alcohol a good deal more than he was comfortable with, and her substance abuse became a serious source of contention between them. Each time they fought about this Connie would agree to cut back, but within a few weeks, her good intentions were clouded by a haze of marijuana smoke or dissolved in an evening of too much wine.

Despite these problems, they decided to marry. Brian felt he was getting too old to start another relationship and wanted to give this one his all, and he convinced himself that marriage would help Connie settle down. Less than one year after their marriage they divorced. The only significant change that occurred that year was that Brian ran out of patience: Connie had made and broken too many promises. With his trust undermined, Brian was left a bit older, wiser, and considerably less hopeful about ever establishing a family.

TESTING THE WATERS

Courtship is comprised of a series of tests which we set up both consciously and unconsciously in order to observe and evaluate our partner's reactions. Is our partner sensitive, caring, and reliable? Do they mean what they say and say what they mean? Do they keep their word or do they make repeated excuses for why they have failed to do so? Do they lie and cover up or do they tell the truth?

It is the outcome of this process of testing that helps us determine whether we want to keep moving forward toward a deeper commitment. Because trust is the foundation of any healthy relationship, distrust and the lack of feeling safe curtails intimacy. With sufficient breach of trust, the relationship begins to falter. With each confirmation of trust, however, we are able to relax a bit more of our guardedness, reveal more of ourselves. If our partner still loves us after we have exposed our vulnerabilities and imperfections, a crucial test has been passed and we have begun the healing process.

Bennett's business began to fail during his courtship. Try as he might, a shifting business climate and an excess of competition made it impossible to turn a profit any longer and he was forced to close his restaurant. Although he had done his very best, he still felt guilty and embarrassed about the unfortunate turn of events; he felt as though he himself were the cause of the failure, and he feared that others would see it that way as well. But Andrea continued to be supportive. She saw his business difficulties as situational, having no bearing on his character, and she repeatedly told him so. Her reaction strengthened Bennett's trust in her and encouraged him to make plans to consider another business venture, one that ultimately proved to be quite successful.

Trust is the outgrowth of reliability, dependability, a measure of predictability, and a correspondence between words and deeds. These attributes provide relief from the energy-draining state of guarded vigilance, the result of wondering whether we are being told the whole truth, whether we can count on having our partner's loving support when we need it, and whether things will turn out as we had hoped they would. Will our partner be willing to compromise some of her or his own needs to assist us with ours? Will he or she rise to the occasion when an occasion arises?

"I had been going out with Stuart for about a year," said Jenny, "and while I was very much in love with him, there was always this cautionary voice inside. There were these peculiar ways in which he didn't come through, but nothing I could put my finger on. And then one day I had to work late and there was no one around to pick up my daughter so I called him and asked him if he would take her to dinner that night. Stuart was a dentist. He said he couldn't take my daughter because he was behind on reading his dental journals. Suddenly, something clicked inside me. I knew it was over. It was like an epiphany. His priorities were so different from mine. I understood why I never trusted him completely. I just didn't think I could count on him coming through for me."

A reasonable courtship period should also allow sufficient time to see how you weather your first big fight. Serious differences of opinion or a clash over style or attitude will occur before too long, even between two people who are very well suited to one another. How these frictions are resolved, however, will influence the viability of the relationship.

"When Patty and I had our first major argument she walked out without giving us a chance to resolve it," said Giorgio. "When I hadn't heard from her by the second day, I had the feeling that she was gone for good. Emotionally, I went nuts. I felt nauseous and I was quivering with anxiety. I said, 'Oh my God, I've opened my heart to her and now she's going to walk off just because we had one fight.' And *she* was the one who always said that as long as we could talk about things the relationship would make it."

But Patty's actions spoke louder than her words, as actions inevitably do. When she did talk to Giorgio some days later, it was to tell him that she hated emotional confrontations and she didn't think she could handle the relationship after all. Giorgio felt duped and was furious, but ultimately he was glad that he had learned this about Patty before the relationship had progressed even further.

Compulsive Testing

Since each of us has been hurt by various experiences and disappointments in life, none of us goes wholeheartedly and unguardedly into a relationship. The step-by-step testing that we carry out is a normal part of courtship and, in fact, quite often continues well into marriage, but it can be carried to the extreme. While scrutiny and analysis must play a role in evaluating a relationship during courtship, it should not play so large a role that it ends up killing the love that is there. And some tests can be so severe and dramatic that they do precisely that.

For instance, there are occasions when a woman may accidentally get pregnant as a way of testing her partner's commitment. In some cases such a pregnancy is the result of an oversight dictated by unconscious feelings or needs. But such a test can be so destructive that it can negate any positive potential and jolt the relationship into oblivion.

Eleanor, for instance, was absolutely certain that she couldn't possibly become pregnant on that Tuesday when she and Nick made love on the deserted beach where they had picnicked; she persuaded herself that it was a "safe" time and didn't bother to go back for her diaphragm which she had left in her travel case in the car. Nick and Eleanor had been dating each other exclusively for over two years, but each time Eleanor brought up the subject of getting engaged Nick would dodge it or tell her that he wasn't quite ready to make that move just yet, but soon, soon . . .

After Eleanor learned that she was pregnant, she told Nick, hoping that he would greet the news positively. Needless to say, he didn't. He was extremely upset and accused Eleanor of trying to trick him into marrying her. Of course, he was as responsible as she was for being negligent about using contraception, but he refused to see it that way. As one might expect, their relationship went rapidly downhill from there, with each of them feeling enraged because their trust had been betrayed. Eleanor eventually had an abortion and Nick never saw her again. Perhaps this dramatic and painful test put an end to something that was already doomed. Perhaps not. Eleanor and Nick would never know.

Some people come from backgrounds that taught them to be profoundly distrustful of anyone who wants to become emotionally close. Their personal histories, both recent and distant, have predisposed them to be exceedingly wary of intimate connections. In an attempt to quiet their distrust they create a seemingly endless series of tests that eventually overwhelms even the staunchest and most steadfast of lovers. These tests escalate in severity and difficulty until their partner inevitably "fails" in one way or another. This confirms what the tester "knew" all along: he or she was correct to be so distrustful.

This exaggerated testing is common among people who were abused as children or whose parents were alcoholics. At base, they feel that if they really allow themselves to be vulnerable or dependent upon someone, they are likely to be left in the lurch or injured in some other way. As a child Tara had been repeatedly sexually abused by her grandfather. "I think there's programming in my head that says that men are not to be trusted —*all* men," she confided. "I learned this while growing up, along with the notion that somehow I'm not really lovable. So I test it all the time. I say, 'How difficult can I be without him leaving me?' Ultimately, my partner gets fed up and leaves. I'm the one who's causing the problem, I know. But I can't seem to stop myself."

Obviously, this kind of compulsive testing is pathological and self-defeating. While it can be used to reconfirm the idea that no one can be trusted, justifying a return to the secure place of isolation that was inhabited during childhood, it precludes the development of real intimacy, which, paradoxically, is the only thing that can truly heal early wounds.

Are you chronically testing your partner because you have been consistently let down by others in your own life? Are the tests fair ones? Can they be "passed" or are there secret answers which only you can decipher? Do you require your partner to read your mind in order to prove that he or she truly loves you? Must your partner be virtually devoid of human imperfection and fallibility before you feel safe to love him or her?

Sometimes it is difficult to tell whether you are being unreasonable in your testing or whether your partner *is* really untrustworthy. In this case, repeated testing may express a desperate desire to give your partner the benefit of the doubt, even going so far as to stack the deck in his or her favor in the tests you set up. By decidedly providing ample opportunities for your partner to come through at least occasionally, you actually may be making a strenuous attempt to justify a relationship with someone who, in truth, is really unable to be there for you in the ways that you desire.

Donald had become infatuated with Karen, a vivaciously

beautiful dancer. Though something within him told him that he would end up being hurt, he refused to listen to that voice. Attempting to prove his intuition wrong, Donald continued to make small requests of Karen. "Please pick up some coffee on your way over tonight." "Schedule in Saturday afternoon for my niece's second birthday." Sometimes Karen would come through, but usually she wouldn't. When Donald was finally prepared to take a good look at the relationship, he realized that most of the time his requests seemed to "slip" Karen's mind, or else some "emergency" arose at the last minute that took precedence. Finally, he was left with little confidence that Karen could be relied on for any plans they made. Donald could no longer ignore his intuition, and he reluctantly said goodbye to one of the most exciting, yet at the same time infuriating, love affairs of his life.

THE DIMENSIONS OF COMPATIBILITY

During the courtship phase while you are exploring the issue of trust, larger questions concerning your basic compatibility can and should be examined in some depth. Discuss your future plans and life visions together. How do you see your lifestyle? What kind of income is necessary to support it? What kind of work do you plan to be engaged in? Where and how do you want to live? What are some of your most important likes and dislikes? What about children, avocations, travel? What are your time frames for attaining your various goals? Making your expectations and desires explicit requires thoughtful reflection about the picture you hold for your life. Even if many of your aspirations fail to materialize or are revised many times, these discussions will provide you with a clearer picture of the person who may become your life mate.

As a part of this dialogue, for instance, you may discover that your partner has always wanted to live in the country, and while living the big-city life now, is arranging for an early and peaceful rural retirement. Do you see this as an option for yourself or would you die of boredom reading in a hammock and tending the garden? You may both want children but with further discussion discover that one of you feels that a child should have a full-time stay-at-home mother while the other believes that a mother should have an active career as well.

If there are discrepancies between your two points of view, further discussions give you an opportunity to see how your partner thinks, how amenable each of you is to the kind of compromising that will be necessary as you create a life together. It gives you time to grow accustomed to certain ideas which at first may cause concern or consternation. You may, in fact, be surprised to find yourself comfortably embracing some of these ideas and enjoying them as much as if they had been your own to begin with.

Don't avoid bringing up "touchy" but important subjects even if you believe that they might disturb your partner somewhat and cast a temporary pall over the relationship. It is far better to deal with these issues now rather than later. If you delay a discussion of bothersome issues for too long, you open the door to further complications: feelings on both your parts can become exaggerated and facts can become distorted with the passage of time.

Heidi and Dick realized early in their courtship that religion was going to be a source of difficulty for them. According to Dick, Heidi was an "unquestioning Catholic." He himself had long been disenchanted with religious orthodoxy and was not willing to have their children raised as Catholics. Despite his opposition, Heidi eventually persuaded him to attend some classes in Catholic religious instruction—purely as an intellectual exercise, she assured him. Secretly, she hoped it would bring him back to the fold.

After attending a number of classes together, a curious thing happened: for the first time, Heidi began to feel uncomfortable with some of the tenets of Catholicism, especially the idea of original sin. She found it impossible to be at peace applying the concept to the children she hoped she and Dick would have. Her growing disenchantment with Catholicism, however, left her still longing for a spiritual orientation that she and Dick could share. Dick then began to explore Unitarianism, and as Heidi read the literature he brought home she felt herself drawn to the ideas expressed there. Eventually they both decided to become Unitarians and they married soon afterward— in the local Unitarian church.

What was remarkable about this couple was their willingness to be open and flexible in an area where they had substantial differences which potentially could have threatened the survival of their relationship. Each of them tried to remain open to the other's point of view even though it was not originally their own, and in the process a mutually satisfying resolution was arrived at quite naturally.

THE LABORATORY OF COURTSHIP

In the precourtship phase when you are simply dating, compromise is limited to fairly trivial issues, such as which movie to attend or whether or not you will split the bill for dinner. On the other hand, questions about religious differences, the ideal number of children to have, where and in what style to live, and so forth, may require negotiations of a major order. As you negotiate, you are not only provided with information about your partner's values and points of view, but, of equal importance, you are given the opportunity to observe the negotiating process itself. Is there give and take? How well do you listen to each other? Do you each respect the other's right to have different opinions and needs?

Since differences between people are inevitable, negotiation is a necessary and ongoing activity in the life of every couple living together, and unless you can successfully negotiate differences between yourself and your partner, these differences will become a barrier that will eventually block the development of intimacy. Creating opportunities to address difficult issues establishes a basis upon which trust can be built.

If you envision courtship as the "laboratory" for a relationship, you can use it as a place to conduct critical "experiments." Being your most authentic self, "warts and all," is the only real way to behave in a laboratory if you are each to learn what you need to know in order to make the most informed decision about your compatibility as life partners.

It is fairly easy to get disillusioned during the testing stages of courtship. Our expectations for having instant or thorough harmony with our partner may be very high—and very unrealistic. Relationships portrayed in the media are usually glamorized and present us with false images of marriage. In addition, many of our parents, in the desire to protect us from the harsh realities of life, hid their conflict behind closed doors, thereby adding to our distorted view of how a couple ought to function. We may come to believe that a happy and successful relationship can develop only if there is virtually no conflict or perhaps only the slightest amount. The greater the discrepancy between our initial expectations and the reality we are confronted with, the more unhappy and disappointed we are likely to be. But the problem lies less in the amount of conflict than in whether the resolution of the conflict is effective. Encountering difficulties which then get resolved is actually a positive sign of relationship durability.

FORECAST FOR THE FUTURE

The patterns of interaction which are established during the courtship period can affect the entire future of the relationship. If our approach is to sweep issues under the rug as fast as they appear, we are likely to create a superficially harmonious courtship leading to a later relationship during which that same rug is pulled out from under us.

Bella, now married almost fifty years, told us about an incident that occurred during her courtship with Adam that set the tone for their marriage. "Adam's father," she said, "was a handsome, tyrannical Russian whose way of controlling his feisty, beautiful wife was to turn stonily silent whenever there was a hint of conflict between them. Early on, when Adam and I had one of our first big quarrels, Adam turned his back on me and absolutely refused to discuss the matter. An image of his father passed before my eyes. I knew that I couldn't go through life with someone who would behave that way, but I was very much in love with him, so I said, 'Look, if we can't talk, we can't get married, because I won't marry you unless I know that whenever we come up against the hard places we can discuss them and work them out.' He knew I meant it. And even though talking is not easy for him, and he usually needs some time to calm down and get his thoughts straight, we have been able to talk things through ever since—if not immediately, then soon enough."

Adam and Bella had established a way of communicating that served them well throughout their married life. Early in their relationship Bella decided not to ignore the crucial issue of Adam's refusal to discuss things that were difficult. She confronted Adam with her feelings and thoughts while at the same time respecting his need to have time to come to terms with his own feelings first. Because she didn't attack him and provoke his defensiveness, he was willing to look at the problem at hand and make the necessary changes to alleviate it. Today they have a relaxed and loving relationship, the result of the healthy communication patterns established during their courtship period.

When he was eighteen, and only hours after he had first met Cindy, Ted told his mother that he had met the woman he was going to marry. This "love at first sight" relationship soon fell on hard times, however, and these difficulties inevitably loomed larger once the couple started living together. Cindy found Ted to be quite inconsiderate, apparently expecting her to do all the cooking and housework, despite the fact that they both had full-time jobs. And he frequently stayed out late after fencing practice without informing her of his plans.

Ted also felt dissatisfied with their relationship. Rock concerts, parties, and sporting events were activities that he enjoyed immensely, but Cindy was often resistant to going to them or frequently wanted to leave early when she did attend. Cindy hated crowds, and in fact was slightly claustrophobic. Ted felt hemmed in by her hang-ups. Both of them were seeing sides of the other person that hadn't presented much difficulty before they started living together.

One day, after a heated argument, Cindy informed Ted that she was moving out. Ted was relieved at first. He thought that at last he would be free to do what he wanted without having to be concerned about Cindy's reactions and her perpetual complaints. But within the first week after she left he felt a growing sense of loneliness and a longing for her. Cindy, who had been living temporarily at her best friend's apartment, had been morose and insomniac all week. Finally she called Ted and they had a long and tearful talk. For the next few days they discussed their feelings openly and listened to each other more seriously than they had ever done before.

When they began living together again, Ted made a vow to do more around the house and to spend more time doing some of the things Cindy enjoyed. Cindy, in turn, agreed to go to more of the music festivals and larger social events that Ted enjoyed. She noticed that her claustrophobic feelings were less of a problem once Ted promised that they could leave if she began to feel too uncomfortable.

Now, nearly twenty years later, Cindy and Ted would agree that what was a crisis during their courtship had become transformed into one of the mainstays of their relationship: the ability to listen better and respond more sensitively to each other's needs.

Trust: The Keystone of Intimacy

Trust is the very basis, the *sine qua non*, of intimacy. Being honest and forthright with one another, even when it is embarrassing or awkward, leads to the development of the deepest trust between people.

What we mean when we speak of trust within a relationship is nothing less than the capacity to be deeply vulnerable, open, and defenseless. When we trust someone we are most profoundly able to relax in their presence. We are unguarded with them. We feel safe. The epitome of trust occurs when we are able to be most *ourselves* in the presence of our loved one without having to put on airs or pretenses. We feel secure in our partner's love and in the knowledge that they will protect and care for us as thoroughly as they care for and protect themselves. And only to the extent that we *mutually* feel relaxed and secure are we able to be intimate with one another. Being truthful is central to establishing this trust.

For Phyllis and Sid, the issue of trust was broached on their first date. Sid told the story:

"I remember that we were having dinner at one of my favorite restaurants that first evening and we were discussing Watergate. Nixon, his lousy gang, and their dirty tricks were being exposed daily on TV. Dean had just finished testifying. Phyllis was talking about how appallingly easy it was for people in government to get away with lies. This eventually led to a discussion of duplicity in personal relationships as Phyllis spoke of how uncomfortable she was relating to a friend of hers who was conducting an affair behind her boyfriend's back.

"It was a strangely heavy discussion for a first date," said Sid, "but oddly enough, I found myself saying that I never wanted her to lie to me—and that I never would lie to her. I guess we knew somehow that the relationship had a future. Anyway, we established some very important ground rules then and we've been practicing them ever since—they're the backbone of our relationship: no one gets punished for telling the truth—even when it hurts."

Truth or Consequences

A most important point: if we are expecting the truth from our partner we must do all we can to make it safe for them to express it. Even when the truth is disturbing or painful, it helps to remind ourselves that it is better than carrying around the destructive emotional baggage that is produced by lying. Each person bears equal responsibility for keeping the truth alive as one of the highest priorities in a relationship.

Sometimes our insecurities tempt us to color or withhold the truth. We may try to hide our frailties, our fears, our areas of incompetence. We may not have learned to trust our partner with our imperfections because we fear rejection, easily among the most universal of fears despite the fact that many of us feel even *more* loving of our partner when we become aware of their foibles. We can choose to see our partner's minor flaws as endearing; often they allow us to be helpful in ways that make us feel good about ourselves, and simultaneously give us permission to accept our own deficiencies.

But it is one thing to know and accept our partner's "feet of clay" and quite another to discover that we have been duped or deceived. Deception and lies are *the* most corrosive influences on love and intimacy.

Expectations play an important role in this regard and can have a great effect on a relationship's promise and prospect. If we expect much more than we are given, either because of our own romanticized vision or due to our partner's salesmanship, we are apt to be far more disappointed and hurt in the future than if we know, at least in a general sense, what we can honestly expect from the beginning. The more honest we both are, neither overstating our abilities or good qualities nor diminishing or exaggerating our faults, the less likely either of us is to be disappointed in the end.

When Wyatt first met Emmy he learned that skiing was one of her passions. On their first date, he implied that he enjoyed skiing immensely, although he hadn't had much experience. In fact he had never skied in his life, but he was a good athlete and believed that he could learn the sport easily enough. He was very eager to impress Emmy in any way he could, so he quietly disappeared and took skiing lessons in Colorado for a week. He practiced hard every day and came back fully equipped and able to navigate a slope of medium difficulty.

A few weeks later, the two of them went off skiing. They had a great time and Emmy looked forward to skiing as one of their shared activities. Unfortunately, during their third trip, when the novelty had worn off, Wyatt realized that this was just not his sport. He felt irked by the high cost involved and all the fancy gear it required; he didn't like the cold and he was impatient with his progress. In addition, he felt competitively inferior to Emmy on the slopes.

When Wyatt started making excuses not to go skiing, Emmy felt duped. Had he initially told her that he had never skied but was willing to give it a try, she would have been prepared from the start to accept a relationship in which skiing might not be high among their shared activities. Rather than appreciating how desperately Wyatt wanted to please and impress her, Emmy was left with the feeling that she couldn't really trust what he told her. She began to wonder what other unpleasant surprises lay in store and began, self-protectively, to pull back from him.

In general, game playing, petty dishonesty, and other forms of deviousness can cause serious injury to any relationship, but especially to a new and developing one. Be wary of partners who ask you to cover for them with others; chances are that they will find others to cover for *them* as they deceive you. It is usually dangerous to believe that you will be the significant exception to the patterns your partner has established in previous relationships, especially if he or she was dishonest in them.

The Dances of Courtship

The dance of courtship moves irregularly back and forth as it progresses through the inevitable maze of exploratory tests. When successfully negotiated, each challenge brings the couple closer. When qualities or attributes are discovered which do not fit one's fantasied image of the perfect partner, or when tests are failed, or, quite often, when the intimacy becomes too great or the relationship develops too quickly, a retreat from intimacy occurs. This dance of moving closer, moving apart, two steps closer, one step back, is the most common ritual of courtship, a natural process in which two people begin to discover each other, gradually overcoming their inhibitions and learned distrust as they strive to resolve their past hurts and allow the relationship to deepen.

The person who is most cautious and who moves most slowly, will ultimately establish both the pace of the relationship's development as well as the level of commitment, a level the other cannot surpass without jeopardy.

Problems can occur when each person's pacing is different, when one wants to move to a greater depth of intimacy more quickly than the other. Although men and women are equally likely to determine the pace, at least on the overt level, it has generally been more common in our culture for the man to take the role of the pacesetter initially: he being the pursuer, she being the pursued. Some men feel uncomfortable, even threatened, if they sense that the woman is taking over this unconsciously assumed domain.

Sandy was quite a confident and self-assured person. She was the president of her own business and was used to taking command of situations and making decisions for herself and others. She was no shrinking violet when she saw a man she was attracted to, and she didn't hesitate to call or invite him to a particular event once it became clear that mutual interest had been established. Over the years, however, she learned to temper her natural enthusiasm, since she had been criticized on a number of occasions for exerting too much control over the relationship. Though Sandy's style may have been too assertive for some men, at least part of the negative reaction it generated was due to an idea that most children in our culture learn while growing up: in any dance, the dance of courtship included, boys lead and girls follow. Interfering with these role expectations can be problematic on a gut level for both sexes, even though they may be intellectually enlightened about stereotyping and sex roles.

Sometimes both partners collude in preventing the relationship from deepening. It is no longer two steps forward, one step back, but what we would call the Dance of the Middle Distance—a maneuver in which both people work in tandem to maintain a constant or fixed position vis-à-vis one another, neither too intimate nor too distant. As one person puts up roadblocks or becomes less available, the second pursues or behaves seductively or invitingly. Then, when the first person moves forward again in response, the second person retreats. In this way neither substantial progress nor regress occurs. The most salient feature of the dance of the middle distance is that the partners are rarely or never in the same place at the same time with regard to their feelings about the relationship. Each person may feel intense love for the other but this usually occurs when the other is least available or least interested. Over time, the roles continue to shift back and forth, as each takes her or his turn as both pursuer and pursued.

Maurice had led quite an active social life since his divorce nearly five years earlier. He had just completed his last alimony payment to his ex-wife and had been dating a number of attractive women, yet he began to grow increasingly weary of the dating game.

When his cousin introduced him to a realtor in her office he thought that at last he had met the woman of his dreams—he was captivated by her beauty, charm and intelligence. Nola was crazy about him, too, and their relationship took off briskly. Before long they were spending weekends together and seeing each other fairly exclusively, though they hadn't really formalized their relationship.

It was a puzzle to both of them that despite what seemed to be a close and passionate relationship, they fought regularly and tempestuously over relatively trivial matters.

On one occasion, Maurice was enthusiastically planning a special birthday weekend out of town for Nola when he learned that she had just accepted a dinner date from a new agent in her office. Even though they had not agreed to date exclusively, Maurice felt hurt and jealous. He canceled the weekend plans and they quarreled for days.

Nola was incensed at his reaction. "You don't own me," she said. "And besides, every time I try to get more serious you evaporate and I don't hear from you for days." Maurice knew she was telling the truth. And while he was quite convinced that he loved her, his own behavior puzzled him.

Nola, too, shared many of the same perplexing feelings. She told her best friend that she wished Maurice would ask her to marry him, yet each time he started getting "cozy," talking about their future, a strange discomfort would rise within her and before long, she would find herself starting another quarrel, flinging epithets, slamming doors, until they ended up going their separate ways.

After a time the dust would settle. Both of them, beset by growing feelings of loneliness and longing, hoped the other would call, and one of them inevitably did, on some pretext or another. Apologies would be made, tenderness would reemerge, they would make passionate love . . . and in a short while they would be embroiled in yet another painful altercation.

Both Maurice and Nola were quite unaware that they were colluding in the dance of the middle distance. After two years of this on-again, off-again behavior they decided impulsively to "solve things" by getting married.

Within four months they were separated. For the first time

in years they were in agreement. Their relationship was not meant to be. Unfortunately, like many couples, they needed to get married, in order, finally, to separate.

Whether it is only one person who is reticent, or whether both people are working together to prevent the relationship from progressing, a relationship that does not progress will soon begin to atrophy. As Woody Allen once said, "A relationship is like a shark; if it doesn't keep moving, it dies."

After a sufficient time of doing the "middle distance waltz" one partner will usually pressure the other either to move forward or to end the relationship. Some people seem to require this kind of ultimatum in order finally to make a commitment. Others need encouragement in order to decide to leave a relationship that is not quite right. In time the courtship period must come to an end as the couple either moves forward to a deeper commitment, backward to concluding the relationship, or laterally, by transforming the relationship from a love relationship into a nonromantic friendship.

A Courtship of a Different Color

Most of the courtship patterns we have been describing thus far are typical of love affairs that open with powerful intensity, a thrilling infatuation that is magnetic and enrapturing. However, couples who first get to know each other as friends, with the romantic and sexual elements well in the background, unexpressed or not even experienced, often conduct the testing phase quite differently. In these situations a caring friendship has an opportunity to flourish without the common anxieties or intensity of passionate romance. The two people spend meaningful time together, confide in each other, and come to trust and rely on one another, as good friends do. Gradually and without much pressure, they become familiar with each other's character and relaxed in each other's presence.

Then, at a later date, the relationship, surprisingly, may become suffused with the excitement of courtship: the passion that was waiting in the wings moves to center stage. A new depth of connectedness is revealed. Because the friendship is already well developed, these relationships often achieve a degree of intimacy with fewer dramatic or disturbing adjustments. When the qualities of friendship and companionship are combined with those of sexual and romantic passion, we have the very best of all possible worlds. Such occurrences are not all that rare. Many couples who start out as friends wonder how they could have been so oblivious to—or only fleetingly aware of—the chemistry between them.

Since expectations often determine outcome, if we are only concerned with experiencing the intense and captivating passion of falling head over heels in love at the start, we may overlook a very promising relationship opportunity because it doesn't begin with a bang.

As Carla confided, "Blake and I had a genuine friendship. We shared a sense of humor, and we trusted each other deeply. Even our sexual relationship was good. But I was very young, looking for something more flashy, something new and mysterious, and, I confess, I was a bit of a junkie for stormy, dramatically romantic connections. I think that the problem was timing. If I were to meet Blake today, I would be delighted with the relationship."

Obviously, not all friendships can be transformed into love relationships. For some people, the spark, the chemistry, the possibility of sexual connection, is just not there—not even latently. Yet we can rarely be absolutely sure in advance that the potential for this kind of transformation doesn't exist. If there is a possibility, it may well be worth considering: the most satisfying and enduring relationships are those between people who truly feel that they are each other's best friend.

Above all, we should not move forward into marriage or its equivalent with anyone who is *not* at least our dear friend, and it is supremely foolish to cheat ourselves of the time it may take to develop a deep friendship with our mate-to-be *before* we make a commitment to spend the future together.

For most of us, at least the lucky ones, the future is a long, long time. Spending it with someone who is not a trusted friend can make it seem like a miserable eternity.

4

You Say Tomato,
I Say Tomahto

The Roots of Conflict

. . . mature love is union under the condition of preserving one's integrity, one's individuality.

—ERICH FROMM,
The Art of Loving

In the first months of a relationship when love is abloom and we are viewing our partner through rose-colored glasses it is hard to imagine that life won't always be this way: a dream come true and a bit of heaven on earth. But it is only a matter of time before this honeymoon phase of the courtship period comes to an end, and as elements of the real person behind the fantasy image are gradually revealed, reality replaces the dream.

During the courtship period, when we are creating that third entity called "a couple," we each bring our own personal baggage to the venture: our values, comforts and discomforts, defenses, points of view, anxieties, distortions, habits, and the like, to bear on every aspect of the new partnership.

More often than not, we discover things about our partner that we hadn't anticipated, both positive and negative, attractive and unattractive. Certain of these qualities transport us to new horizons, expanding our possibilities, stimulating our growth; others, of course, may prove to be the root of potentially serious conflict, especially that class of conflict which is the most basic and common to intimate relationships: power struggles.

POWER STRUGGLES

Differences in attitude and personal style are a function of both heredity and learning. Once these personal patterns are set—and they continue to become more firmly set throughout our lives—we tend to use them as standards to which we expect our partner to conform. But our partner inevitably resists this pressure to change, for they, too, are steadfastly trying to make us more like they are. It is the process of handling these differences—differences in needs, style, personal philosophy, ways of handling money, sex, and so on—that becomes the source of the most frequent and destructive strife in relationships. Consequently, negotiations over control, or power, or say-so, are *always* involved in the process of forming a couple, and these negotiations, obviously, are most difficult where the differences between the two people are greatest or least reconcilable.

For example, Dean grew up in a family where money was tight; every penny was accounted for and no one ever spent it frivolously. Melody's family always had more than enough money, and spending it on pleasures was a way of life; no one thought twice about indulging their whims. Melody and Dean had roughly equivalent incomes, and since they had agreed to split expenses, deciding on such simple matters as marketing for food or what to do on an evening out became a ready source of tension and conflict. They often found themselves engaged in a power struggle over whose desires would prevail. Dean was more comfortable with an inexpensive restaurant and a movie; he didn't want to be made anxious by what he considered to be overspending, pushing his budget too close to its limit. Melody preferred the symphony or the theater and a fancier restaurant; she felt deprived and irked by what she considered Dean's miserly approach. Each person had an elaborate set of rationalizations justifying their own point of view. But their basic disagreement could not be resolved by debate because the issue really revolved around each person's historically based comfort level regarding the spending of money.

Differences between partners necessarily exist on many levels. Fireworks can easily occur when a person who is predominantly controlled and logical is coupled with an emotional, intuitive partner, an introvert with an extrovert, a homebody with one who much prefers the outdoors, a risk taker with a cautious one, a spontaneous person with one who is deliberate and methodical. And, of course, there are the perennial arguments between the fastidious person and the slob, the optimist and the pessimist, or the one who craves sex once a day versus the one who tolerates it once a week.

Since these disparities between people can cause problems, it might seem that the ideal solution to marital happiness would be to find a partner who is most like one's self in as many ways as possible. But that is actually far from true. For one thing, when partners have very similar personalities there is an increased potential for their weaknesses to combine and create exaggerations or destructive imbalances within the relationship, such as when both people are fiscally irresponsible or when both people are prone to impulsive temper outbursts. As one man said, "If we were both like I am, things would never get done, and if we were both more like she is, we would constantly be at each other's throats." In addition, sameness can also more easily lead to boredom and its inherent problems.

CORRECTIVE MEASURES

For the most part, it is not whether the partners are similar or dissimilar that accounts for the ultimate success or failure of the relationship; it is how these differences are understood and managed that determine whether they will lead to a broader and stronger relationship rather than a morass of endless pain and conflict.

Vive la différence

As two individuals embark upon a life together, room to express each of their needs and personalities must be made within the relationship if intimacy-destroying power struggles are to be eliminated. Accomplishing this goal requires both people to accept a new point of view. Rather than seeing differences between ourselves as threats that need to be reduced and removed, we need to focus on the color and richness these differences add to our lives and appreciate how the expression of diverse opinions and viewpoints can invigorate a relationship.

While an overabundance of fairly radical differences can easily lead to serious problems, marked differences can also be stimulating, enabling both people to learn from each other. The relevant question becomes: How can the ways in which my partner and I differ play a useful role in our relationship?

Donna was a travel agent who was getting bored with her work. When a new job became available, one specializing in arranging innovative tours, she spent months agonizing over its pros and cons. Each time she saw Mark she would obsess over the details involved in the job change. Mark hated listening to Donna's endless picayune analyses. He couldn't understand why she didn't just decide to do it and work out the problems as she went along. He felt impatient and irritated with the way she labored over decisions.

Contrastingly, Mark's impulsiveness created the most distressing anxiety for Donna, like the time he decided to buy a duplex without obtaining a contractor's report in advance. She didn't sleep well for weeks as she imagined all the structural defects that might surface later.

This dichotomy of behavioral styles was a major source of conflict between Mark and Donna for the first year of their relationship. However, once they learned to appreciate the benefits of the other person's approach, the differences became assets. Mark found it helpful to bounce his ideas off Donna for her closer examination and, with Mark's support, Donna found the courage to take more chances with her life.

Jean and Elliot met while working in the same small business. They, too, were quite divergent in their approach to life; Jean was an eternal optimist, almost to the point of being a Pollyanna, while Elliot was convinced that danger lurked around every corner. Their differences were highlighted when they played bridge. Jean thought that Elliot almost always underbid his hand, and Elliot constantly accused Jean of overbidding hers. But when Elliot got bogged down with business problems, Jean's optimistic outlook reenergized him; when Jean's optimism was unrealistically high, Elliot's ability to foresee potential problems helped them avoid a number of bad business deals. They did find other partners for bridge, however, a relatively small sacrifice in the grand scheme of things.

In the best of all worlds, the individuals in a couple complement one another. Their differences enhance the relationship. When we are able to appreciate the potential gain that can result from variations in personal styles, and we acknowledge each person's respective contribution to particular areas of the relationship, we reduce the destructive battles for control. A more cooperative spirit can then emerge, one which may eventually lead to a refreshing and generative balance between partners.

The viewpoint we are espousing here is similar to that of "hybrid vigor" in genetics. Individuals with differing qualities combine to produce a more vigorous and, in many ways, superior result. For example, there are certain trees that produce abundant amounts of fruit, but the fruit is not particularly sweet. A second tree produces sweet fruit, but in meager amounts. By crossing the two trees a variety is produced that yields copious amounts of flavorful fruit. (Sometimes, of course, experiments backfire. A scientist, crossing a herring with a jellyfish in the hope of creating a boneless herring, ended up with a bony jellyfish!)

Healthy relationships embrace differences, find room for their expression, and appreciate the unique and helpful contributions that can be made by a partner who is not one's clone. There are trade-offs, each person contributing his or her separate strengths to the whole: he rarely cooks, but when the car breaks down, he fixes it; she assumes responsibility for planning the vacations and keeping their social life active, but he arranges for a good deal of their entertainment, buying tickets to shows and making reservations at restaurants.

"Keeping score" of contributions to the relationship is a destructive process because as "scorekeeper," your point of view is likely to be biased in favor of yourself, and your analysis is almost certainly going to reveal that your partner is giving less to the relationship. It is unreasonable to judge your partner by measuring her or him against *your* strengths; evaluate your partner according to his or her own strengths if you want to avoid painful conflict. Each of us wants to be appreciated for our specific contributions, and no one benefits when their weaknesses or shortcomings become the principal focus of attention.

Luke and Susanna, for instance, were both rather strong-minded and controlling in their own ways, so their collaboration on the book they were writing could have become a nightmare of impeded efforts and quarrels over the endless decisions about what to say and how to say it. Instead, it turned out to be a relatively pleasant task because they recognized their individual strengths and areas of interest and divided the writing accordingly.

Susanna could deal with great quantities of diverse information, consolidating and organizing it logically and coherently. She enjoyed writing the first draft but hated the details of endless rewriting. Luke, on the other hand, loved working with words, honing each sentence, thinking about the proper punctuation, yet confronting the blank page caused him a good deal of anxiety. Luke was strong on theoretical issues; Susanna excelled at providing practical illustrations that illuminated the concepts being discussed.

While collaborating, Luke had to refrain from criticizing Susanna's sentence structure; he was grateful and appreciative of the fact that he was given a draft from which to work. For her part, Susanna had to keep complaints about Luke's reorganization to herself and simply rework his revision, appreciating his attention to the details of language and theory.

The Attraction of Opposites

We may be drawn to a particular person mainly *because* they possess a quality we admire which is either absent or not very well developed in ourselves. On some level, we may hope that a bit of that very quality will rub off on us—perhaps we will become more intellectual, more organized, or have a broader social life if we connect with them. Additionally, our sense of security may be enhanced by seeking out a partner who is more responsible, or more stable, more emotionally alive, or more financially savvy than we know ourselves to be.

Later in the relationship, however, it is quite common that the very attributes that drew us to our loved one in the first place become irritants. Take the man, for instance, who guides his life by what he believes to be the rules of logic and careful reasoning. He picks his opposite, a woman who operates principally by way of her feelings and intuition. Both have a great deal to learn from one another, and that is part of their mutual attraction. As the relationship progresses, however, she becomes infuriated when he dismisses her feelings as being irrational and foolish, imploring her to be more logical. He, on the other hand, becomes incensed when she argues that he is more like a computer than a human being, and criticizes him for not showing more spontaneity.

Jeffrey and Lacy provide a good illustration of the way opposites can both attract and repel us. Jeffrey was captivated by Lacy's lively, passionate nature. He found her to be delightfully unpredictable in ways that stimulated him. "I think I'm a little constricted in some ways," he reported. "I know it's a bit of a stereotype: overcontrolled man and wild woman, but I'm afraid there's a lot of truth in it as far as our relationship goes. She's the emotional vice president, if you will. But there are times when her emotionality can drive me up the wall. She'll *hate* a movie or someone we've met at a party and she'll go on and on about it. It makes me squirm when she gets intense like that so I'll try to quiet her down, and before you know it she's even more worked up, turning some of that anger on me."

Remembering to appreciate what it was that attracted you to your partner in the first place can help you to respond in ways that are more accepting, ways that promote healing and reduce conflict. For example, if Jeffrey could find a way to contain his anxiety and just let Lacy express herself fully rather than "help" her learn to control her feelings better, her anger might dissipate rather quickly. Jeffrey's attempt to control Lacy actually fuels her intensity. She feels criticized and Jeffrey feels frustrated, and no one benefits.

Small differences can become exaggerated as they play off each other. Belinda and Andy continued to confuse and hurt one another before they fully understood the destructive process within which they were enmeshed. When Belinda was upset she tended to withdraw into herself, becoming emotionally unavailable and distant. Andy's natural response to being upset was just the opposite: he would feel a great need for contact, verbal as well as physical. Belinda repeatedly felt suffocated by Andy's need for closeness at times when things were strained between them, while Andy felt abandoned by Belinda's need for distance at those times. A vicious cycle would then result: Belinda's withdrawal provoked Andy to move closer, which then made Belinda close down even more; this then caused Andy to become more demanding, until the mounting tension would eventuate in a violent argument. At times these disturbances could take a week or more to resolve.

Once Belinda and Andy understood and accepted the radically different ways in which they dealt with emotional anxieties, they became much less threatened by these differences, and the quality of their relationship improved dramatically.

"Upsides" and "Downsides"

To change the way you view differences within your relationship, try looking at all the dimensions of your mate's personality with an open mind. Rather than being judgmental about your partner's "faults," concentrate on identifying your partner's *strengths*. Then see if the behavior that you find irritating is actually the "downside" of a behavior or personality component that you like or appreciate (its "upside"), even one that may have attracted you to your partner in the first place. For example, in Belinda and Andy's case, Belinda may have been attracted to Andy partially because he was so nurturing and physical; Andy may have chosen Belinda partly because her self-sufficiency made him feel more secure.

Nancy had a generous and giving nature that delighted Barry, making him feel special and well cared for, but when a local charity drive became, for a time, the major beneficiary of her generosity, Barry felt deprived and was peeved with her.

Madge loved William's sensitive and gentle manner, but found herself angry because he didn't wield power in ways that typified the more traditional male role, which would have made her feel more protected.

Lewis was certain before he met Dahlia that he wanted to be with an independent woman who had her own career, but he was upset when she had to reschedule their time together because of her work commitments.

Caitlin loved Jacob's athleticism and his adventurous, go-for-it attitude, but she found herself exhausted and irritated as she tried to keep up with him when they hiked, golfed, or played tennis together.

Ari felt secure because of Leslie's loyalty, protectiveness, and strong affection, but her possessiveness drove him crazy.

Jody felt comfortable with Jason's quiet demeanor; it allowed her time to think and find her own center. But when he wouldn't bring up issues that were bothering him until they had totally gotten out of hand, she wanted to wring his neck.

Viola admired Wayne's business acumen, but hated his conservative nature.

It stands to reason that any individual trait which is strongly represented in a personality is very likely to preclude the presence of certain other traits that are in opposition to it. No one has it all, not on this planet anyway, and no one can possibly give us *everything* we want or need.

It would be folly, for example, to expect someone for whom a successful career depends on the excellence of their analytic skills and their adversarial power to be uncritically accepting of the ideas of others when they get home. The carefree, spontaneous person may be more irresponsible than we'd like; the focused, practical, down-to-earth careerist may come up with few romantic suggestions for that special occasion.

Every personality style has positive as well as negative components. For example, whenever Tamara packed for a vacation, she spent weeks thinking about it, becoming totally consumed by the task. The level of stress she experienced was considerable, but she anticipated every item needed for their vacation. Don, on the other hand, had a *laissez-faire* attitude that led to a stress-free packing experience, tossing things together at the last minute, but when he arrived at his destination he often discovered that he had forgotten a number of items that he wished he had taken.

It helps to remember that if your partner were different in the ways you would prefer, they would also be different in ways that you would *not* prefer, losing qualities they now possess which you hold dear. For example, when Pete was asked what he would like to change about Sylvia, he replied that he wished she were more tactful and less direct. But after thinking about it a moment longer, he reconsidered. "Her blunt honesty puts some people off, but they tend to be people who are not very honest themselves," he said. "So maybe that's good protection for me, because I'm gullible enough to believe anything."

Feet of Clay

Taking stock of our own liabilities helps to keep our partner's weak points in perspective. A sign we recently saw stated, "When searching for faults use a mirror, not a telescope." We all have "feet of clay," however; despite our own imperfections we each still feel that we have the right to a partner's love and support. Our partner has the same right. As one woman said about her lover, "He's somewhat overweight, but so what? I believe everybody has one 'give-me' and I guess that's his. I mean, if that's the only thing I have to 'give' him, I consider myself lucky. You have to expect to put up with certain things when you love someone; there are always trade-offs to be made."

The capacity to accept information and learn from our partner requires a degree of self-assurance and an ability to acknowledge our *own* weaknesses and imperfections. If we cannot do this, if we are embarrassed, guilty, or ashamed about a part of ourselves, we may try to bolster our own image by attempting to prove our partner wrong in circumstances where there really is no "right" or "wrong," only a set of varying approaches. When this happens, everyone loses.

VULNERABILITIES AND SENSITIVITIES

In addition to difficulties which may arise out of our differences, each of us has sensitivities that can become sources of conflict. Personal vulnerabilities and physical or emotional frailties can lead to problems if they are ignored or dealt with insensitively.

Certain of these limitations are probably based in our biological makeup. Cleo was very appreciative of Judd's attitude about her handicap: "I'm dyslexic," she told us, "which means that I had a lot of self-doubt while growing up. My brothers and even my son tease me, but Judd never does. He never takes advantage of my difficulties. When I have trouble pronouncing certain words, he is patient and tries to help me—I don't feel criticized, I feel supported."

Some of us are quite easily affected by our changing physical states—becoming very uncomfortable or cranky when we are too tired, too cold, or too hungry—and we need to have these needs attended to without being judged and made to feel as though there is something wrong with us. Many women suffer from extreme premenstrual symptoms. If the symptoms can't be alleviated, it is helpful for the couple to keep a calendar with the next distress period highlighted so that allowances can be made for certain physiologically based emotional reactions that may occur during that time.

Men and women both have mood swings and bad days at the office, become irritable and exhausted, and need their share of tender loving care and forbearance. Allowances must be made for each and every one of us from time to time.

Hot Buttons

Many areas of vulnerability reflect deeper psychological issues that have their foundation in one's early life. Martha seemed to be ultrasensitive when Tad was late for dinner. At work there was a tendency for things to come up at the last minute. Tad was inclined to underestimate his arrival time, but this was actually the by-product of his desire to be home early and to please Martha, so he had a hard time understanding the intensity of her response when he was late.

Despite constant rehashing, this issue was not resolved, and it appeared to be on the verge of destroying their young relationship. Finally, Martha realized that the intense feelings she experienced while waiting for Tad were oddly familiar ones. She recalled that her father, whom she considered to be a workaholic, would often return home very late from his office. She remembered feeling abandoned by him as she waited for his arrival each evening, often having to go to bed before he ever made it home. Ultimately her parents divorced and her father married his secretary. It's not difficult to see how this part of Martha's personal history colored her reactions to Tad's tardiness. Once Tad understood how his behavior triggered Martha's insecurity he took greater care to be more realistic about his expected time of arrival.

If your partner becomes inordinately or chronically upset by a particular behavior on your part it is a clear signal that serious thought and attention need to be given to the deeper roots of these reactions. Even though your behavior appears to be benign, you are probably touching off one of his or her "hot buttons," a sensitivity that cannot be dismissed or ignored without causing harm to the relationship.

In the year and a half that they had been dating, Jay and Vanessa had taken three vacations together. During each one of these they had a quarrel on the second or third day that resulted in their going off in separate directions for a number of hours and talking only minimally to each other for the following day or so. When they finally began to discuss the pattern that had emerged and the feelings behind it, Jay came to realize that he started each vacation by trying to accommodate to Vanessa's needs, many of which were quite different from his. His own preference was first to get settled, staying close to home base and relaxing, but instead he would accompany Vanessa, who preferred to go out exploring and sightseeing first and to settle down later. After a few days of this, Jay would start to feel desperate, fearing that the vacation would soon be over without his having had time for himself. He had grown up in a poor family and had never even taken a vacation until he was in his late twenties, so time away was particularly precious to him. Once Vanessa understood this she made sure to keep the first few days of the vacation available for Jay to relax while she occupied herself in other ways. With his vacation needs taken care of, Jay not only lost his feeling of desperation but was much more emotionally and physically available to Vanessa for the remainder of their time together.

CORRECTIVE MEASURES

Because our limitations and areas of sensitivity are usually not under conscious control, they are difficult to change. When our partner measures and appraises our behavior and reactions against their own standards, we usually feel criticized, which makes us even more defensive and therefore less likely to change. Genuine and effective change is the by-product of a healing attitude, and healing is not promoted by coercion, judgment, threat, insult, or invidious comparisons.

Only when we feel safe can we begin to lower our defenses enough to explore the issues at hand. It is worth remembering that each area of sensitivity has its own idiosyncratic cause and rationale. It cannot simply be dismissed. Discovering the *basis* of the sensitivity is what is needed, so that both partners can be more understanding. This humane attitude then becomes the prologue to change.

Serena had repeatedly asked Patrick to fix the door to her apartment, and even though he had agreed to do so he continued to procrastinate. Finally she lost patience and angrily criticized him for being lazy, for not keeping his promises. She was surprised when he responded angrily in return: she had expected him to be apologetic and contrite.

"I really don't know how to fix the damn thing," he confessed, "but you always expect me to know these things just because I'm a man!"

As they talked further, Serena discovered that not being able to live up to someone's expectations was a very charged issue for Patrick. Both his mother and father had made many unrealistic demands on him during his childhood, and punished him by coldly withdrawing their affection whenever he was unable to meet them. Consequently he had a great fear that if he disappointed Serena she would no longer care about him.

Once Serena understood this part of Patrick's background she was able to alter her approach when making requests of him. She would, for instance, give him an "out" by suggesting that she call in a repair person first. And if he took the project on, she would be pleasant and affectionate with him just for trying to help, regardless of whether or not he succeeded.

Joe grew up in relative affluence. Inherited money coupled with his father's successful business permitted him and his siblings the indulgence of charging expenses to a credit card which they each were given on their eighteenth birthday. Georgia's family, though not wealthy, was comfortably well off until her father died and her mother had to go back to work in order to make ends meet. Hard times had followed her father's death, but with a new frugality the family managed reasonably well.

Whenever Joe decided to buy things by borrowing against his credit line, Georgia experienced a pang of discomfort. Joe's considerable indebtedness was a great concern to Georgia and actually was a deterrent to her becoming more committed to the relationship. Joe was unperturbed by his large monthly interest payments. To him, her concerns seemed totally unfounded and exaggerated. "After all," he argued, "being in debt is a cornerstone of capitalism."

One issue that they continued to argue about had to do with

a beat-up old car that Joe owned, which barely ran and which he seldom used. Georgia wanted him to sell it. She thought keeping the car and paying insurance on it was a waste of money, while its sale could help Joe reduce his indebtedness. Joe, however, felt that he had more important things to do with his time than sell the car. It wasn't until he understood how Georgia's history was connected to her financial anxieties that he decided to offer to let her sell the car for him in return for splitting the profits, a solution that provided additional money for both of them while at the same time eliminating the basis for a major ongoing quarrel.

Claire was chronically irritated and frustrated by Ben's difficulty with decision making: he would spend an inordinate amount of time deliberating over the most insignificant matters. It wasn't until she met Ben's mother and saw how incredibly controlling she was—still making decisions for him, constantly telling him what to feel and think—that she could appreciate why Ben had as much trouble with decision making as he did.

Sid could never joke about sex or be playful in bed. This annoyed Valerie, who considered him to be unbearably "uptight," until she learned that his ex-wife had frequently humiliated him by sarcastically demeaning his sexual performance in front of friends.

Empathy

Empathy provides the key to understanding our partner's sensibilities, opening the way for compromise and growth.

Empathy results from a process in which we willingly suspend our own viewpoint momentarily and enter into the other person's world, trying to see things as *they* see them, operating under *their* assumptions, crediting *them* with as much right and reason as we usually credit ourselves. The willingness and ability to put aside what may be our own opposing and often strongly held beliefs and judgments in order to enter the other person's world is not always easy to achieve, but it is necessary if we hope to give genuine validity to the way our partner feels and thinks.

Empathy is the most profound form of loving another person: the very core of love. It is not to be confused with *sympathy*, in which you feel *for* someone, rather than <u>*with*</u> them. In sympathy you are outside the other person, looking in at them. In <u>empathy you are "inside" the other person, looking at the world through their eyes.</u> Empathy is what the French call *"la participation mystique,"* the mystical sharing.

When you can empathize with your partner's position or feelings, even though, perhaps, you consider them to be rather exaggerated, inappropriate, or even erroneous, you help your partner to feel more understood, cared for, secure, relaxed, loved.

Ironically, one of Max and Ginette's running arguments arose out of Ginette's extremely empathic nature. She could readily empathize with nearly anyone, sometimes to the extent of losing her own point of view. Whenever they went to a movie together and the film focused on a character's emotional pain, Ginette would identify so strongly with that character that the only way she could relieve the tension for herself was by talking, distracting Max and interfering with his enjoyment. Max began to dread going to the movies with her. He would testily warn her in advance not to talk. Despite her best intentions, however, the words just seemed to slip out as the film's tension mounted. When Max finally understood that Ginette's talking was an indication of her genuine emotional discomfort, he felt his angry impatience subsiding. Her talking didn't bother him any less, he just handled it differently. Instead of angrily hushing her, he silently patted her gently on her knee whenever she spoke, or he held her hand. Max's new response was comforting to Ginette. She, in turn, made an effort to find a way of reducing the tension she felt so that she wouldn't annoy him, ultimately discovering that if she talked silently to herself she no longer felt the need to voice the words aloud. In this way, empathy formed the basis for change.

The human mind is naturally inclined toward seeing itself as the center of the universe. As a result, both people in a relationship frequently distort or interpret what is going on in their immediate environment as being directed specifically with them in mind. This self-indulgent point of view can be the source of endless strife. However, when empathy becomes an integral part of daily interactions it can free a relationship of the serious and frequent conflict that arises from these commonplace distortions. Then, rather than interpreting our partner's behavior as being designed to hurt or provoke *us*, we can see that it probably has little to do with us at all.

Natalia, for example, would occasionally lapse into silent periods during which she would be reflective and self-absorbed. Mason believed that her retreat was designed to punish him. He believed she was giving him the cold shoulder and she felt shut out. His mother, he later recalled, actually did punish him by withdrawing when she was displeased, so Natalia's behavior brought up old feelings. Numerous and excruciating arguments had resulted when Mason would, with total conviction, accuse Natalia of being angry with him and refusing to admit it. Natalia would be confused by these seemingly senseless accusations and would protest that she wasn't doing what Mason said she was, wasn't acting out of anger at all. But Mason's own vulnerabilities and the distortions that arose from the punitive withdrawals he had experienced in his early life made him feel absolutely certain about the accuracy of his interpretations.

Actually, Natalia had grown up as an only child in a family where her every move was under the scrutinizing gaze of her two very controlling and overprotective parents. She had simply learned to retreat into herself in order to get some privacy when she needed it. When Mason learned more about the basis for her reveries he no longer felt threatened by them and jokingly began to refer to the episodes as Natalia's being "lost in the interior."

Of course, empathy, like any positive trait, can have negative consequences when it is exaggeratedly or inappropriately applied. When a person repeatedly *over*empathizes with their lover to the extent that they lose themselves in the process, the relationship soon develops problems as a result of the imbalance.

For example, Mason might have been so empathic that he neglected his *own* needs for intimacy in order to support Natalia's needs to flee into the interior. To avoid conflict and make a relationship work, *both* people must be able to empathize with their partner's position while not selling themselves down the river in the process.

Nay Saying

When the desire to please and impress a partner is especially great, you may have a tendency to overextend yourself and make promises which you are not able to keep. Repeated failure to pick up the cleaning, fix the window, or keep an agreed-upon meeting time breeds distrust, even when intentions are honorable. The disappointment resulting from broken promises creates a serious impediment to the development of intimacy.

It is most important, therefore, to agree only to do favors or provide services for your partner that you are virtually certain you can accomplish. When in doubt, qualify your agreement: "I'm not sure I'll have the time to do it right away. If it's important, maybe you had better not count on me." I don't want to make a promise and then let you down. Maybe you had better make other plans."

If you are not certain, it is better to respond conservatively, thereby freeing your partner to take the appropriate steps to insure that his or her needs will otherwise be met. Of course, if you later find that you are able to carry out your partner's request, you can let them know at that time. Ironically, learning to say "no" when it is appropriate to do so permits you to say "yes" and mean it.

Since you probably *want* to please your partner, you may feel a bit petty or somewhat guilty when you say "no." Therefore, confronting your partner's disappointment can take some getting used to. However, when compared to bearing the brunt of your partner's anger at being let down in the end, this initial discomfort is really a small price to pay.

By extension, it is unreasonable and unfair to *badger* your partner into agreeing to do something for you and then to be angry with them when they fail to come through. A healthy relationship must make room for *reasonable* refusal, otherwise it has not made room for *genuine* acceptance.

The Presumption of Innocence

The presumption of innocence is not only a humane foundation of our legal system, it also should be a humane foundation of our relationship system. Rather than jumping in with harmful and negative assumptions, *no matter how certain we are of them,* it is vital for us to learn to suspend judgment for a moment. In order that we may discover whether other motives could possibly underlie the behavior we are convinced was designed to hurt us, *we first must assume our partner to be innocent.*

In the bedroom, for instance, we often see differences in the frequency of the desire for sex interpreted as evidence of the less interested partner's lack of love, or an attempt to punish the more interested partner by rejecting him or her sexually. But it is entirely possible that these differences might be physiologically based variations in libidos, attributable to a discomfort one partner has with sexual contact in general, or some other alternative explanation. As one man told us, "Sure, I wish Janet were more physically expressive, hugging and touching me more, but I've learned to accept her as she is. I know she makes an effort at times, but basically I don't think it's in her nature."

Shaking Hands with the Inevitable

Seeing your partner's actions as an expression of personality, character style, or history, rather than being aimed directly at you, can make the behavior easier to understand and accept. Couples who do well over the long haul realize that in certain ways they simply must be willing to take their partners as they are, giving up fantasies of transforming them. They have the maturity to realize that they themselves expect to be loved despite their imperfections, and their partners deserve no less. Rhonda was bemused as she told us, "Ward always has to be cajoled to go to social events, and that's a bit hard on me at times. But I know that I haven't made myself into exactly what he wants either. I guess we have to accept each other the way we are."

In all areas of life we must learn where, when, and how to make the changes we can make, and, as ancient wisdom tells us, we must also learn when it is most appropriate simply to "shake hands with the inevitable." Every difference does not have to be reconciled; each peculiar sensitivity cannot always be overcome.

If your partner has a particular way of behaving in certain settings that drives you crazy, it may be more constructive at those times to turn your attention to caring for your own needs rather than focusing on the irritating behavior. One man we know couldn't bear his girlfriend's indecisiveness, so when they were in a situation where she had a hard time making up her mind—in a store trying on clothes, for example—he would take a short walk, window-shop, or go for a cup of coffee and read a magazine, having arranged to meet her at a later time. This effective strategy reduced the tension between them and gave them each a way out of potential conflict.

Accepting your partner as he or she is will open you to discovering a way to remain close to one another emotionally even while you are separately occupied. If your partner, for example, doesn't want to join you at tennis, see what it's like if he or she reads a book on a grassy knoll by the courts while you play with another partner. Or, if your partner is a terrible cook, he or she could be seated at the kitchen table, writing a letter or paying bills while you prepare the meal.

Agreeing to Disagree

In areas where your opinions decisively differ from one another, you can agree to disagree. The choice of agreeing to disagree is useful and necessary when two partners have different, strongly held religious persuasions, political orientations, styles of decision making, opinions about an issue, or approaches to problem solving. In such instances you could listen endlessly to the reasons why your partner holds to a particular point of view without being persuaded by them. Until and unless your own direct experience of life convinces you to change your viewpoint, you will probably retain it.

A healthy relationship is not the result of a blurred merging of two personalities into one homogeneous mush; it is the by-product of a respect for diversity and independence. It is also a place where two individuals feel free to be themselves while simultaneously creating a third path which they agree to travel together for their mutual comfort and advantage.

In most good relationships, however, political differences, religious differences, and even certain differences in style become less extreme over time. Each person's outlook affects that of the other as they live together. There is a natural tendency for their separate styles to accommodate and consolidate to an extent, with both slowly acquiring some attributes of the other and the two of them moving more toward the center. The optimist begins to notice potential problems and the pessimist learns to move forward despite them. The introvert feels more comfortable in groups and the extrovert feels more comfortable spending time alone. Even activities and interests change: a bookworm may find himself or herself enjoying outdoor activities while an outdoor person discovers the virtues and pleasures of spending the day reading in front of the fire; a conservative may become somewhat more liberal and a liberal more conservative. Couples find that even their choice of clothing and home furnishings changes as they indirectly influence each other's tastes, at times evolving into a style that, while having elements of both, is different from what either person might have chosen alone.

One man told us that over the many years he and his wife had been together, "We've become more and more alike. She's moving more toward spontaneity and I'm moving more toward structure. It continues to be the yin and yang of our relationship."

Once a couple learns how they can agree to disagree without anger or hurt, many irreconcilable differences can be allowed to persist while exacting a negligible toll, if any: they are simply accepted benignly, with good humor and the always necessary touch of forbearance.

BREAKDOWNS IN COMMUNICATION

Given that you and your partner are likely to be two very dissimilar human beings—different, perhaps, in pacing, or in certain values, interests, tastes, sensitivities, or even in personal philosophy—clear communication between you becomes a necessity if you are to live together in harmony. Miscommunication, therefore, is bound to be another major source of conflict within a relationship.

Most of us communicate less clearly than we think we do. We may hide our vulnerability, mask our anger, avoid discussions of sensitive issues, send out double messages and in other ways make it difficult, if not impossible, for our partner to know what is really on our minds and in our feelings.

Oblique and confused methods of communication are often the result of having witnessed faulty communication within our families of origin. Many of us grew up in families where we were taught that it was inappropriate to express our feelings directly, so we learned to suppress them or express them indirectly. In far too many homes children are expected to be seen but not heard, or their feelings and thoughts are minimized, dismissed, or dealt with rather mockingly, as if they were silly or insignificant. In accordance with long-standing prejudices—many of which are very subtle—about what is "acceptable" masculine or feminine behavior, male children may be discouraged from expressing their fears or sensitivities, and female children may be discouraged from expressing their strengths or competencies.

A large part of the adult male population has systematically been taught how to avoid expressions of tenderness or vulnerability because these either are considered to be signs of weakness or have been identified as "feminine" emotions. For fear that his partner will think less of him, or else in an effort to protect his self-image, a man may cover up these feelings with aggressive behaviors or a macho denial that anything is wrong, and this can be totally baffling to his partner. On the other hand, women are too often taught not to rock the boat and to keep their feelings of dissatisfaction hidden; as a result they may have an especially difficult time directly expressing anger. One consequence of this is that their partners may feel genuinely perplexed as to what they have done to warrant the cold shoulder or "sniping" remarks.

Dodging or denying your feelings prevents your partner from learning how to become more sensitive, supportive and helpful to you. For example, out of false pride or a misguided attempt to hide your vulnerability, you might choose to pretend that a slight or oversight on the part of your partner didn't hurt you in the least. Whatever the reason, however, denying the impact your partner has on you leaves her or him confused and unenlightened about your needs, and it sets the stage for future misunderstandings and a progressive alienation that can eventually destroy the love you once shared.

Geraldine was offended by Sal's tendency to be inattentive to her at times when she needed him most. Rather than telling him directly that she was hurt by the way he was treating her, she flirted provocatively with an acquaintance of his, hoping to make Sal jealous and to draw his attention back to her. Having no idea that Geraldine's flirtatiousness was in reaction to his own behavior, Sal felt confused, angry, and betrayed. Not wanting to appear vulnerable, he covered up his own feelings and escalated matters by having an affair with one of his co-workers. Geraldine discovered the affair, and even as the relationship was disintegrating, neither Geraldine nor Sal was aware of the destructive impact caused by their failure to discuss their needs and feelings openly in the first place.

Since most men and many women in this culture have received little encouragement for expressing their feelings openly and honestly, initial forays into this unfamiliar terrain can be awkward and unrewarding, particularly when the couple is embroiled in a controversy.

Knowing what you feel and becoming familiar and comfortable expressing your feelings takes time. However, simply trying to talk more about the way you feel helps you to become more *aware of what you feel.* Enriching your expressive language enhances both your feelings of being alive as well as your ability to convey your experiences more accurately to your partner.

Bedouins, for instance, have seven hundred words to describe camels. Because their lives depend on these beasts of burden, they are able to perceive qualities and components of camels that would probably go unnoticed by most non-Bedouins. This descriptive vocabulary has very practical and adaptive significance for them, just as being able to communicate what we are feeling and thinking is critical to anyone in an intimate relationship.

Double Messages

Discomfort with the direct expression of feelings eventually leads to the use of double messages. These confusing communications occur when a person is expressing two quite contradictory messages at the same time, usually through different modalities. Thus, the words being uttered may say one thing, but the voice tone may indicate something quite different. Perhaps the words are conveying messages of tender love, but if there is no eye contact and the posture of the body is pulled away or unyielding, or the touch accompanying the words is tentative or perfunctory, the sincerity of the words becomes questionable. And conversely, as in the line from an old song: "Your lips tell me 'No, no' but there's 'Yes, yes' in your eyes," your body may betray your hidden desires even as your words pretend another truth.

The sender of a double message is almost always either conflicted or confused, although he or she may not be aware of it at the time. This lack of clarity is then transmitted to the other person, who is left uncertain as to how to react.

When Paula picked up her boyfriend after work, she asked him how his day went. "Fine," he said, but his voice was clipped and terse and he didn't smile. Paula was perplexed. Should she have acted as if she believed his day truly was fine and not inquired any further? If she did, his irritated manner would probably continue. If, instead, she responded to his tone and expression and asked why he seemed angry or upset, she would risk a response such as, "I just told you it was fine. Get off my case!" If she bit at either "bait" she would get nowhere. Accepting only one part of a double message leads to a no-win situation.

The only solution to the dilemma presented by a double message is for the respondent to admit confusion, comment on *both* components, and ask for clarification: "I feel confused. You've said your day was fine yet you seem tense and irritable. What's up?" This encourages a constructive dialogue, which is likely to lead to the revelation of important details and feelings that, if left undiscussed, could cast a pall over the time spent together.

Suppressed Feelings

Feelings are a form of energy. As with all other forms of energy, they follow the law of conservation, which states that energy can be neither created nor destroyed. Energy can only be transformed from one state to another, as electricity can be transformed into heat and heat into light. This means, in effect, that all feelings find their expression one way or another. Feelings that are not directly or overtly expressed are at times turned against the self, causing indigestion, bad dreams, anxieties, increases or decreases in appetite for food or drugs, and so on, or they can be stored up, much as a battery stores energy, and vented later, usually in indirect and confusing ways or displaced onto innocent "targets."

For three solid months, Ned had been working on proposals and marketing strategies to help him land a major local account for the advertising agency at which he was employed. Although he was quite optimistic that he would be given the account, at the last minute it went to another firm. He was devastated, filled with feelings of disappointment, anger, inadequacy, and hurt. Because he took this frustrating turn of events as a mark of personal failure, he felt embarrassed and unwilling to tell his girlfriend, Jan, what had happened.

That evening when they were at dinner he picked a fight over an innocent comment she had made about the restaurant's decor. Jan was shocked and puzzled by his exaggerated reaction, and when she asked if anything was wrong, Ned became furious. "Nothing is wrong with *me*. What's the matter with *you*?" he responded harshly. The communication between them degenerated further and further as the evening progressed until they were barely speaking to one another at its end. Neither of them understood exactly why things had turned so sour. Ned would have had a difficult time believing that his earlier disappointment, which he had covered over, was at the root of the evening's conflict.

The longer feelings remain suppressed, particularly feelings that are in response to a partner's actions, the more havoc they seem to wreak. Small grudges can build and fester, coloring and eroding the entire relationship.

Claudette reported this story: "When Ezra has even a little cold or any illness at all I wait on him hand and foot. I bring him chicken soup, breakfast in bed, or try to think of nice little things to do for him. Anyway, I had recently gotten home from having my appendix out and I was feeling a bit better, but not well enough to climb the stairs. So when Ezra came over to give me a hand, I asked him to get me a glass of orange juice from the kitchen downstairs. I waited and waited, but he never returned. When I got up, half an hour later, I found him watching football on TV. I had asked him for one little thing and he couldn't get it for me. Actually, when I think of it, I carry around a lot of these grudges against him. I generally just stuff them, but they sit there and build and I never really forget about them. I have a little scorecard in my head and when other things like this come up, they get magnified because there are so many other unresolved issues."

Indirect Communication

Ultimately, when feelings that have been stifled for some time do find expression, they are likely to come out in exaggerated, distorted, or devious ways: we burn the meal we are cooking; we forget something we have promised to do for our partner; we are late to meet them; our manner becomes cold and aloof; we behave flirtatiously with others while feeling sexless with our partner; we start a fight over something trivial or irrelevant. These are examples of what is termed *passive-aggressive* behavior—behavior which expresses anger through passive, or indirect, forms.

When feelings of anger that were stifled get expressed indirectly they inevitably manage to hurt or anger our partner, which is often the unconscious intent. However, if our partner has no understanding as to why they are being treated that way, has no idea that our behavior is actually registering our feelings about their own past behavior, they are probably going to feel confused, and in their irritation they may retaliate in kind. In this way a destructive escalation can readily develop, resulting in an emotional climate that is cold, unpleasant, and alienating.

"Hinting" is another indirect and problematic form of communication that is often the result of being taught early on that direct requests or statements of needs are somehow unacceptable and will not be met. The indirect "hint" can be used as an attempt to protect ourselves from possible rejection. The problem is that the hint is often not picked up, so that we are actually less likely to get what we want, leaving us feeling unimportant and frustrated anyway. It is also likely that the recipient of such hints, feeling manipulated, may actively resist picking up on them.

When we hint or otherwise express our feelings circuitously, we are, in essence, requiring our partner to read our mind in order to discover our intent. In fact, some people, unfairly and unwisely, consider their partner's ability to read their mind as a test of true love. The problem is that mind-reading is not something we humans are generally very good at (more often than not we are actually reading our own mind and projecting this "reading" onto the other person). The more indirectly we express our feelings, the more impeded and unsatisfying our relationship is likely to become.

When our partner speaks in an especially loud voice, speaks harshly to us, appears cool or distant, it is only natural to take it personally. Are they upset with us, or are they only expressing the tension from having had a bad day? With no additional information to clarify the behavior, we are left to our own devices, making interpretations that are most likely based on our own past experiences and point of view. We then react in accord with what we ourselves would have been feeling and thinking if we had behaved in a similar manner. Of course, our analysis may in no way reflect our partner's intentions. Under these circumstances, distortions abound, leading to all sorts of misunderstandings.

Lloyd had gone to great lengths preparing for a romantic evening at home: a wonderful meal, flowers, candlelight, and fine wine. But Jeri's attention was elsewhere all evening. Lloyd felt hurt. He thought that Jeri was taking him for granted, but he didn't feel comfortable expressing this because he felt embarrassed at needing her approval and attention. As the evening wore on he became increasingly cold and aloof. Jeri, it turned out, had had a painful falling-out with her sister earlier in the day. She knew that Lloyd didn't like her sister very much so she felt reluctant to tell him about it, not wanting to stir up more negative feelings. Jeri had no idea that her preoccupation with her sister was affecting her own behavior with Lloyd; she experienced his withdrawal from her as yet another punishment from a loved one.

Lloyd didn't tell Jeri that his feelings were hurt, and Jeri didn't mention that she was upset because of her fight with her sister. Both simply experienced the other as being unloving and unsupportive. Finally, Jeri made an excuse to go home right after dinner and they parted on an unfriendly note, both of them feeling alone, hurt, and self-pitying.

CORRECTIVE MEASURES

There are many ways that Jeri and Lloyd's evening could have been replayed, so that both of them would have ended up feeling loving and relaxed instead of at odds with one another.

As we indicated earlier, the presumption of innocence plays a key role in preventing breakdowns in communication. By presuming Jeri innocent rather than supposing she was purposefully slighting him, Lloyd might first have told Jeri how he was feeling: "I'm a bit hurt—you don't seem to be very appreciative of my efforts." Then he could have mentioned that she seemed distant and not really "present." This approach might have been more likely to open the door to a discussion in which both of them were able to express their unspoken thoughts and feelings. Incidentally, it is always important to say *what you are feeling first*, before telling your partner how you are experiencing *them*, and certainly before you dare to make any interpretations of their behavior. By first sharing your own feelings you encourage your partner to relax their defenses, enabling them to be more open to what you have to say.

Be Curious, Not Furious

Even though your partner's actions may have hurt you, until you are absolutely certain otherwise, give them the benefit of the doubt. It is reasonable to assume that they are ignorant about the impact their behavior has upon you, and they require education, not castigation. To prevent conflict, try replacing accusation with inquiry: "What did you mean when you said that (or did that)?" "How were you feeling when you acted that way?" "What were you trying to accomplish, or convey?" Be curious rather than furious.

Fiona had agreed to meet Kevin for dinner at his house at eight o'clock. Eight o'clock came and went. Kevin grew increasingly angry, and by the time Fiona arrived, at a quarter to nine, he was seething. Rather than lashing out at her as she entered his apartment, he controlled himself, told her he was angry, and asked her what caused her lateness. He learned that she had been virtually glued to her computer terminal for almost ten hours, working on a knotty problem that she was unable to solve. She was feeling terribly guilty and inadequate because she had promised a client that she would have a certain analysis ready and she was already four days overdue. Her boss was on her case and the client was threatening to take his business elsewhere. She felt that her job was on the line. Her distress was quite evident, and Kevin sympathized with her plight, but he told her how her being late had worried and upset him. He implored her to call him if, in the future, she was going to be delayed. Fiona apologized for her thoughtlessness and as they continued talking, Kevin was soon pleasantly surprised to find that his anger had dissipated. Fiona, relieved at not being reprimanded and made to feel additionally guilty and inadequate, was able to relax into the supportive and caring arms she so desperately needed.

The Courage to Be Honest

Honesty is absolutely essential if you are to avoid miscommunications with your loved one. Basically, people lie most often when they fear the consequences of telling the truth—punishment, embarrassment, scorn, or a guilt-inducing reprimand—or when they don't feel good about themselves because their actions, or sometimes even their thoughts, don't measure up to the expectations they have set for themselves. For example, some people will lie about an innocent meeting they had with another person if, in their mind, they had fantasies of its being less than "innocent."

If we feel inadequate we may try to compensate by exaggerating the truth, trying to impress our partner with our tales. Our partner, in effect, becomes our mirror. We fiddle with the image we project so that the one being reflected back to us is the one we would like to see, or the one we think our partner would find most impressive.

In an ongoing relationship lies are very likely to be discovered, sooner or later. Because intimates are connected on many subtle levels, dishonesty usually triggers a warning signal through our intuition, and this causes us to shift to a state of heightened awareness. Without any concrete data to rely upon, however, this heightened awareness may look initially like paranoia.

When the lie isn't ferreted out, *many* actions on our partner's part may become grounds for suspicion. This state of suspicious vigilance, though it may be somewhat misplaced, is usually founded on at least a grain of truth. "Even paranoids have enemies," as the saying goes.

Oliver and Abby had been dating exclusively for six months when Abby became concerned about Oliver's commitment to the relationship. He seemed to be less available, more easily distracted, more taken up with his work. Something was bothering her about all this, but it was nothing she could quite put her finger on. Nevertheless, she finally decided to tell Oliver about her feelings and observations. Oliver told her that he still loved her and that there was nothing to worry about. But things didn't change, and Abby couldn't quiet her concern no matter how hard she tried. She kept asking for reassurance, getting disproportionately upset when he broke a date, prying into his work activities. Finally, Oliver said that he couldn't take her paranoia any longer and in a burst of anger he broke off the relationship. Abby didn't understand her own behavior and blamed herself for having driven Oliver away. Never before had she experienced this kind of anxiety in a relationship.

After many weeks, quite by chance, Abby learned from an office mate that Oliver had been having an affair during the last few months of their relationship. Finally, as she was able to put two and two together, her "paranoia" made sense to her.

If you continue to feel oddly disquieted or disconcerted about your partner's behavior and this feeling persists despite a lack of supporting evidence, it is probably not simply a figment of your imagination. Unless you know yourself to be exquisitely hypersensitive, something real is more than likely accounting for your discomfort, and although it may not be what you think, an explanation must exist. In such instances, where your intuition is telling you that something more is going on than you have been made aware of, it is both necessary and wise to pursue matters further until the mystery is clarified and your suspicions have been laid to rest.

If your partner appears to be increasingly suspicious of you,

examine your own behavior, searching for your possible contribution to the disturbance: find that *grain of truth* in your partner's concerns. Reveal and discuss it before the situation further degenerates. It often requires a degree of courage to
respond truthfully and forthrightly in these instances but it is
well worth the effort. The discovery of a significant lie or a
serious discrepancy between word and deed can damage a relationship at its very core. If your partner discovers that you
have been lying in one area, it makes trusting you in other
areas more difficult and provokes your partner into being suspicious and protectively vigilant, attitudes that are antithetical
to intimacy. Pretending that there is absolutely no substance
whatsoever to your partner's disturbance when in truth there
is, will only add to his or her confusion, suspiciousness, and
self-doubt. This is what is known as "gaslighting," a term derived from the Bergman/Boyer movie *Gaslight*, in which a man
tries to drive his lover crazy by pretending that her true perceptions are merely figments of her disturbed imagination.

As we have noted previously, a corollary of the requirement
that the truth be told must be that when someone does reveal
the truth he or she should not be punished for it, even if it is an
unpleasant truth. Certainly, you need not be happy with the
content of the revelation, but if truthfulness is to be a value it
must be encouraged—even if it brings pain.

"I" Statements

When you can talk about the issues that are bothering you *as
they arise*, they can be resolved before they assume outrageous
proportions. If you express your thoughts and feelings rather
than cover them up, you have overcome the first hurdle. If you
listen to your partner and try to see things from his or her
point of view you have conquered the second. "I" statements
facilitate both.

In an "I" statement you tell your partner how *you feel* in
response to his or her actions. After all, *you* are the world's

foremost expert on the subject of *your* feelings. "I felt hurt when you didn't say anything about the flowers I got for you." "I feel afraid when you withdraw into silence. I'm concerned that I've done something terribly wrong and that you'll leave me." "I feel unloved when you book your schedule so tightly that we can't see each other more often." "I feel asphyxiated when you call me two or three times a day at work." These "I" statements *invite* conversation. Because they are neither attacking nor attributive, they are less likely to engender defensive feelings and behavior. They encourage openness and responsiveness and set the tone for the most productive discussions, and they promote dialogue with a partner who, after all, should be as concerned about your feelings as they would like you to be about theirs.

Contrast these "I" statements with "you" statements such as: "You don't care about how much effort I put into things." "You don't think about anyone but yourself." "You think that your work is more important than I am." Predictably, these latter statements soon lead to unproductive arguments. They are basically aggressive in nature, and will, in all likelihood, provoke counteraggression and defensiveness. "You" statements are attributive—they discourage meaningful discussion and promote angry refutation.

You are *not* the reigning expert, no matter how long you've known someone else, on what is going on inside them. So if you begin a discussion by expounding on an analysis of your partner's behaviors, faults, motivations, thoughts, feelings, and the like, you are almost certainly going to provoke that person and close them down. No one enjoys someone else's uninvited presumptuous "expertise" about who they are, what they think and feel, and what they really mean. Your interpretations of your partner (mind reading out loud) are likely to be inaccurate at best, and at worst, downright insulting.

"I" statements also permit you to present information that your partner might otherwise be quite sensitive about receiving. Statements like "I feel overwhelmed when you accept so many party invitations in one weekend" or "I feel embarrassed when we are having dinner with friends and you chew with your mouth open," can be a starting point for negotiations in areas where there is no clear right or wrong, just matters of personal sensitivity. None of these statements cast blame, and therefore they allow you and your partner to discuss a problem and its possible solutions as a team, not as adversaries.

Feelings cannot be argued with in any reasonable way: feelings simply exist and must be taken at face value. From your partner's point of view, for instance, your feelings may seem exaggerated or inappropriate, but since they are your feelings, they have a basis in *your* reality. That alone is sufficient to have them taken seriously. Feelings do not have to conform to the rules of logic or to someone else's standards of appropriateness. The object of making "I" statements is to enable you to become more aware of your partner's reality and to have your partner become more aware of your own.

When each of you knows a good deal about how the other person feels—even if you each feel quite differently from the other—you are then equipped with both the information and, one hopes, the inclination to be generous spirited, working mutually to change certain behaviors that may lead to an improved tone in the relationship that you are building together.

It must be emphasized that "I" statements describe *what you feel, not what you think*. Notice that statements such as "I feel *that* you never want to know my opinion about things," or "I feel *as if* you are always eager to criticize me" or, "I feel *like* you don't understand me," are actually sentences that describe *thoughts* masquerading as feelings; they are attributive statements disguised as "I" statements and they will lead to trouble. Correctly restated, they would say, "*I feel angry* with you—you rarely ask my opinion about things. Aren't you interested in hearing what I have to say?" Or "*I feel frustrated* because I can't seem to get my point across to you." Or "*I feel threatened* when I am criticized so frequently." Thoughts are important too, of course, but they are usually based on inferences about what you are perceiving, or they are attempts to make rational sense out of your feelings. They are one step removed from your feelings.

Feelings are your most direct, personal reactions to your experience, good, bad or indifferent. Taking them seriously at face value, rather than arguing about them or dismissing them, is essential if an intimate relationship is to prosper and grow. Thoughts and interpretations, *not feelings*, are the proper subjects for debate. This is not merely a picky academic analysis, it is a practical and necessary distinction which, if understood and implemented, will make a genuine difference in your communication. If you actually are expressing your thoughts or interpretations and posing them as feelings, you can expect your partner to feel provoked or attacked and to dig in her or his heels as an argument soon unfolds.

Don't Begin to Work Until You Are Hired

Your partner lives in a subjective universe very different from your own. This is an obvious but humbling idea well worth remembering before you consider making pronouncements about your partner's character or behavior. Even if your opinions are correct, they are likely neither to be useful nor welcome unless they have been requested: *don't begin to work until you have been hired*. Your partner's betterment is not your responsibility. The insights you may have to offer are of value only when they are seen as valuable by the one being offered them; therefore, it is essential that you ask your partner if he or she is interested in hearing your "words of wisdom" *before* pronouncing them: "Would you like my input as to how you can do that an easier way?" or "May I tell you what I've noticed?" And remember, if your comment is going to be a criticism, make sure that you mention it at a time when your partner can benefit from the information. Nothing is more infuriating than being told something when it is too late to do anything about it.

Gerald and Brenda lived a few miles from each other. They

had been invited to a dinner party some distance away and were enjoying an animated conversation en route. Just before they arrived, Brenda noticed that Gerald's pants and shirt didn't match and told him about it. She knew he was color-blind so she often made helpful suggestions on his choice of clothing, something for which Gerald was usually grateful. This time Gerald became angry with her, not because of what she said but because she had waited so long to say it. If she had told him when he had first picked her up he could have returned home and changed, but now it was too far to go back, and his embarrassment over his mismatched outfit would only make him self-conscious and interfere with his enjoyment of the party.

Certain behaviors, of course, cannot be commented on at the opportune moment and may be more satisfactorily revisited afterward, but it is wise to reflect carefully on your intentions before you do so. Many things are simply not worth mentioning if nothing constructive is likely to come of it.

Selective Containment

Practically speaking, there are times when withholding certain information is exactly the right thing to do. We might call this "selective containment." While we have been advocating the importance of open communication and describing some of the problems created by its absence, there are definitely times, as in Gerald and Brenda's case, when it is most appropriate to say nothing at all.

Tact, that great virtue and social lubricant, is too often underemphasized in intimate relationships; perhaps its absence accounts for some of those instances in which "familiarity breeds contempt." There are probably aspects of your partner's personality which, while somewhat annoying to you, are not likely to change. You might deal with them more effectively on your own, working to release their hold on you and accepting your partner as he or she is, rather than nagging about them.

Withholding a discussion about something until you have had time to think about it, to get your bearings or to obtain the necessary data to back your position, can be crucial to a good relationship. Furthermore, it is not unreasonable to want to wait until your partner is in a more receptive mood before you bring up a controversial subject.

Contrary to what some people have been led to believe by pop psychology, not everything needs to be talked about. It is possible to *generate* problems through *over*communication. Exposing every little nuance of life to scrutiny can rob it of its mystery, reduce its intensity, and be tedious and off-putting. Since all relationships have their good and bad days, it is not necessary, for instance, to keep your partner abreast of those times when you are a little less in love. As one woman said, "If life together seems boring, I simply don't tell him. I know it will look different soon enough."

Many people find that having small secrets, little areas that they keep totally to themselves, can have a positive and invigorating impact on their relationships—it reminds them that they are individual human beings, distinct and separate, not simply a part of a couple. Of course, we are not referring here to keeping a destructive and guilty secret such as an affair, but rather to such things as a brief and innocent flirtation with a passing someone who was attractive to you at the lunch counter, or the decision to treat yourself to a midday movie, or buying some small extravagance that pleases you. Everyone wants to have part of themselves that they can call their own, something about which they have to answer to no one else.

There are times when it is also best to withhold information that is unimportant but which you think might make you look ridiculous in your partner's eyes or which you find to be somewhat embarrassing, like bouncing a number of checks because you balanced your checkbook incorrectly. As one man said, "I might just not want her to know that I had been a horse's ass." This kind of withholding does no harm; the withheld information is not germane to the functioning of the relationship.

However, withholding certain facts in order to protect yourself from your partner's anger when you know the information is important to your partner is patent dishonesty and is likely to eventuate in serious, unpleasant repercussions before very long. Lying by omission is quite different from the innocent containment we are talking about. Most people, when they are willing to be honest, can easily tell the difference.

It is well to remember that even with the healthiest communication in the most loving relationship, occasional conflicts are inevitable. There will be times when your fuse is especially short, times when you will respond defensively despite your best intentions, when you are unable to stand back and see the situation from your partner's point of view, or when you don't see how the relationship can possibly survive the problems you are currently experiencing. Even then, there are more effective and less effective ways to handle things, ways that can salvage the relationship and bring you closer together and ways that can cause irreparable damage. In the next chapter we will discuss the skills necessary to help you handle the clashes that occur in nearly every intimate relationship.

5

Conflict

The Clash of Separate Realities

What power has love but forgiveness?
In other words
by its intervention
what has been done
can be undone.
What good is it otherwise?

—W. C. WILLIAMS,
From *Asphodel, That Greeny Flower*

A most unwelcome surprise: the dreaded first fight bursts upon the scene accompanied by a rush of disturbing feelings. Fear, anger, self-protective withdrawal, confusion, and uncertainty are only some of what we must contend with when the first serious conflict is upon us. Perhaps we are also revisited by bitter or sad memories of other relationships that fell apart, that broke our hearts. We worry about what the fight portends. Is it only the tip of the iceberg? Are there deeper, irreconcilable problems lurking beneath the surface? Will the relationship weather the storm?

Regardless of what we are fighting about, the worries are often the same—and our point of view is usually fairly predictable. Each of our inner dialogues usually goes something like this:

Question: "Who started the damned argument anyway?"
Answer: "You did."
Question: "Whose memory about the sequence of events leading to the present nastiness is correct?"
Answer: "Mine is."

The problem is, you can't go anywhere with such an analysis. It is rarely illuminating nor is it particularly productive to explore the "objective" elements involved in a conflict, as if the "real truth" of the matter can be unearthed and mutually agreed upon. Every conflict has at least *two* "truths," yours and your partner's. Since most conflict is rooted in subjectivism— your separate views of reality—trying to resolve differences by searching for the objective truth can be a colossal waste of time, energy, and good feelings.

We are reminded here of the well-known poem about the blind men and the elephant. In effect, the first blind man, running his hands up and down the animal's leg, says with great certainty, "This, my friends, is unquestionably a tree." The second blind man, grasping the tail, convincingly disagrees: "No, no, no. You are mistaken. What we have here is a rope." Meanwhile, the third blind man, his hands placed on the huge animal's side, argues vigorously that the large, flat, rough surface he is touching is unmistakably the wall of a building!

When it comes to arguments, we are all blind people dealing with an elephant. Our limited perspective of reality is profoundly influenced by who we are and what we've experienced in our lives, by our backgrounds, expectations, personal prejudices, varying sensitivities and sensibilities.

Rather than quarreling about whose experience is correct,

what is needed is a good deal of modesty as we present our own view of reality, a healthy respect for alternative perspectives, and a willingness to create a new vision that embraces both points of view. Using this blend of wisdom, the three blind men in communication with one another might have realized that they were actually all holding on to different parts of the same elephant.

CONFLICT: BURIAL GROUND OR BREEDING GROUND?

Most of us are well aware that any two people in a partnership are bound to disagree from time to time. Yet this understanding alone does little to protect us from the trepidation and dismay we experience when we find ourselves embroiled in an intense disagreement. It may be of some solace to know that the first fight often inaugurates the shift from the idealized early stage of courtship to the more realistic secondary stage. It is an inevitable and necessary rite of passage.

While growing up, many of us were taught to keep our feelings under wraps, especially the darker ones. If our mothers and fathers maintained a controlled and cool demeanor while in our presence—even if they were screaming at each other out of earshot—we may not have learned that intimates could fight and survive it, continuing to love each other despite their battles. If, on the other hand, our parents had dramatic or brutal arguments in front of us, we may have vowed never to do the same thing ourselves. And if our parents divorced, or if we ourselves have gone through a divorce, we may be convinced that fighting is the prologue to disaster.

Nearly everyone has a personal memory in which a loving relationship was wrecked by frequent harsh emotional storms, where love and good feelings were swept away leaving behind only the ruins of what might have been. Any sensible person who has experienced such pain recoils at the possibility of it being repeated.

There can be no doubt that certain forms of conflict are significantly detrimental to our health and our spirits, in some cases enduringly so.

Provoking a conflict, especially by insulting or demeaning another person, can be motivated by many things, ranging from a misguided attempt to enhance one's own self-worth at the expense of another, to a way of capturing another's attention when certain needs for contact are not being met. At the extreme are those who might be called "conflict junkies," whose pathology leads them compulsively to provoke conflict. They feel most alive when they are embroiled in heated confrontations; otherwise they tend to feel depressed or deadened inside. There are others who seem to need conflict in order to feel sexually excited, so when life becomes a little mundane and the lovemaking becomes a bit tepid they generate a fight in order to activate strong feelings, which are then directed to the bedroom. Still others create conflict when they begin to sense a growing closeness with their partner, a closeness that frightens them. The conflict they stir up creates an increased emotional distance and dilutes the intimacy that is making them uncomfortable.

Granted, conflict is anything but pleasant, but not all conflict is destructive. If a relationship is to deepen and grow, it cannot and must not circumvent problematic moments. If anger is suppressed, it slowly strangles the good feelings and stifles the life out of a relationship. Routinely choosing to restrain our true feelings and beliefs out of a fear of being disliked or causing conflict is a form of passive dishonesty that only temporarily delays, and ultimately exaggerates, the inevitable clash.

When issues arise which are the by-products of our struggle to come to terms with our differences, we learn something about our lover's boundaries and sensitivities. When we ourselves are angry, we become quite vulnerable, exposing ourselves to the considerable risk of being hurt, misunderstood, or rejected by our partner. It is partially through being in conflict that we may learn either to trust or distrust our partner with our most private feelings, and, as we air our differences, our wounds will eventually either be healed or, if we fail the mission, deepened. When we are able to negotiate a conflict constructively, our hope is strengthened that future storms will be weathered as well. Properly conceived of and kept within limits, conflict can actually be the breeding ground for constructive change and the healthy evolution of the relationship.

The Causes of Conflict

To begin with, it is essential that you carefully consider the sources of your discontent. Which of your partner's behaviors are causing you distress? Can you specify them or are you fighting because the person you are with is really a disappointment to you across the board? Are your conflicts based upon a desire for a partner who is radically different, more like the person in your fantasy image?

If you are chronically irritated with your partner for who he or she *is*, for his or her essence, rather than about a particular behavior or two, you are in the wrong relationship and it is never going to be very fulfilling. Generally speaking, it's fair to assume that a person's character style, a person's way of being-in-the-world, doesn't change very much over the years. Your partner may be unrealistically optimistic; they may be compulsive about details, or relentlessly gregarious. They may wear their emotions on their sleeve or be very emotionally controlled; they may have no interest in esthetics or be zealots about sports . . . Whatever the underlying abiding dimensions of their character style, they are part of a person's very nature. They are not areas you are at liberty to change, nor are they areas that are likely to change. Your partner's idiosyncrasies of character simply have to be accepted as such—as you would like yours accepted. The only things worth fighting about are things that *can* be changed.

For example, Ike was about as obsessive-compulsive as they come. Everything in his home seemed to be organized into neat little piles, complete with labels; even the spices on the shelf were arranged alphabetically. Watching Ike during one of his organizational frenzies made Kelly feel very uncomfortable, and she couldn't imagine how they could ever live together. But she loved him and decided to give it a try. Once they moved in together, Ike had to accept the fact that Kelly wasn't a "neatnik" like he was, although she wasn't a slob either. He didn't seem to mind taking most of the responsibility for keeping their apartment as neat as his own had been, and Kelly found a way to busy herself whenever Ike began his compulsive routines. They had each made a reasonable adjustment to their separate styles and lived together quite harmoniously.

The more you are able to accept your partner for who she or he is, limiting your occasional expressions of displeasure to a particular behavior in question, the greater the likelihood that your partner will be receptive to what you have to say.

Take the time to differentiate the *specific action* that irritates you from that of your partner as a person. If you are not careful to present your concerns thoughtfully and with due consideration for your partner's feelings, you will only provoke defensiveness and lessen the chances for cooperative change.

The constructive use of conflict, as we have mentioned earlier, is to *promote change* in certain undesirable behavior—it is *not to punish* the person for what you may believe to be their misbehavior. Punishment is the precursor of resistance. At most it may force someone into an angry and reluctant compliance that eventually kills the spirit of a relationship.

Forms of Fighting

People differ as much in the way they fight as in what they fight about. There are those who present cool, quiet, logical arguments, those who use colorful language, those who cry, and those who jump up and down, yelling at the top of their lungs. Some of us need a bit of time and distance—going off alone to reflect—before coming forward, while others seem to be unable to delay their reactions even for a moment once a troubling feeling comes to the fore.

Regardless of what you are fighting about, physical or verbal violence causes irreparable damage and should be avoided. Except when protecting yourself from physical harm, physical violence to a person or their possessions is *never* warranted.

Verbal aggression can be almost as destructive as physical aggression. Words cannot maim or kill a person but they can cause great injury to feelings and self-concept. Violent language, violent tone, threats, character slander, insulting labels, epithets, invidious comparisons ("You're really an idiot, just like your father") have no place in a relationship where love is expected to flourish.

Violence begets violence. If you absolutely must express raw anger, beat up a pillow, smack a racquetball, go see a violent movie, close the windows of your car and scream and shout until you lose your voice, but use restraint in your relationship. Don't romanticize violence—it is a grim perversion that leads only to misery.

There is another kind of violence, a form more common and more insidious than the kinds we have been discussing: the violence of "guerrilla warfare," where anger is expressed obliquely, through nasty sniping or potshots, or by passive-aggressive actions such as the "silent treatment," sexual withholding, or "forgetting" matters of importance to a partner. Often these behaviors are not consciously intended, yet in their quiet way they may be ferociously destructive.

Samuel and Page had been together for nearly a year. Page had made it quite clear on a number of occasions that when they dined together on the evenings when she had to return to work afterward, it was particularly important to her that Samuel arrive on time.

Samuel had grown up in a household in which, regardless of what he was doing, he was expected to be home promptly at 6:00 P.M., the time when his family sat down to dinner each evening. When they were first dating, Samuel had been late for several dinners with Page, but once he recognized that his resistance to a set dinner hour dated back to the resentment he still carried from his childhood, he put his full attention to meeting Page on time. After three months of impeccable behavior, Samuel was again late for dinner twice in a row. When he tried to minimize Page's irritation by suggesting that his lateness was only due to an unavoidable occurrence, Page became even more angry. This led to a conflict in which Samuel finally revealed that he had been feeling upset with Page for the past few days. He had allowed her to borrow his car in order to pick up some wood for her fireplace, and she had returned it with a mess of wood splinters and dirt on the back seat and floor, and with the gas tank nearly empty as well. Samuel never said anything about this to Page, but clearly his anger was being expressed in a passive-aggressive way, by his being late for dinner. Had he told her what he was angry about when he first felt it, the subsequent blowup could have been avoided. If Page had not been willing to pursue the discussion despite Samuel's original denial, they might never have gotten to the basis of their conflict. Some couples continue such a series of symbolic escalations without ever acknowledging and resolving what is really going on beneath the surface.

For some people the "passive" expression of anger takes on a self-destructive form. They may abuse food and become obese as a way of punishing their partner. They may abuse drugs, endanger their health, or fail in their endeavors. All these ways of turning their anger inward, of course, have an important negative impact on their partnership as well.

CONSTRUCTIVE CONVERSATION

To prevent the buildup of anger and to minimize passive-aggressive warfare, troubling feelings should be discussed as openly and as quickly as possible. However, most of us find it somewhat difficult to express uncomfortable feelings. We may be embarrassed at being perceived as someone who is so sensitive or easily upset. Or perhaps a fear of our partner's response encourages us to postpone the inevitable confrontation. Whatever the reason, suppressing the feelings will not cause them to disappear, and it is a rare partner who is unaware when something is wrong—even if it has not been discussed. For this reason it is often a relief when one of the partners finally makes the first move.

Timing and Framing

Obviously, choosing the right time to discuss sensitive subjects is very important if you want to increase the likelihood that your words will be well received. It is usually a poor idea to bring up difficult material when others are present, for example, and it is wise to postpone such a confrontational talk if either you or your partner is pressed for time or is too fatigued or preoccupied to give it your full attention. The goal of such a conversation, after all, is to resolve the issue at hand as effectively as possible, not to see how many sparks can fly.

There is much to be said for taking a short cooling-off period before a "heart-to-heart" talk. If there is tension in the air, a delay of thirty minutes or so can diffuse it so that the discussion can go more smoothly. Incidentally, many people find that having a serious, emotionally charged conversation is easier when they are taking a stroll together. The act of walking seems to allay certain anxieties and enhance open communication.

Common sense suggests that the way such a discussion is introduced, the way it is "framed," is every bit as important as when it is introduced. We recommend that you begin with a prefatory remark requesting your partner's time and attention, for example, "Something is really bothering me and I need to talk with you about it. Is now a good time?" This kind of request shows respect for your partner's needs and offers them options, helping to reduce the resistance that might arise if they felt pressured into a discussion at a time when they were not prepared to have one. In this regard, one woman explained,

"My fiancé is extremely sensitive to criticism, no matter how slight, so if I have a bone to pick with him, I'll knock on his door and ask him if he wouldn't mind having a short talk. If he says, 'Not now,' I know enough to back off and trust that we'll get to it pretty soon. In fact, just giving him the opportunity to say 'Later' generally opens the discussion."

Once a time to talk has been set, make sure you stick to it. Take the phone off the hook, turn off the TV or radio, create a period of time free from distractions, and remember to begin your discussion with the presumption of innocence that we discussed in the previous chapter. Give your partner the benefit of the doubt and assume that the behavior that upset you was not intentionally designed to do so. A spirit of inquiry, not judgment, should characterize the talk. Certainly you may find this attitude more difficult to maintain if this is the third go-round on the same subject, but people often do make the same mistake more than once—don't you?—and should be given the time they need to change *if* they are working on it in good faith. A mistake, after all, is best construed as a learning opportunity, not as evidence of moral turpitude, hostility, or a flawed character—especially in an intimate relationship.

In fact, doing something incorrectly is actually the first step in the learning process. Behavioral change generally begins retroactively, that is, after the mistake has been made and discovered. First we make an error, then we notice it or it is brought to our attention: *after* the fact. If we are not punished for the error, but instead are *nonjudgmentally* advised of it, we will feel more inclined to be open to correcting it and avoiding future occurrences.

Speaking to Be Heard

Even on the third go-round there are more and less effective ways of approaching a problem. Suppose your partner continues to be late for appointments despite the fact that on numerous occasions you have mentioned that you find it very annoying. Instead of saying, "You just don't give a damn about me, otherwise you would have changed long ago," it might be a lot more instructive and productive as well if you were to say, in a conversational tone, "I wonder how you feel when you keep me waiting again and again, knowing how upsetting it is for me? What goes on in your mind at those times?" This is an inquiry, not an accusation. Chances are that this approach is more likely to lead to increased understanding which will then encourage the hoped-for change.

Remember, too, to use "I" statements, not "You" statements, and confine your part of the conversation to describing *your* feelings and *your* perception of the event in question. Avoid the tendency to criticize your partner's position. It is only likely to lead to more conflict. People are most inclined to alter their behavior because they have been made aware of how their actions make the other person feel, not because they have been "proven" wrong.

Critical information is generally easier to digest when it is presented with some sweetening. Sandwiching a criticism between compliments is often a good idea and leads to a spirit of cooperative openness: "Thanks for volunteering to help my mother with the dishes. I appreciated it. She's pretty fussy about her Waterford crystal, though, so in the future I wouldn't insist on washing it for her—she'd really prefer to do it herself, though I know she was grateful for your thoughtfulness."

The particular language used in a discussion can exert a tremendous influence on its outcome. In addition to blaming statements that point the finger of accusation at your partner, avoid using words that are absolutist or exclusionary. Words such as "only," "always," "never," "all," "just," or "every" tend to be inflammatory because they fail to acknowledge the gray areas. They are terms of emphasis and exaggeration; therefore, they encourage the listener to think of exceptions, while the point you are trying to make gets lost in the process.

Is it true that your lover *always* forgets to return the videotapes? And is it correct to say that you take care of *all* the entertainment plans? Is it wholly accurate that your mate is *just* stubborn—isn't he or she also a lot more than that? Are you really the *only* one who cares about the relationship? Is *every* opinion you offer ignored and are you *never* taken seriously? You will get a lot further in your discussions if, when describing things that have occurred, you make reference to specific situations, refrain from generalizing, and use terms that qualify the description: "seldom," "frequently," "during such-and-such a time," and so forth.

The law of diminishing returns suggests that emotionally charged discussions be kept as brief as possible. It is easy to become overloaded and exhausted fairly quickly during intense conversations, so try to limit the number of points you bring up on any given occasion to the essential few that can be assimilated without causing emotional indigestion.

Beware of the "kitchen sink" error: the inappropriate airing of a batch of complaints that have nothing directly to do with the subject at hand.

Suppose you're angry with your partner for having rudely and frequently corrected and contradicted you at a dinner party. As you get into the car to go home, you launch into a kitchen sink diatribe that goes something like this: "It really infuriates me when you contradict and correct me like you did all evening! Who the hell do you think you are, the world's foremost authority or something? Not only that, but you had no right talking to my brother behind my back about my financial situation. And while we're at it, don't ever ask me to take care of your cat again when you're out of town. I was late to work twice because I couldn't find her to give her those lousy pills."

Talk about overkill! The message you are sending is likely to get lost somewhere between the brother and the cat, leaving your partner reeling with confusion . . . as well as wishing for revenge after having received such an unjust bludgeoning. The *last* thing you are likely to elicit here is the desired change in behavior.

Like the kitchen sink error, the "avalanche of history" error involves bringing a set of extraneous elements into the discussion, but in this case the list of grievances all bear in some way, real or imagined, on the issue in question. "I can't believe you forgot to pick me up for work today. I'm your lowest priority. Last week you stood me up for tennis; then there was the time you made us late for the theater; and remember that Easter Sunday when you arrived so late for lunch with my parents that you barely got there in time for dessert?"

The result of such an avalanche of criticism, however well founded, is to make the listener feel inundated, nailed to the wall with nowhere to turn, except, perhaps, to make a desperate attempt to rationalize the behavior, or to focus the discussion onto an earlier "infraction," one that may have been somewhat justifiable, rather than arriving at a creative solution to the current or larger problem.

Remember that when conflict arises or miscommunication occurs your motive should be to educate, not to punish. Most of us tend to respond in accord with the ways that we are treated. Harsh treatment breeds harsh responses, and the more we are beaten down, ignored, blamed, or pressured, the more inclined we are to dig in our heels and resist. When we are treated with consideration, when our feelings are respected, it is easier to admit to mistakes and we feel more open to change. Our own shame at letting down our partner often has a greater transforming effect than our partner's worst fury.

Attempting to convince our partner to view life through the same set of lenses that we use is among the most common and destructive errors we can make in a relationship. If change is what you hope for, trying to achieve it by arguing someone out of their way of seeing things is sheer folly. Promoting change by first creating an atmosphere of safety and trust through acceptance and empathic understanding is unquestionably the best and most efficient way to proceed.

Norm and Olivia had had more squabbles about oral sex than either of them could count. Oral lovemaking was one of

Norm's greatest delights, but Olivia, who had tried it on a few occasions, found it disagreeable. Norm tried again and again to convince Olivia to change. He was scrupulous about his cleanliness, he brought her all sorts of articles and studies that attested to its normalcy and its benefits. Feeling frustrated, at times he would badger Olivia, until out of sheer exhaustion she would agree to have oral sex the next time they made love. Then, however, she would avoid sex as long as possible, and when they finally did make love she approached the moment as a prisoner approaches torture. Norm's eager and rather unrelenting approach, no matter how it was packaged, was only encouraging Olivia's resistance.

At last, Norm began to see that Olivia's reaction to oral sex, while alien to his own experience, was very strongly entrenched. While Norm certainly wasn't happy about giving up this form of lovemaking, it was obvious that his campaign was causing Olivia enormous discomfort, so he made it clear to Olivia that even if he never was able to have oral sex again, he would continue to love her. Being cared for and respected despite her sexual inhibition, Olivia felt more like returning Norm's generosity. Free at last from Norm's urging, she became more interested in exploring her own restrictions in this area. Through therapy she became aware that her anxieties were directly related to having been sexually abused as a child. As she confronted and worked through her early memories she grew less inhibited about initiating oral lovemaking. Norm was very appreciative of her efforts and put no pressure on her to do more than she was comfortable with. She began to feel that she was in control, and this made her much more relaxed. For the first time she actually was able to enjoy this form of lovemaking, and, although it did not become a central part of their sex life, at least a brief period of oral stimulation became a fairly regular activity when they made love. Empathy and acceptance solved the problem where resistance and coercion had failed.

If your aim is to arrive at a fruitful resolution of your difficulties and not just to blow off steam, even your manner of speaking and your voice tone need to be thoughtfully considered. Many of us are more formidable and intimidating than we are aware of being. As one woman said, "I finally discovered that I actually lose power when I say things too strongly. If I say, 'Honey, when you clean up the kitchen and leave it only half done I just want to scream. Could you please complete the cleanup once you've started it?' he'll say, 'Oh, I'm sorry. I meant to go back and finish.' But if I walk into the kitchen and shout, 'Damn it, you left the dishes standing there and it's been three hours!' and I start slamming the dishes into the dishwasher, he'll either withdraw and stay withdrawn until he can deal with me or he'll shout back, 'Nobody asked you to go into the goddamn kitchen!' or something like that. It's really clear that the way I talk to him has a lot to do with the response I'm going to get, so I always try to cool off before confronting him. Since I changed my approach, we've made a lot more progress."

People respond most favorably when they are dealt with as equals, not as inferiors. The use of intimidation, condescension, contempt, or statements aimed at belittling a partner, especially in front of others, attest to a lack of self-confidence in the person using such tactics. All they promote is warfare and resistance. A woman we interviewed told us, "Sometimes he talks to me like I was born yesterday or as if I were an idiot. It really turns me off. No way am I going to cooperate with him when he uses that approach."

Parental or authoritarian tactics also have no place in relationships between equals. If we try to order our partners around, they will ultimately thwart our attempts to do so. They may gain weight, take up smoking, turn us down sexually, forget to run an errand for us or in some other way prove that we can't control them. The power in a relationship always gets equalized eventually. One way or another, either directly or indirectly, the person who feels less powerful will sabotage his or her partner's attempts to dominate.

While desires for revenge and retribution may feel like sweet recompense for hurts that have been sustained, acting out these desires has no place in an intimate relationship—unless, of course, the interest is in ending it. Such behavior only promotes a cycle of escalating assaults. Instead of defusing and resolving conflict, they enlarge it. The resulting emotional injuries that are sustained along the way are rarely forgotten. The same is true of threats, which are usually a dramatic way of calling attention to how desperate and frustrated the person making them is feeling. Threats are most often used by people who feel fundamentally weak and uncertain about themselves and who attempt to compensate for these feelings through the use of intimidation, a form of posturing. Threats are also a form of violence and abuse; they represent an attempt to exert unfair leverage and they engender fear and rage, not cooperation. They are an ineffective way of letting your partner know that you are angry and upset. When threats are made repeatedly and not carried out, the person making them loses credibility, inadvertently teaching their partner neither to believe nor respect them.

Whenever Ed became angry at Carrie he threatened to end the relationship, and every time Ed threatened to leave her, Carrie would become seriously depressed and withdrawn. Once Ed realized that his threats to leave were really an expression of his need to feel that he had options, rather than something he actually intended to carry out, he stopped making them. He agreed to mention ending the relationship again only if it was something he was seriously considering. As a result, Carrie felt less intimidated and was more confident and interested in working out their conflicts as they arose.

Making requests is far more effective than giving orders. The governing assumption between equals is that either of you has the right to say no to a request if it is unsuitable, and the other must be willing to negotiate or accept the refusal graciously at such times.

Dialogue, not monologue, is the appropriate vehicle for producing change. Pontificating, talking down to your partner as though he or she were an ignorant fool at the feet of a master, will get you nowhere fast. As one man said: "The thing that really gets to me is when she gets very schoolmarmy, and starts lecturing. It makes me feel put down, like I was a little kid, so when she does this I just turn her off." Unless a person has willingly agreed to be your student, that person will almost certainly refuse your efforts to "educate" them.

Talking louder and longer also has a notably poor correlation with being heard and understood. Being more logical and eloquent may pay off in the boardroom, but not necessarily in the bedroom. The object of dialogue is to invite each person to put their thoughts and feelings into the forum so that differences can be recognized, explored, and dealt with democratically. You have not convinced someone merely because, through whatever tactics, you have silenced them. Silenced feelings are not resolved feelings, and any "victory" based on silencing is going to be a pyrrhic one: the conflict is certain to resurrect itself in the future. Consequently, it is important to be sure that both of you are comfortable with your discussion and its conclusions before assuming that the case is closed. And the simplest way to find that out is to ask. Ending important discussions by recapping what has been discussed or decided can eliminate misunderstandings before any further confusion and conflict develop.

Again, beware of mind reading. You may rush to judgment based on assumptions made without ever having taken the time to check out their accuracy or validity—and you may be dead wrong. Nearly everyone has had such an embarrassing experience, both as the accuser as well as the one falsely accused. If you are not careful, in long-term relationships "reading a partner's mind" can become an insidious habit in which more attention is devoted to speaking for your partner than responsibly expressing your own feelings and thoughts. If you habitually speak for your partner, failing to investi̶g̶a̶t̶e̶ own presumptions in doing so, you may be fomentī̶n̶g̶ ber of serious misunderstandings and causing incalculable harm to the relationship.

Humor is an excellent social lubricant and a way to reduce defensiveness, but it does have its limitations. Frequent sarcasm, for example, generally indicates the presence of disguised anger that really needs to be addressed more directly. And humor, at times, can be used to dismiss serious concerns which actually require more in-depth discussion.

One of the things Gabriella liked best about Dave was his sense of humor. He could use his quick intelligence to make her laugh, even when tense or unpleasant situations arose. But his humor and self-deprecating remarks also allowed him to dance around uncomfortable and important issues, like his annoying tendency to make impromptu invitations to include friends on their dates together. Even though Gabriella laughed, she found her anger building as well. Finally, the third time that Dave invited others to join them without asking her permission in advance, she blew her stack and embarrassed him in front of his guests. He never forgave her for her rudeness, she never forgave him for his, and their relationship ended on this sour note.

The Art of Listening

In terms of conflict resolution, the way we listen to information is as important as how we present it. However, attentive listening is not something that comes easily. A history of being ignored, dismissed, or unjustifiably accused, predisposes many people to impaired listening capabilities.

You have not listened to someone merely because your ears have heard their words. Attentive listening is a complex skill that requires giving your partner your full, undivided attention. By this we mean that your attention is not to be diluted by either external *or* internal distractions.

Watching TV, reading a paper, listening to music, or working on a project while trying to listen to what is being said will obviously create impediments to healthy communication. Both the listener and the speaker must then compete with the distraction for full attention. This obviously can lead to misunderstandings. It can also result in increased impatience and irritability as each of you tries to overcome the pull of the distracting element.

Less obvious, however, are the internal distractions that compete for the listener's full and undivided attention: extraneous thoughts may easily intrude on your consciousness and divert your focus from what your partner is saying. You may discover yourself formulating rebuttals, corrections, excuses, exceptions, apologies, and qualifications to what your partner is saying even as he or she is speaking. These internal machinations can readily erode your ability to listen effectively.

It is easy to combat the external distractions, of course: put down the paper, turn off the TV, stop gardening or playing the piano, or set a time to talk when these other activities have been concluded. Dealing with internal distractions is more difficult, but there are a number of techniques that can prove useful. It helps to look directly in your partner's eyes while he or she is talking: facial expressions will not only reveal additional information, but will help you to focus on what is being said.

If you feel anxious, guilty, or otherwise uncomfortable while listening, try to relax by taking a few deep breaths. Remember that this too shall pass, and remind yourself that you have something to learn from what your partner is telling you. Stay open to what he or she is saying by avoiding the common mistakes of interrupting, contradicting, qualifying or changing the subject.

As a listener, your verbal expression should be limited to requests for clarification or for specific examples, so that you can understand your partner more fully and more precisely. Otherwise, try to be silently attentive.

Only one person should talk at a time. Even when you believe a factual error is being made, it is best, whenever possible, to correct this *after* your partner has finished or, if the correction is absolutely necessary for the conversation to proceed, make it gently, briefly, and unthreateningly.

Remember, rather than trying to control your partner, dismiss or minimize their worries, or prove them wrong, your objective as a listener is to encourage the fullest expression of your partner's concerns in an attempt to arrive at the deepest understanding of their point of view. Since there is rarely an absolute right or wrong, just two different perspectives, a working solution cannot be arrived at without having all the relevant data. The data can only be gathered by listening assiduously to what your partner has to say.

So when you are listening to a criticism or complaint, do everything in your power to avoid the pitfall of evaluating everything being said with an eye to searching for errors, issues you can disagree with, or points you can invalidate. Instead, look for the validity, the grain of truth, the one thing that you *could* learn from, that could better your relationship. As one man told us, "Even when I think that I didn't do what she is accusing me of, if she is taking the time to bring it to my attention and it is obviously upsetting her, there is usually something I need to learn. She doesn't get disturbed for no reason at all."

Active Listening

The technique of "active listening" ensures that you not only hear, but really *understand* what your partner is trying to tell you. Often, resolving the differences between two people becomes difficult because, without being aware of it, you may actually be arguing about two different things. Perhaps you have been so busy evaluating your partner's statements and planning your own rebuttal that your attention strayed while your partner was talking; perhaps you projected your own interpretations onto what was being said and without realizing it made certain assumptions that differed substantially from what your partner meant. Active listening can correct these misunderstandings as they occur and prevent them from developing into greater problems.

In essence, active listening consists of paraphrasing your partner's words, repeating in your own words what you believe your partner is trying to communicate to you. It is a process of checking to make certain that you and your partner are truly on the same wavelength, and it is a way of confirming that you understand both the thought being expressed as well as the feelings that underlie the thought.

Nicole and Chad had a disturbing fight as they returned from the Christmas party at Nicole's office. Chad was hurt and angry that Nicole hadn't paid much attention to him, especially because she hadn't made a sufficient effort to introduce him to her co-workers. Nicole thought that Chad was being jealously possessive simply because she was enjoying the innocent company of other men at a social function. She felt irate at what she thought were Chad's accusations.

Nicole and Chad might have avoided their painful argument. By using the principle of active listening, their discussion might have gone more like this:

CHAD Why did you bother inviting me to the party if you didn't want to be with me?

NICOLE You think I didn't want to be with you? But I *did* want to be with you.

CHAD You say you wanted to be with me, but it sure didn't seem that way to me. You ignored me all afternoon and it looked like you were having a great time with your other friends!

NICOLE You thought I didn't want you there because I didn't pay enough attention to you?

CHAD Sure. You hardly introduced me to anyone. I felt awkward, almost invisible.

NICOLE Were you jealous?

CHAD No, I just felt ignored.

NICOLE   Oh, I'm sorry, I didn't realize that you felt alone and awkward. It seemed that you were having a good time and making contacts on your own. I guess I was just caught up in the office gossip. So you weren't jealous?

CHAD   Well . . . a bit. I thought you were feeling like you'd rather be with someone else.

NICOLE   No, I wasn't interested in anyone else. Although, it's funny, I did notice that every time I talked to one of the guys, you suddenly appeared at my side. I thought you were being jealous and possessive, so I veered away from you.

CHAD   You thought I was being jealous when I appeared at your side? Maybe a little, but I was mostly trying to get connected! I really didn't want to cramp your style. I just needed more contact than you were giving me. Maybe it would help in the future if we touched base more often when we go to social events.

NICOLE   Sure. And I'll be more careful about introducing you to others. I can see why you felt the way you did.

To minimize the listener's potential confusion, keep your statements short and to the point. Remember that the speaker is the sole judge of whether he or she has truly been understood. If the listener hasn't understood, the speaker should try again, using different words. Continue the dialogue until a satisfactory understanding has been achieved.

Here's another example of active listening:

HE   I wasn't sure what you were trying to tell me this morning. I thought you wanted to make love, but once we started you seemed to be rushing things, just going through the motions as quickly as possible.

SHE   You didn't know if I really wanted to make love or not?

HE   Right. I didn't know how to react. In fact, I just about decided to roll over and go back to sleep, but that didn't seem right either.

SHE   Well, I can see that I might have been sending out a mixed message. I really did want to make love, but I had a date with my mother, and last week she was really upset with me because I kept her waiting, so I promised her that I wouldn't be late again. I was afraid that if we made love I wouldn't be on time to meet her.

HE   Sounds to me like you didn't know what you wanted to do so you wanted *me* to make the decision.

SHE   No, I didn't want you to make the decision. But I was confused, which is probably why you were confused. I felt pressured to go, but I didn't want to disappoint you either.

HE   Oh, so you really didn't know what you wanted? You were worried about being late and also about disappointing me?

SHE   I think that's right.

HE   Well, why didn't you just tell me what you were feeling? I'd be happier to take a rain check than to be rushed along.

SHE   You'd rather have me tell you "no" than feel rushed, even if it meant that we didn't make love?

HE   Yes. It's not worth it the other way.

SHE   I didn't realize that. Thanks. Knowing that takes a lot of pressure off me.

Validation

If we do not feel that our partner has heard us, we will generally repeat ourselves, perhaps using a louder tone of voice, perhaps at another time, but we are likely to continue to reiterate our point of view until we feel that we have made an impact. However, once we feel heard, understood, and acknowledged, we are able to ease off. In fact, validating a partner's point of view is probably the most salient factor in resolving a conflict.

Validation consists of giving credence to our partner's universe of experience, a universe different from but no less valid than our own. For most of us, being validated is as important as obtaining the outcome for which we are lobbying. In fact, from a psychological perspective, it may be even more important.

We may not necessarily agree with what our partner is saying, but by validating them we are acknowledging that we recognize the worth of their subjective experience; we bear witness to it even though we may find it at odds with our own. We are indicating by this recognition that there will be room in the relationship to encompass more than one perspective. For example, your partner says, "It's cold in here. Will you put up the heat?" You respond by saying, "It's not cold in here. I only have a T-shirt on and I'm warm." This is an invalidating response because it assumes, based on your own subjective point of view, that your partner is incorrect. However, if instead you said, "Although I'm not cold, I can see that you are," you have a place from which to start negotiating. At that point you can agree to turn up the heat or you can ask your partner if he or she wouldn't mind putting on a warm sweater instead, so that it does not become uncomfortably warm for you. Or, perhaps, you could turn the heat up just a few degrees and your partner could put on a light sweater. In any of these instances, the solution is based upon a cooperative attitude, one that takes both points of view into account.

All of us want to be treated with consideration for our feelings and thoughts, especially by those closest to us. Validation is the key to expressing respect and consideration. It can also make or break the process of conflict resolution.

In essence, Shane felt that she was the social director of the relationship: if she didn't make the arrangements, they would rarely go out or visit with friends. Even though Eugene had made it quite clear early on that he was not comfortable initiating these social contacts, Shane still got irritated periodically at the inequity. On those occasions, Eugene let her know just how much he appreciated all that she did, and then proceeded to make a social plan or two on his own initiative. Even though Shane knew that things were not likely to change dramatically in this area, Eugene's willingness to recognize her feelings meant a great deal to her and, without resentment, she once again resumed her role as social chairwoman.

It is essential to validate your partner's feelings *before* putting
your own feelings out on the table. If this sequence is not followed and this acknowledgment is not given, trouble, in the
form of escalation and competition, is likely to follow. For instance, if your partner says, "I feel really angry when you raise
your voice at me that way," and you answer with, "If I didn't,
you wouldn't pay attention to what I'm saying," you have
started the escalation process. If instead you first validate your
partner's feelings by saying, "Sorry—I guess I was talking too
loudly," you then can go on to say something like, "It was
because I didn't think that you heard me. I'd like to have your
attention when we're talking." At this point it would then be
your partner's responsibility to ratify your point of view and
acknowledge responsibility for having been inattentive, if that
was the case.

It is easier for most people to own their role in a conflict
when their partner owns theirs. When our partner contradicts
our reality we feel dismissed and discounted. If we don't get
the acknowledgment we need, we only try harder to get our
partner to see our point of view and in this way we become
even further entrenched in our own limited reality.

Mara provided us with a good example of how this sequence
of validation averted an argument. "After dinner last night
Nigel and I went to my apartment," she said, "and the first
thing I did upon entering was to listen to my answering machine to see if I had any messages. Nigel followed me, saying,
'Nothing earth shattering happened; just leave it alone,' or
something like that. Anyway, it made me fume. 'I'll listen to
my answering machine anytime I want to,' I retorted. 'If I
wanted to be with someone who was going to tell me what I
should and shouldn't do I would have married my father! Stop
nagging me.' I was really surprised when he said, 'Sorry—
you're right; it was really none of my business to tell you how
to deal with your phone messages.' You could have blown me
away with a feather. And that was the end of it. My anger was

gone and we had a nice evening. As long as I know that he hears me, I can let go of it."

Another all-too-common signpost of unhealthy communication, and a telltale introduction to what will probably turn out to be an invalidating remark, is the phrase "Yes, but . . ." At first, this phrase sounds as if it will be supportive and sympathetic in that it starts with the word "yes." The word "but," however, is exclusionary; it is defined in Webster's Dictionary as *"always* adversative," that is, it is used to refer to adversarial relationships, not cooperative ones. The "but" therefore discounts and cancels the effect of the "yes," and the recipient of the message ends up feeling placated or dismissed. For example, if you say, "Yes, I know you've been overworked, *but* I need your attention now," you are, in effect, dismissing the validation or support pretended by the word "yes," setting up a kind of challenge, and increasing the likelihood of conflict.

On the other hand, the conjunction "and" is *inclusionary.* Saying, "I know you have been overworked *and* I still need your attention now," validates each of your positions and needs, allowing both of them to co-exist, thus lowering the likelihood of conflict. "And" invites, "but" rejects; "and" opens, "but" closes. This, we promise you, is not merely a hairsplitting distinction: using "and" rather than "but" creates an atmosphere which is far more conducive to resolving the issues at hand. Of course, merely using the word "and" is insufficient in itself. You also must *mean* what you say, inviting your partner's feelings and thoughts to stand democratically alongside your own.

An egalitarian relationship is the one that can lead to the profoundest intimacy, and validation is a fundamental element of all such relationships. When each of you takes care to validate the other's experience, no one's welfare is compromised.

THE RESOLUTION OF CONFLICT

Many couples agree never to go to bed feeling angry, having made a commitment to work out whatever problems exist between the two of them before the day has ended. While this is generally an excellent approach, there are times when a dogged insistence on grappling with a conflict can be destructive—for instance, when you are both tired and your flagging energies cause your attention to stray and lapse, or when you find yourself at a stalemate, repeating the same irksomely unproductive approach to the problem. At other times the anxieties and pressures of having to get up early for work may give you reason to agree to continue your discussion later the next day. It is perfectly acceptable to say, "I'm sorry, I'm too tired to go on with this right now. Can we continue it tomorrow (or in a few hours, or at some specific time in the very near future)?"

Certainly, you don't want your partner to feel dismissed, ignored, or otherwise hurt by your inability to be fully present for an important discussion, but it is far better to have a satisfying conversation when you are both fresh and attentive than to continue to plug away at it with diminishing returns. Taking a break may provide you with a new perspective and help you to resolve the impasse. It must be emphasized, however, that if one of you needs to get some distance, some time alone to reevaluate your feelings or point of view, it is incumbent upon *that* person to assume responsibility for reestablishing the discussion, and it is most helpful if you can agree upon a particular time when it will be resumed.

There are times when a conflict may span several days before it is resolved, times when other issues surface that lie beneath the one you've been discussing. The important thing is that you continue to talk, keeping the lines of communication open, until a resolution has been reached that makes both of you feel more at peace.

If either person in a relationship is defeated, the relationship itself is diminished. Trying to "win" an argument (trying to defeat your partner as if he or she were an opponent) is a destructive model for conflict resolution in an intimate relationship. A relationship is *not* a zero-sum game in which one person "wins" and the other "loses." There are either *two*

"winners" or *two* "losers" at the end of any conflict. Ultimately, feeling good and loving toward each other is unquestionably more pleasant and rewarding than holding on to being
"right."

The Art of Apology

A positive outcome to conflict can be accomplished only
when both people take the risk of saying what is difficult to say,
especially choosing to apologize if and when they are wrong.
Making the first move toward reconciliation can be difficult,
because when you expose your vulnerabilities to your partner
you leave yourself potentially open to attack. Taking the first
step toward reconciliation doesn't necessarily mean accepting
total responsibility, however. Indeed, such false humility can
misdirect the relationship into an additional morass. Yet, when
one partner genuinely takes the lead in reconciling, it is easier
for the other person to follow suit. It requires a person with a
strong ego to take the first step toward apologizing. It is the
more *in*secure person who must appear to be "right" at all
costs.

It goes without saying that each partner has a profound responsibility to make it *safe* for the other to admit to error in
whatever form it may have occurred. Too many people leap
upon their partner's admission of error as a perverse opportunity to extract the proverbial pound of flesh. Statements such
as "It's about time you finally admitted that you were wrong"
or "I told you so" or "Maybe next time you'll listen to me"
have no place in a relationship that is striving to achieve loving
intimacy. Any rejoinder that underscores a partner's guilt or
attempts to take revenge by embarrassing the partner is fundamentally misguided and destructive. Again, it will produce
only alienation, resentment, defensiveness, and a markedly reduced likelihood of admitting to error in the future.

It is far more constructive and encouraging if, instead, you
express your appreciation and support to your partner for hav-

ing apologized by saying something like "Thanks for being willing to own up to that" or "I appreciate your honesty." The more people are rewarded for extending themselves in this way, the easier it is for them to do so in the future. It is no sin to have erred or acted with poor judgment, although not apologizing for your errors when you know you've made them can seriously diminish trust and love in a relationship. Once an apology is made and appreciation expressed, it is important to drop the issue; don't bring it up later for rehashing.

Even if you don't realize your contribution to a conflict until a day or two after it has occurred, it is still essential to apologize. Wendy and Jake got into an argument about his returning to school and studying law. "Don't you remember how unhappy you were when you went back for your business degree?" Wendy reminded him. "You were always bitching about money, and this will cost even more and take a lot longer. You'll have to cut way back on your work, so how will you meet your expenses?" "I only wanted your support," he retorted, "not an analysis of my financial life. I think it's a good idea and I'm going forward with it." They fought back and forth about it for hours before they finally let it drop.

When Jake awoke the next morning he went for his usual run before going to work and found himself pondering the issue as he ran. He often did his best thinking during these morning workouts, and as he reflected more dispassionately on the matter it became increasingly clear to him that Wendy was absolutely right: the financial pressure would be extreme if he cut back at work to go to law school, and he didn't feel at all comfortable with the prospect of three more years of struggle. After his run, Jake wrote Wendy a note acknowledging that what she had said was correct. They both considered the matter resolved and no more was said about it by either of them.

Reestablishing Intimacy

Reestablishing intimacy after a conflict can sometimes be awkward, especially when one of you prefers to make love in order to reconnect and the other needs more time to talk, to do things together, or even to be alone, before feeling ready for physical intimacy. This common difference can itself become the basis for further conflict: the partner who initiates lovemaking may feel rejected when not responded to positively and the other partner may feel rushed or invaded. Quite suddenly the resolution of the difficulty, which was within easy reach, is once again far away.

When such a disparity exists between yourself and your partner, the person who is feeling most wary or vulnerable about resuming lovemaking should be allowed to have greater control over when and how it is resumed. This person may, for instance, require a brief period of time alone before being able to reconnect. Yet, it is essential that the partner who wants the more immediate emotional connection be given solace as well. Words of reassurance such as "I need some time alone now, but I'll be back before too long," can bridge the emotional gap. When the couple reunites they might spend some time being tender with one another, doing something together which is pleasant and encouraging to their friendship, which relaxes their defensiveness and allows love to flow between them once more.

Healthy conflict resolution is usually accompanied by a rebirth of loving feelings as our defensive, self-protective walls crumble. There are other reliable signposts which indicate that a conflict has been successfully resolved. Negative feelings should dissipate and you should be well on the way to forgiving and forgetting. In fact, most people *do* forget the particulars that led to a conflict that has been well resolved. As one man said, "I know we've had times when we were in agony over something or other, but for the life of me I can't remember what they were about." In addition, as we develop an increased confidence that we can get through difficult times without splitting up, trust is enhanced. As another woman told us, "My boyfriend now knows that it is even possible for us to have really terrible fights and that I'm not going to leave him, that I'm not going to betray him like his ex-wife did."

THE EVOLUTION OF CONFLICT

Conflict is never likely to disappear completely—not even in the healthiest of relationships—but in a good relationship you should expect your fights to change over time, with less blaming and a greater feeling that you are on the same team trying to attain goals that will be of advantage to the both of you. As a relationship successfully journeys toward greater intimacy and deeper love, the frequency, the intensity, and the duration of serious conflict should be decreasing.

However, if you find that your conflicts are *not* getting less frequent, less intense, and shorter, you need to have a talk with your partner at a time when you are free of the very conflicts you are trying to explore to see if you can unearth any basic themes underlying your strife. Many couples find that one or two repetitive themes run below the multitude of issues they fight about.

Most commonly, conflicts center around the issue of control. When there are differences in personal style (for example, spiritual-material, intuitive-logical, ordered-spontaneous), whose personal style will win out? Who is going to call the shots about the many decisions a couple must make? These themes can manifest themselves in such diverse situations as choosing a restaurant, deciding what to do on Sunday, or even how to wash the dishes.

Frequent arguments about how often you get together, how much time you spend together, and other matters concerning the depth and pacing of the relationship's development may indicate a discrepancy in your levels of commitment. This, of course, must be openly discussed and resolved before the relationship can deepen.

Don't be alarmed if you have to return to an issue a number of times before it is ultimately resolved. A conflict may be partially resolved only to reemerge after a few weeks or months. When things deteriorate, you need to confront the issue again, and with each successive attempt the resolution may be more complete. As one woman told us, "If there is something important to me, he'll get it. He might not get it right away, but past history has shown that if I stay with it, gently and patiently, he'll ultimately understand what I'm trying to convey."

A man we interviewed summed it up this way: "I believe a good relationship is a lot like two rocks with rough edges that are in a bag together. Over time as they come into repeated contact, bumping into one another, chips are knocked off each of them, rough edges are smoothed out. Eventually you get two pretty smooth stones with polished surfaces, but it does take a while."

6

Influence

Pathways to Change

The Art of Progress is to preserve order amid change and to preserve change amid order.

—Alfred North Whitehead

The habits of behavior and ways of thinking that we have developed over the years and have grown comfortable with, that have come to work pretty well for us, are sometimes the very ones that cause problems for our partner. Our partner, after all, has spent a separate lifetime learning and practicing entirely different ways of dealing with many of the same life issues.

The insouciant optimist, the indefatigable bundle of energy, the obsessive-compulsive controller, the inveterate cynic, and other fundamental styles of behavior are usually what we refer to when we talk of someone's personality: a way of being-in-the-world. Regardless of their genesis, be they genetic or learned, these personality configurations are unlikely to change to any significant degree after we reach maturity, and even less so as we continue to grow older.

If we are relentlessly unhappy with our partner's way of being-in-the-world, we should not be with that person: it is as simple as that. As we mentioned in the last chapter, it is not only futile, it is oppressively unfair to expect and pressure our partner to transform who he or she is, to attempt a personality makeover. Unfortunately, this truth doesn't deter some people from holding onto the fantasy that with a bit more time and effort they could change their partner into becoming another person, the person they honestly believe their partner would even be happier being. The road to hell is paved with such "good" intentions!

THE MECHANISMS OF CHANGE

While taking on the transformation of our partner's personality is a preposterous project, influencing certain behavioral change—especially in areas that directly affect us—is not. *Within limits*, there are ways in which we can and do influence each other's behavior for the better (and, of course, sometimes for the worse).

Unfortunately, the methods most commonly used in attempting to induce change—complaining, cajoling, sweet-talking, nagging, guilt induction, anger, and other forms of emotional leverage and manipulation—don't work very well. They convey dissatisfaction and criticism and, predictably, they lead the person on the receiving end of these messages to feel judged, unloved, and angry—the very antithesis of an emotional climate that fosters change.

Fran considered herself to be a visual perfectionist. She was thoroughly jarred by disorder, whereas neatness and order, especially in her apartment, gave her a sense of peace and a quiet esthetic delight. When Ken would come to stay overnight he would sometimes leave the kitchen chairs awry or a few dishes out after eating breakfast or he would not replace a magazine on the pile from which he had taken it. She knew that he was much less concerned about how things were arranged in his own apartment. He usually had dishes in the sink, an unmade bed, and a pile of laundry on the floor of the closet, so when she came to his place she did him the "favor" of tidying it up a bit.

After a number of months, Fran's relentless and persuasive logic about how things *should* be arranged managed to convince Ken to become more scrupulous about the way he kept his own apartment . . . when he expected her to visit. Before Fran would arrive he would engage in a tidying frenzy in order to avoid her nagging criticism or the silent judgment implied as she put his dishes away, emptied the ashtrays, and aligned the books on the bureau near his bed. However, he noticed that before long his desire to make love ebbed away, the costly by-product of his unconscious anger.

No one is powerful enough to change someone else against their will unless, through coercion and abuse, their will is broken. And then what have you? An angry, defeated, half person; no one you can love and respect. Certainly no one who will love and respect you. The more vigorously you try to change your partner's personality style, the more likely your partner is to resist and frustrate your efforts, and before you know it an escalating battle of wills is under way.

The key to eliciting a change in your partner's behavior lies in a totally different process: one based upon changing *yourself.* Since you are the designated authority over only one person, *you* are the only person you can effectively change. However, when your intentions and efforts are creatively and consciously *self*-focused, the *incidental effect* on your partner's behavior can be decisive.

Homeostasis

A relationship is a system, meaning that the parts—the two people and the way they express themselves—are interactive and interdependent: each person necessarily affects and influences the other all the time. Within a system it is not possible to alter the functioning of one part without causing an alteration in the functioning of its counterparts.

All living systems operate in accord with certain fundamental principles, one of which is the principle of *homeostasis*. Homeostasis refers to the fact that a living system tends to move into a state of equilibrium or balance. In relationships, this means that when there is an *excess* on the part of one person in the system, an excess that is problematic, you are likely to find a *deficit* in the counterpart of the system expressed by the other person.

For example, let's say that your partner is considerably less helpful or responsible in a certain area than you believe to be fair. As you continue to pick up the slack yourself, you try to convince your partner to lend a hand, doing everything from asking politely to badgering. Regardless of what you say, however, you find that it is still you alone who does the work, albeit grudgingly. Unknowingly, you have actually become a coconspirator of sorts, colluding with your partner in sustaining the very problem you wish to resolve.

If you are putting too much energy or effort into a particular aspect of the relationship and your partner is putting too little into it, changing the equilibrium of your relationship system by *reducing your own input* will tend to create a vacuum that, *after a period of time has lapsed,* your partner is more likely to fill.

Julie had always assumed the bulk of the responsibility for planning their vacations together because, left to his own devices, Oscar never seemed to get around to it. During this particular time as she set about making arrangements, she also encountered an emergency at her job. Even with giving the problems at work her full attention, it was touch and go as to whether she would be able to leave for vacation at all. Any significant planning or preparation on her part was out of the question. She just had no time available.

Julie was very frustrated; Oscar still wasn't lending much of a hand despite the fact that she had asked him to do so a number of times. "I finally got really angry about it one day," she said, "and I told him that if there was any possibility of us going on vacation, it was going to have to be up to him. I didn't say another word. I just focused my energies fully on the problem at work. Well, I was amazed to discover that Oscar actually handled the whole thing. And we had a great time, even if he did forget the toothpaste and the snorkel equipment. We just bought new stuff when we got there. It was a relief to know that when I really let go, I could count on him."

At first you may find Julie's approach and the solution it produced hard to believe. Your greatest fear may be that if *you* do less, *nothing* will get done at all. And in all likelihood, if your partner has absolutely no interest in the area in question, it is likely to remain your primary responsibility. But, if your partner can derive some personal benefit from making a contribution, he or she will gradually do more *because* you do less, filling the gap created by your absence. The transition, like most transitions, will take some time and patience—systems almost never change instantaneously.

Relinquishing Control

The ability to influence the relationship system by changing yourself rather than trying to change your partner is among the most effective ways of sidestepping conflict and achieving the goals you desire. Sometimes, however, people find it difficult to change their behavior because of their own discomfort in giving up control, and a willingness to give up control over certain areas is necessary if real change is to occur.

With some couples, one person consistently plays the responsible "parent" role and the other assumes the irresponsible "child" role. Because of a system's tendency toward homeostasis, when either person too fully occupies either one of these roles it actually tends to *force* the other person into assuming the opposite role. This balance is maladaptive because it is so polarized and rigidified. However, it cannot change until the "parent" is willing to relinquish control, because no matter how hard the "child" tries to be more responsible, he or she cannot succeed until the "parent" has made room for change to occur by switching to a supportive rather than a controlling stance.

Learning to give up controlling power is often a good deal more difficult than learning to wield it. We are inclined to equate active control with strength and to assume that the power of surrender or yielding is the mark of a weak person. This is actually far from true, for it takes a good deal more internal fortitude and self-confidence to be able to relax one's usual vigilance and yield control. Allowing ourselves to be guided by our loved one despite our own desire to be the guide is a hallmark of a trusting relationship between equals and indicates that being vulnerable within that relationship is possible.

Many of us never experience the genuine pleasure of healthy surrender because, in order to keep our anxieties manageable, we must always retain control. In maintaining this control, we prevent our partner from making the very changes we say we would like them to make. We may say we want our partner to do more around the house, for example, yet our demands are so exacting that we leave them no room for their own creative input, or we respond to their own way of fulfilling the task by being critical and dissatisfied and, eventually, resume control of the responsibility once again, feeling rather like a martyr: "If I don't do it, it will never be done properly" (as if we alone define what is proper).

If your partner's job is to load the dishwasher, for example, but you continually tell them just how to do it, you will soon notice that you are doing more and more of the dishwasher loading yourself. If you want your partner to share the cooking, but always find fault with their meals—the meat is overdone, the pasta lacks salt, there is no salad—your partner will become less and less excited about meal preparation. If you want your partner to be more informed about and conversant with current world events, but you point out how misinformed they are or sharply criticize any factual errors when they express their opinions, they are likely to give up the endeavor, or at least stop talking to you about what they think.

Often, the controlling person initially sees his or her behavior as being only generous and beneficial rather than controlling and problematic. About a year after Billie and Charles started going together in college Billie had a devastating diving accident. For a while it was thought that she might remain paralyzed for life. During the time of her long convalescence Charles became her primary caretaker; he had to feed her, drive her around, and help her with her studies. Billie was very dependent on Charles, and their situation naturally encouraged a system to develop in which Billie became somewhat of a "child" to Charles's "parent." They were both irritated with their roles, but couldn't seem to break out of them no matter how hard they tried. Finally, the stress proved to be too great and they split up. During the nine months they spent apart Billie discovered that she could be more and more independent, and as her healing progressed so did her capacity to take renewed control over her life. When they started dating again, however, Charles fell into his parental role once more and Billie began to regress to her childlike role. When they noticed this pattern recurring they began to work decisively on resisting it, good-humoredly helping each other to notice their respective slip-ups, and eventually they moved the relationship into a healthier, more democratic, balance of power.

By changing yourself, you will eventually create a new balance in the relationship—one that may work better in the long run. But there is a tendency in all systems to resist change—to maintain the *status quo*. Therefore, it must be emphasized that you have to *persist*—overcoming the resistance to change takes time, and then it takes additional time for the new behaviors to become well established.

Even when you do change your own behavior, there is no guarantee that you will be successful at significantly influencing your partner's behavior in the ways that you would like. Instead, however, changing your own behavior may affect your attitude in such a way that this attitudinal switch effectively resolves the problem. Lisa and Jack were temperamentally quite different. Lisa's pace was rapid: she was quick at completing tasks, often doing two things at the same time, quick at making decisions, at formulating her ideas and conclusions. She was quick tempered as well. Jack, on the other hand, was quieter and more deliberate. He tended to be rather low key, reflective, emotionally calm, cool and collected, perhaps even a bit phlegmatic.

Whenever Lisa tried to make Jack move faster he only seemed to dig in his heels and resist. When, at last, she realized the futility of trying to get Jack to speed things up, Lisa needed to find another way to handle her frustration. She decided to concentrate on slowing down, trying to relax about tasks that had to be done. This was something she *could* accomplish with moderate effort, and although she still felt annoyed from time to time at the disparity in their pacing, her newly developed attitude made her relationship with Jack much less frustrating.

In this instance Lisa's change did not seem to alter Jack's behavior at all, but their relationship system was improved. The long-standing conflict between them subsided, to their mutual benefit. Furthermore, in the process of downshifting, Lisa grew more comfortable with Jack's methodical style and began to appreciate more fully the ways in which it made a positive contribution to their decision making.

There are certain risks involved when the behaviors within a relationship shift. For instance, we may find that particular qualities we liked ("upside" qualities) are lost along with the ("downside") qualities we didn't like: a person becomes more responsible, but less playful; more independent, but less available. And sometimes, to our great surprise, we may even find that when our partner actually does begin to change in the precise manner we had been hoping for, our reaction is more of fear than delight.

Heather's father was an alcoholic. While growing up she never knew what to expect from him, and since she had no control over him, she tried to control nearly everything else in an attempt to create the consistency and security she needed.

When she first started dating Greg in college she noticed that he drank a fair amount of beer, but neither of them considered the possibility that he might be a budding alcoholic. When Greg started dental school the problem became more noticeable, especially when they went out socially. After a number of drinks, he would either become more aggressive and rude, or he would fall asleep. Everyone chalked up these behaviors to how hard Greg was working. Heather would kick Greg under the table when he was drinking or quietly beg him to stop, but nothing seemed to change.

One morning, Greg's hangover and trembling hands affected his dental procedure and he finally had to acknowledge that he had a serious alcoholic problem. He decided to join AA in order to do something about it, but rather than being relieved by this positive turn of events, Heather was surprised to find that she was actually quite disturbed by it. Numerous fears surfaced: if Greg were more competent and in control of himself maybe he would realize that he didn't need her and he would leave; maybe he would fall in love with someone else.

Heather grappled with her fears. She didn't want to end up like her mother, married to an alcoholic, so she gradually began to abdicate a number of responsibilities that she had previously assumed in the relationship, and as Greg stopped drinking he began to take over some of them. These developments measurably increased Heather's trust in Greg, and their relationship began to change. Among other things, she noticed that she was "allowing" herself to have orgasms with him, something she had always had difficulty with before.

If a couple succeeds in altering their system in a fundamental way, the switch in their balance of power may entail an emotionally distressful period of transition. Rather than things immediately getting better, they may actually worsen for a while as the old rules are discarded but before the new rules are in place. In certain ways this is similar to what might occur if you wanted to improve your tennis game and began taking lessons. Initially you would become aware of many of your bad habits, ones you have been using for years. As you begin to make changes in your swing, you first feel awkward and inept. Most likely you have even more difficulty hitting the ball with the new, improved swing than you did with your old one. For a time your game actually worsens. However, after a period of difficulty and little success, you integrate the new skills, and as they become familiar, your game slowly begins to improve, soon surpassing anything you had previously achieved. The same kind of time and practice is necessary for new and more effective patterns of interaction to become established and integrated into the routine of a relationship.

One of the more problematic aspects of achieving structural changes in a relationship centers on our tendency to play watchdog. Because of our anxious concern about our partner's ability to follow through on their contribution, we may be more attuned to their possible backsliding than we are to our own progress. By focusing our attention on our partner, we foster their resistance. As we have noted, the swiftest and surest way to change the relationship system is to dedicate our energies to working on transforming our *own* roles within it.

Action and Reaction

An important concept that can be used to augment change is derived from the physical principle of action and reaction: for every action there is an equivalent and directionally opposite reaction. When applied to relationships, the concept of action and reaction essentially refers to reciprocity: actions on your part will tend to promote equivalent reactions on the part of your partner back toward you. Aggressive actions ultimately beget aggressive reactions; generosity usually breeds generosity. Consequently, it becomes possible, to some extent, to shape behaviors of your partner by consistently treating him or her in the way *you* would like to be treated.

If, for example, your partner errs and you one-up them with an "I told you so," you are certainly not going to promote positive feelings and a willingness on your partner's part to support you when you err in the future. And you *will* err. When you do, you are likely to get an "I told you so" in return.

Generous-spiritedness, on the other hand, can continue to pay positive dividends long into the future. We interviewed a couple who had been married over fifty years and who continued to enjoy a vital and loving relationship. The man recounted a story about their dating days during the Depression when, despite his training as an engineer, he could get only low-paying jobs as a draftsman. Additionally, on one occasion, he had been fired and his ideas were stolen and developed by his employers, leaving him feeling crushed and hopeless. Meanwhile, his new love never lost faith, sticking by him and supporting him emotionally as well as financially until things finally turned around for them. After a time of hardship and economic privation he found a good-paying job and eventually received a sizable settlement for his stolen inventions. "By being so supportive, Doreen built up enough credit during that period," he said, "to last a lifetime."

Allowing a partner to be in a bad mood without making them feel guilty about it is another form of generosity. We all have our gloomy days and should be permitted to deal with them from time to time without having to cope with external pressures to put on a cheery face. Of course, this does not give us the right to take our bad moods out on our partner, but a generous-spirited partner, one who allows us the time we need to work through the personal issues we are dealing with, helps us to return more fully and more rapidly to the relationship.

Nora's friends would have described her as a rather moody person; in fact, her close relatives reported that dark mood swings had punctuated her life since early childhood. These episodes had always caused problems with her boyfriends because they tended to take her moods personally, as if she were expressing dissatisfaction with *them*.

When Nora met Gary things went quite differently. Gary found it quite easy to accept Nora's occasional emotional shifts as long as he knew that she was not upset with him. When they occurred he would quietly leave her to herself, checking in periodically and unobtrusively to see if she needed anything. Nora felt a relief that she had never before experienced. Not having to manufacture a friendly facade in order to deal with Gary permitted her to get through her own disturbance more quickly. When her mood lifted, her gratitude made Gary feel good about himself: a winning solution for the both of them.

A relationship can easily begin to go downhill when one partner becomes too parsimonious with time, affection, or support. This reduction in nurturance usually leads to the other partner's withholding as well, saying in effect, "I'm not going to give unless I get, and I'm not getting!" Soon a cycle of negative reciprocity takes hold, leaving both partners feeling cheated, alone and closed off: quite contrary to the generous-spirited attitude we have been describing.

It is possible, however, to turn such a negative cycle into a positive one without too much effort. The trick is to react swiftly and nonpunitively to your partner's lapse, once again by changing your own behavior and *giving more* at such times instead of protectively withholding. Your generous-spiritedness is likely to be disarming, thereby reducing your partner's defensiveness and increasing her or his desire to return the favor. An enhancing cycle is then set in motion, similar to that which characterized your early courtship, when mutual thoughtfulness was part of your daily fare together.

Support and Positive Reinforcement

Building on the idea that you can catch more flies with honey than with vinegar—that kindness breeds kindness, and criticism and judgment promote a return of the same—we can now explore how these attitudes can be used not only to support the general atmosphere of love and well-being in a relationship, but actually to *create* specific behavioral change.

The process of positive reinforcement involves two steps: first, pay careful attention to any behavior being expressed by your partner that you wish to *encourage* or *increase*, and second, give your partner immediate verbal approval, recognition, or other forms of appreciation when any positive change has been made, no matter how small. This process is the antithesis of complaining as a way of encouraging a partner to change.

Negative reinforcement, defined as the removal or withholding of "goodies" in an attempt to augment change, is usually destructive, and tends to make people feel hurt, angry and infantilized. Positive reinforcement makes people feel good about themselves, encourages cooperation while diminishing resistance and other forms of defensiveness. It spurs the motivation for becoming open to change, and induces a more relaxed relationship climate.

Kate had grown up in New York City and had never learned to drive. After living in San Francisco for a while, she met Larry and they eventually decided that they would live together in his apartment in Sausalito, across the Golden Gate Bridge, even though both of them worked in San Francisco.

With patience and loving attention, Larry taught Kate how to drive and she got her license. But, being a novice driver, she was still quite insecure and uncomfortable about driving to the city alone. One Friday afternoon, shortly after she arrived home, Larry phoned, telling her that he had totally forgotten about an important business dinner scheduled for that evening. There wasn't enough time for him to take the bus home so that he could drive back with her. Would she drive alone? He really wanted her to accompany him.

"I was agonized," Kate said. "I expected him to be really impatient and irritated when I hesitated and told him that I didn't feel comfortable driving across the bridge. I was ready for a deluge of criticism, and I even felt that I deserved it for being such a baby, but he was surprisingly supportive and understanding. He gently told me that he knew I could do it if I tried. He told me that I was really quite a good driver even though I wasn't a very experienced one, and he suggested that I could just drive to the parking lot at the other side of the bridge and take a taxi the rest of the way. His support and acceptance gave me courage somehow, and I surprised both of us by driving all the way to the restaurant."

Every human being likes to feel competent and successful. When we are backed by positive recognition we are encouraged to perform better in all areas, to extend ourselves and go the extra mile. Recognition and approval tend to stimulate excellence, reciprocity, and generosity, and when two people love each other they want the best for each other as well as for themselves. Positive reinforcement makes excellent, practical sense as long as it is genuinely felt and reasonably given.

Modeling

Human beings, children and adults alike, learn more from observing others' model behavior than they do from any pedagogical pressure. We learn more from witnessing deeds than we do from hearing words. Consequently, rather than persistently attempting to explain to our partners the error of their ways, it is far more effective for us to model the methods, responses, and emotional reactions that we think are more desirable. For example, when he was under pressure, Theo would become increasingly anxious and frenetic, rushing about trying to do six things at once—and doing none of them very thoroughly or well. Sonja, on the other hand, could be under the same pressure yet never accelerate her pace.

At first, Theo would observe the contrast in their styles and grow resentful at Sonja, assuming that she wasn't pulling her share of the load, feeling that too much of the responsibility was on his shoulders. Then it dawned on him: "I'm not part of an army that's rushing across Russia to get to our destination before the first snowfall," he said. "I realized this by Sonja's example. She kept a steady pace and stayed calm. I looked at her and asked myself, 'Who would I rather be, this uptight frenzied person or her?' And that was when I began to cool out —and nobody died or anything and the work eventually got done."

Theo wasn't trying to become another Sonja. He liked who he was, but he was flexible enough to know that his life could be enhanced by taking a leaf from Sonja's book and learning a particular skill from her that worked better than his own did under certain circumstances.

Each person's approach may be equally effective, but under different circumstances. If you rigidly hold on to your own way of doing things irrespective of the situation, and fail to appreciate the particular benefits of your partner's methods, you could be shortchanging yourself in the long run. For example, Bill generally had a rather rebellious nature, whereas Becky tended to be a good deal more compliant. Becky usually would complete a project as instructed, but Bill preferred to figure it out on his own. This difference between them often caused conflict when they were involved in a task together.

Because of their willingness to learn from the other's way of operating, Bill realized that there were certain situations in which it was a lot more efficient to read the directions first, and Becky began to appreciate the flexibility of Bill's more creative approach, which could be a real lifesaver when the situation warranted it.

If you would like to see your partner change her or his behavior, you would be well advised to reflect first on whether you yourself have been providing a good role model for the behavior in question, one from which your partner could learn. Again, you may find that by changing your own behavior and, in this case, providing a good role model, you can most quickly and easily help your partner change in the ways you desire.

Lightening Up

Humor is another powerful tool that can significantly reduce defensiveness and promote cooperative change. Using humor in a way that shows your acceptance of what you deem to be your partner's shortcomings is usually quite endearing, and can enhance the overall atmosphere of the relationship. Furthermore, it should come as no surprise that your partner is more likely to get the message when it is offered in a friendly, humorous manner. We are, of course, not referring to the use of bitterly sarcastic humor that is designed to wound, but to the good-natured kind that allows people to laugh at themselves or at the absurdity of the situation.

Natasha, for instance, had the habit of going off in her thoughts to such an extent that, at times, even if she was in the same room with you, she was *not* in the same room with you. Francis initially found this behavior very annoying, especially when Natasha didn't respond when he talked to her. He knew that her behavior was not aimed at excluding him, but was a result of her concentrated focus, which in other circumstances was an asset. This realization, however, did not cause Francis to dislike Natasha's response any less, but rather than getting angry with her he handled such moments by smiling, waving his hand in front of her face, and saying, "Hello, remember me? I'm your date, Francis Mansfield." This would snap Natasha out of her reverie. They would both have a good laugh and Francis would have gained Natasha's willing attention.

Letting Go

The ability to cut a partner some slack by letting go of small issues is an essential ingredient in any healthy relationship. Overlooking minor "infractions," rather than nitpicking every point, is a form of grace and leads to greater peace and harmony.

One woman told us, "The most important thing I learned in my relationship is to put more 'fat' on my giving—not to be so lean with him, so demanding—and if he makes a mistake or he's rude or whatever, not to impute all these crazy motivations to him all the time. If I don't react so strongly and I can say things in a gentler way, he's a lot nicer and more loving to me and we have much better times together." Another man concurred: "We have decided that talk is cheap and action is what counts—being nice to each other. We used to be long-winded about every little detail, every disappointment or mistake. Now when she uses my razor for her legs I just pop in another blade and forget about it—it's no big deal—and she won't complain about my bringing some dirt into the house from the garden; she just sweeps it out and nicely asks me to take my shoes off. I don't mind: life has become a lot smoother and easier since we've lightened up on each other."

To many of us who are independent and self-sufficient to a fault—traits that in other circumstances may lead to success—it can be difficult to believe that by changing our own behavior and "letting go" we will actually help to facilitate a behavior change in our partner. But the truth is that even if it doesn't immediately lead to the desired response, the change in our own attitude will have a significant and positive effect on our relationship and the happiness we derive from it. After all, the content of most arguments is rather insignificant in the greater scheme of things, yet the argument itself can generate a disproportionate amount of ill will and even long-standing damage. While petty irritations are the source of the majority of our fights, the emotional residue can be anything but petty. Consequently, the value in learning how to lighten up and let go becomes apparent.

One man told us, "Earlier in the relationship I would consistently counter things she said that I didn't like. Actually, I wasted a lot of energy on it because there seemed to be so many issues that I could sink my teeth into. Now I just let it go much of the time. I say to myself, 'I won't get suckered into this one.' For instance, a couple of weeks ago she was complaining that I always act too fast, without thinking things through. Anyway, she went on to say, 'It's because of you that thus and so happened'—I can't remember just what it was. What I *do* remember is that I just decided to drop it. There have been times when I would have picked up on it and really blasted her, but this time I just bit my tongue and went out for a walk. When I got back we talked a bit more about it, but the charge was gone. I think that after I left she also became aware that it made no sense to make a mountain out of a molehill. We let bygones be bygones."

One woman told us that when she feels herself getting angry, she takes a step back. "I stop to think for a minute about just how important the resolution of the conflict or the issue we're confronting will be to me tomorrow, or in a week or even in a year. If it's not going to matter much, I just let go of it."

The healthy ability to let go of occasional small issues in a genuine way should not be confused with the act of merely suppressing feelings. In the latter case harmful consequences are more likely to follow, as martyred feelings find expression in other ways. In the former case, however, the principal considerations are those of proportion, an assessment of the relative importance of what is at issue in the conflict. On some level it is a judgment call: is the issue a major one or a minor one? And if it is minor, can you drop it and go on to other things?

We are talking here about the very practical ability of being able to restrain ourselves appropriately instead of acting impulsively—a measure of moderation and reserve. In this regard one woman told us, "I used to bark at him and he would get terribly upset and then I would feel remorseful. I simply learned to moderate my responses, to be more charitable."

Making changes in our own behavior—letting go, lightening up, yielding some control, being more generous, positively reinforcing rather than criticizing—all have a significant impact on a partner's behavior and therefore, cumulatively, they can alter the very nature of the relationship itself. These are things we can do entirely on our own, without first consulting, convincing, coercing, cajoling, or in some other way obtaining agreement from our partner. Whether or not our partner initially responds in kind, our generosity will be repaid, although it may be at another time or in some other way. There are few things as rewarding and effective as an overall attitude of generous-spiritedness in transforming a relationship. This is nicely illustrated by the following example:

A couple who had been living together for two years were on the verge of splitting up. For the previous six months their quarreling had escalated to the point that hardly a day went by without an altercation. The man realized that he had become very preoccupied with figuring out how to leave the relationship. At about this time he attended a personal growth workshop that made a major impact on him, shifting certain of his long-held beliefs. "I became less hung up about being right all the time; more relaxed somehow. I'm not even sure how this happened to tell the truth, but something dramatic occurred: I could let go of things in a way that I never could before. I just dropped this whole shitload of baggage that I was carrying, and I felt like I did when we first started going out together. And her willingness to join me in opening up and not punishing me felt like such a gift. We were both very relieved to be free of the sniping warfare that we had been engaged in for all those months."

Rather than waiting for problems to surface, if both you and your partner make regular use of the suggestions and techniques described in this chapter you will be doing a great deal to ensure the likelihood that your relationship will be a loving and harmonious one, developing in ways that are beneficial to both of you.

7

The Third Way

The Art of Negotiation

A great part of all the pleasure of love begins, continues and sometimes ends with conversation. A real, enduring love-affair, in marriage and out of it, is an extremely exclusive club of which the entire membership is two co-equal Perpetual Presidents.

—ROBERTSON DAVIES,
The Pleasures of Love

One of the fundamental truths about human beings is also the basis for one of the knottiest problems in relationships: every one of us tries our damnedest to arrange a life that requires the fewest possible adjustments and compromises to what pleases us . . . but what pleases one person often doesn't please another. The obvious corollary of this is equally true and equally knotty: in a relationship, each of us secretly hopes that our partner will go along on *our* ride.

The trouble is, of course, that there are *two* people driven by these demons and only *one* relationship.

Our differing personalities, needs, and priorities become most clearly illuminated whenever a decision must be made that affects both people and where each person has a vested interest in its outcome: such decisions as how to spend free time, make love, deal with financial matters, when and with whom to socialize. Conflicts around these and other issues may erupt soon after a relationship is formed.

As a relationship develops, the number of decisions that must be made proliferate and the potential for conflict rises. Consequently, the *process* by which the two people negotiate, in light of what may be their competing needs and viewpoints, is of paramount importance in determining whether a relationship will ultimately be able to go the distance.

With these factors in mind, we have developed a number of strategies to help a couple successfully navigate these sensitive occasions in their relationship.

THE POINT OF VIEW OF THE RELATIONSHIP

In a healthy relationship, a basic principle underlying constructive negotiation is that *all decisions should be made from the point of view of the relationship itself.* This means that your partner's desires need to be considered as thoroughly and carefully as your own, as you each agree to design an alternative that will favor the entity of the relationship. Learning to make decisions from the point of view of the relationship, as opposed to those that favor one or the other person, marks a couple's ability to think and act as a unit.

In this culture we are taught much more about individualism, competition, personal and financial achievement, than we are about the importance of cooperation, community, and a social consciousness that leads to good feelings because one is working for the welfare of a greater whole. One of the few areas where we sometimes learn such attitudes is in team sports. A few outstanding athletes may be sufficient to win some games, but rarely the championship. A team wins consistently only when the members play well *together*, emphasizing each player's particular strengths: the whole becomes greater than the sum of its parts.

A relationship, like a team, is best understood as if it were a single complex organism. It has its own needs that require attention just as each partner within the relationship has his or her individual needs. A well-functioning couple implicitly operates according to the principle that each partner must attend to the other's happiness and contentment if his or her own is to be assured.

This principle is illustrated in the following vignette: After knowing Brett only six months, Shawn left her hometown and moved five hundred miles to live with him in the city where his restaurant was located. Soon afterward a crisis developed in the business. His manager quit and Brett had to fill in for him temporarily. This meant that he wasn't arriving home until well past midnight, leaving little time for him and Shawn to be together. After nearly three weeks of this schedule and a number of increasingly heated discussions that led nowhere, Shawn announced that if Brett did not find a new manager by the end of the next week she was moving back home. Brett was not too happy with Shawn's ultimatum, but a few days later he did hire a new manager. He would have preferred to have had more time to pick a better one, because the one he chose was rather inexperienced and he didn't expect him to last very long. However, Brett knew that even with a mediocre manager the restaurant would survive quite well, and he wasn't willing to jeopardize the relationship over this decision.

By his willingness to make this important concession, Brett was accommodating to the basic requirements that were needed to sustain the relationship, just as Shawn had done earlier by her willingness to move. By valuing the relationship's needs above their individual concerns, each of them had made their decision from the point of view of the relationship.

When a couple is capable of going the distance together, the two partners are team members working together toward the greater goals of the unit. As in team sports, there is always room for an individual to show his or her unique skills and please the crowds, but when the needs of one player interfere with the ability of the team to work together as a whole, the team itself falters and ultimately fails.

Some married couples continue to operate predominantly as two singles cohabiting under one roof, living parallel lives and never combining their intentions and efforts in a way that would bring them the benefits of mutuality. If and when accommodations are made by one or the other person, careful tallies are kept, as if a contest were taking place. Since we rarely have the same excellent memory for the concessions our partner has made as we have for our own, before too long we are apt to feel unfairly taken advantage of, as if we have been doing the serf's share of the giving while our partner has been receiving the king's share of the spoils. This point of view inevitably leads to resentment and the withholding of affection. As our partner reacts and withholds in turn, an escalating and destructive spiral of tension is created.

As Joseph Campbell said, "You don't sacrifice for the other person, you sacrifice for the relationship." It makes no more sense to be angry with your partner for the personal sacrifices you have made for the good of the union than it does to be angry with your garden for the demands it has made on your time, money, and energies in order that it produce food for your table or flowers for your delight.

Couples who have been happily married for many years reiterate similar refrains: in essence, they talk about considering the needs of their partner and family first when making decisions. An attitude of "what's best for all concerned" governs a fair share of each partner's thoughts. When both people feel that their own needs are being considered, they are each more interested in meeting their partner's needs. Therefore, if you want your partner to be more considerate of your needs, the place to begin is by being more considerate of your partner's needs. This is practical common sense, but it is easily and often overlooked.

Ramon and Inez had been living together for two years when Ramon finished medical school in Chicago and began applying for internships around the country. He applied everywhere but Chicago, since he hated the winters there and was looking for a change in climate. Inez was deeply troubled by his unilateral decision making. Most of her friends and family were in Chicago and she had just begun to explore some attractive career opportunities there. She was firm: "I told Ramon that he would be on his own if he put the inconvenience of suffering a few cold winters before a fair consideration of my needs. I had already sacrificed enough to put him through med school. Actually, to be fair, Ramon really had no idea of how important it was to me until I showed him how strongly I felt about it. As a result, he agreed to apply for internships in the Chicago area as well, and because he was willing to respect my needs I secretly knew that I would be willing to accompany him somewhere else if he wasn't accepted in Chicago, although I prayed that it wouldn't come to that."

STRATEGIES FOR NEGOTIATING

Making decisions from the point of view of the relationship requires an examination of the particular needs *underlying* each person's separate point of view. It is *not* the by-product of merely analyzing the surface pros and cons of the two alternatives. The process we are referring to is a *cooperative* one. It may be the very antithesis of the *modus operandi* frequently used by people who are caught up in the *competitive* work world where "winning" plays an essential role for eight or more hours every day; therefore, it can be more difficult to achieve than it sounds. In addition, those who have been single for a long time usually are not accustomed to deliberating about the concerns of another before making a decision. And finally, figuring out what a new partner requires is actually quite complicated, at least initially, when each person is just getting to know the other.

The Third Way

Once the two people in a relationship become better at knowing and communicating their needs to their partner, it becomes possible to come up with an alternative that represents neither *his* way nor *her* way, but one we call the "third way," a solution that accommodates each individual's most essential needs.

Jeremy wanted to hire outside help to clean the apartment that he and Kimberly shared. He made a decent salary, disliked housework, and was tired in the evenings and on weekends. He preferred to relax when he had free time. Kimberly wanted them to continue doing the housework themselves. Her salary was more modest than his, and she preferred to spend her extra money on things other than household help. She also was a very particular housekeeper and actually found housecleaning rather therapeutic, although she clearly didn't want to assume all the domestic responsibilities.

They reached an impasse in their discussions, and their arguments over the matter were causing serious tensions, as each of them tried to sway the other to their point of view. Neither of them, however, was persuaded; they were caught in the grip of "dichotomania": the either/or approach where one person or idea "wins" and the other "loses." They needed a new approach to break the stalemate they had reached, a "third way."

In this instance Jeremy's need was to have time for leisure; money wasn't of great concern. Even though Jeremy offered to pay the entire cost of household help, Kimberly wasn't satisfied, since she wanted to continue doing a significant part of the housekeeping herself. Finally, Jeremy came up with an idea that took both their needs into account: although they would continue to share the shopping and cooking, he agreed to pay Kimberly for doing his share of the housework. In this way

Kimberly would not have to give up control of the housekeeping and with part of the money Jeremy paid her she could occasionally hire someone to do the more arduous household chores that she found distasteful. This solution also gave her extra spending money and it gave Jeremy the extra free time he desired. They had discovered a third way that resolved their dilemma in a manner that was satisfactory to both of them.

Clive and Robin used to argue about Robin's jogging routine. Because of a back injury, Clive was unable to jog with Robin, so she would run with different partners—often with other men—and this irritated Clive. At times she would have to get up as early as five-thirty in the morning in order to meet her running partner, disturbing Clive's sleep. Clive wanted Robin to give up jogging on mornings after they had spent the night together. Robin was quite committed to her exercise program and did not want to interrupt it so frequently. They argued back and forth for weeks until they realized that the conflict was starting to erode their relationship. Neither of them wanted that to happen, so they began to search for a third way. Robin suggested that they go for a vigorous walk on the mornings they were together. This met her need for exercise, enabled both of them to sleep a bit later, and gave them some additional time together. Now Robin enjoys walking almost as much as jogging, Clive enjoys getting the exercise as well, and they have developed another activity they can enjoy together.

Creating the third way requires that you have a dialogue in which each of you does the best you can to define and clearly describe the needs you are trying to meet by taking your particular position. It also entails specifying the *precise elements* of your partner's solution that make it unacceptable to you. This process not only sheds more light on the issue at hand, but enables you to get to know each other better as a result. Remember, this is an ongoing process; don't expect instantaneous results. In determining the third way you will probably discard a number of unworkable solutions before arriving at one that is acceptable to both of you.

When you have this kind of dialogue, you may be surprised to discover that what you had assumed to be absolutely essential was not really so after all, and that some other factor that you had not even been conscious of was actually of paramount importance. For example, Myra and Fritz had planned a road-trip vacation to the Southwest. After all the plans were made, Myra decided that she would rather not fly to the place where they intended to begin their car trip but would prefer to take a train instead. She had recently been inspired by a travel article touting the luxurious joys of train travel. Fritz refused on the grounds that it would take too much time to go by train. When they explored his refusal they discovered that what he *really* objected to was having to organize a whole new set of travel arrangements. He had spent considerable time and effort arranging their original plans and in an unspoken way had been the one to assume responsibility for carrying out their vacation scheduling. Once Myra offered to take care of the change in plans, leaving Fritz with no further work to do, he found himself quite amenable to this new approach to their trip.

Compromises

Couples get into trouble when one or both of them feel that their needs are too frequently being subsumed by the needs of the other. Though resolving matters by arriving at the third way might be the most ideal solution, there are times when another form of conflict resolution is more appropriate.

Whereas the third way involves the design of an entirely *original* solution that satisfies both partners, a compromise is essentially the result of taking the two alternatives posed by the partners and agreeing on some point roughly midway between them, approximately the average of the two alternatives. For our purposes, compromise involves a negotiation in which the two parties stay *within* their original parameters but each person yields to a certain degree.

Jonathan was a psychotherapist who worked late Monday

through Thursday evening, usually until eight or nine o'clock, a schedule that gave him little time to spend with Amalia except on weekends. Amalia complained, but Jonathan's pressing financial needs prevented him from making any significant concessions: he was paying a fair amount each month in child support and alimony and did not see how he could afford to cut back on his practice. In fact, in order to make ends meet he would often extend himself and see an extra client after nine o'clock.

At first, they battled over their conflicting needs, with Amalia saying, "Your work is more important to you than I am!" and Jonathan responding with, "You're totally insensitive to the pressures I'm under. Many of my clients have jobs that only enable them to see me in the evening!" Finally, they reviewed their needs and decided on a compromise. On Tuesday night Jonathan would end work at six o'clock. Unless there was a dire emergency, Tuesday night would be sacrosanct, with a standing date for the two of them to be together. On the other evenings he could work as late as he deemed necessary. This solution took both their needs into account equally, given that if Amalia could have had it entirely her way she would have wanted to spend several weekday evenings together, while Jonathan would have preferred working late on Tuesday as well, in order to boost his income still further.

In all effective compromises, each person has to give a little in order to get. It is important to remember that in a successful compromise negotiation, each partner feels initially somewhat *dissatisfied* with the solution, since they are really getting only part of what they want. But then again, half a loaf is better than none, and an intimate relationship is inconceivable without compromise.

Trade-Offs

While you each get only about half of what you want with a compromise, with a trade-off you may get nearly all of what you want—but you get it only about half of the time.

When you pick the movie tonight and your partner picks it next time or you go to the ballet this month and the ball game next month, you are engaged in a trade-off. In this way each of you gets to have your "selfish" (that is, uncompromised) desires satisfied from time to time—a necessary indulgence, we think, in every happy relationship.

Allison and Quinn had worked out a trade-off in two areas. Allison loved the opera and the symphony and enjoyed dressing up for a night on the town. Quinn was often bored by these events and liked to dress casually when he wasn't at work. Quinn agreed to attend some cultural events with Allison as long as she agreed not to buy season tickets, as she preferred to do, but to select individual performances carefully and with an eye to what Quinn might enjoy most. She also agreed to go with friends to those events she didn't want to miss but which were not at all Quinn's cup of tea—Wagnerian opera, for example.

Quinn, on the other hand, loved fishing. Allison tried it a few times and decided that there were few things in life more uncomfortable or boring. As part of their trade-off Quinn eventually exchanged his boat for another that Allison found more comfortable and they agreed to ask friends to join them whenever possible, something that Allison enjoyed. At other times Allison would bring a book or a project to work on while Quinn fished.

In the strategy of a trade-off each person can expect that they will have a significant portion of their needs met, if not today, then next week or next month or next year, depending on the issue being decided. Each person comes to trust that, in the long run, they will not be deprived of what is personally important to them in order to sustain the relationship.

Yielding Control

All successful conflict negotiations—the third way, compromises, trade-offs—require us to be willing to forgo a certain amount of control over decisions. And for some people, abdicating any degree of control can be rather difficult.

An exaggerated need to control the actions of our partner is most often a defense against the anxiety experienced when we believe that our personal autonomy is being jeopardized by our partner's needs, wishes, feelings, or decisions. Even when the need for some form of negotiated settlement is obviously necessary and reasonable, it can still produce anxiety. The tendency of one partner to exert more control as a way of coping with those anxieties can excite the anxieties of the other. The relationship then moves into a stage of distress because it is no longer working as a unit but has split into two solo entities vying for control. Consequently, the capacity for both partners to be able to *yield* appropriate control is vital to any healthy relationship.

In the relationship between Sasha and Joyce, Sasha seemed to rule the roost. He imposed his will on most of their joint decisions: when they would get together, where they would eat, what movie they would see, who they would socialize with, and so on. However, his rather tenacious control was accompanied by a stream of complaints about how little initiative Joyce took and how unfair it was that he "had" to assume all the responsibilities or otherwise "nothing would get done."

Yet, whenever Joyce took the initiative Sasha would inevitably find fault with her choices and critically pick them apart using a form of "logic" that Joyce felt unable to counter effectively. She often felt beaten into submission by the intensity of Sasha's controlling and critical ways. She found it very difficult to find a way to exert a reasonable portion of her own control in the relationship. Although she loved Sasha, she often felt frustrated by him and angry with him. Soon she began to gain weight, and despite dieting and Sasha's entreaties and "helpful suggestions," she seemed unable to control herself. Of course, her weight was finally something that Sasha couldn't control, and that was exactly the (unconscious) point. Now the shoe was on the other foot and Joyce had the power, albeit a self-defeating power at best.

After a brief course of therapy both Sasha and Joyce became aware of the roles each of them played in their relationship, and they discovered how interdependent their behaviors were. As Sasha began to relax control and learn more about the benefits of yielding, Joyce began to make more decisions. As she did so, she gradually lost the weight she had gained. Sasha actually came to feel relieved at not having to do so much himself as he experienced Joyce's competence in areas that previously were his exclusive province.

Learning to yield control, to relinquish power and render ourselves partially subject to the decisions of another, can be quite a difficult skill to master, one that takes time, trust, and determination to achieve. It also involves a willingness to accept graciously an outcome that we may consider to be less than perfect.

If we happen to be in a partnership in which one of us is quite easygoing while the other needs to maintain a good deal of control, we may have a most fortunate match. But, more often, the greatest potential for compatibility and for achieving the deepest intimacy exists in a relationship where the power is distributed more equally.

Division of Labor

One way to circumvent power struggles over decision making between equals is by making use of the concept of division of labor, with each partner assuming the predominant responsibility for decisions made in their particular areas of expertise or special concern.

The advent of the Industrial Revolution dramatically increased the efficiency and productivity of the workplace, and one of the ways it achieved this was through the division of labor, in which a complex multifaceted task was broken into component parts, each assigned to a different person. This process simplified things considerably and led to the creation of a class of specialists who could perform their jobs very well indeed and who made their separate and valuable contributions to the whole.

This form of organization is especially necessary with two-career couples for whom the time in a day seems barely sufficient to carry out even the necessities of life. Since the responsibilities each person assumes, whenever possible, should be closest to his or her own strengths and interests, a division of labor can make for a more pleasant, less burdensome, domestic atmosphere in which each partner comfortably relinquishes control in certain areas in return for having more free time.

For example, because of Colin, shoes get shined, the house looks great, and when something breaks down, it gets fixed. Lana takes care of social arrangements, and does most of the food shopping and the cooking.

Naturally, dividing up tasks requires a measure of trust, especially in the early stages of a relationship where you may feel reluctant to yield control over certain matters for which you have habitually assumed responsibility. Over time, however, as you learn more about your partner's way of working and her or his special interests, you should be able to relax and begin to share duties that were previously yours exclusively, even giving some of them up entirely to your partner when it seems appropriate.

Marjory had a garden at her house which she loved but really didn't have time to care for adequately. Amos loved gardening and actually was quite knowledgeable about it, but since he lived in an apartment complex, he had no garden of his own.

At first, Marjory and Amos did a good deal of the work and decision making about the garden together, with Marjory's wishes generally predominating. After a couple of months, however, Marjory began to have a deeper trust of Amos's horticultural abilities and found herself abdicating much of the gardening to him. As Marjory surrendered control, Amos grew more confident and comfortable making independent decisions about the garden, bringing to it what he thought was needed without consulting Marjory on every occasion. This did not mean that Marjory's input was no longer welcome, it was just that Amos's enthusiasm and competence encouraged Marjory to trust his judgment, and on the rare occasion when she did not agree with one of his decisions, she usually said little about it. She was happy with the end product: a wonderful garden that she had only minor responsibility for maintaining.

One of the benefits of traditionally assigned sex roles was that particular areas of control were rather clearly delineated. The fundamental problem with that tradition, of course, was that these tasks were usually rather rigidly assigned according to one's gender rather than to one's particular interests and abilities.

With greater freedom from that rigid sex role stereotyping comes the new burden of having to decide who is going to do what. Initially, this may create a period of uncertainty and stress until our individual talents and enthusiasms gradually begin to make themselves known and we come to trust our partner to handle certain roles and responsibilities that were previously ours alone.

Roles should not be ironclad, of course, and where there are tasks that are distasteful to both people, they can be assigned alternately. Sometimes assuming responsibility in an unfamiliar area can lead to valuable new learning. For example, taking over paying the household bills may give you a totally new perspective on the overall budget and on deciding what can and cannot be purchased at a particular time; ultimately it may familiarize you with the workings and language of economics: mortgages, interest rates, matters of taxation, and the like.

Interim or Temporary Solutions

Even when realms of responsibility have been fairly well divided, there will continue to be areas in which the two of you remain equally concerned, and where there is a fair degree of competition for shared control. Interim solutions, because of their temporary nature, are very useful in instances when you are at loggerheads over an issue. They entail an experimental attitude, a wait-and-see approach that frees both of you from being overly invested or identified with the outcome, the results of which are often unforeseeable. If, after a period of evaluation, either of you is still dissatisfied, the interim solution can be abandoned and other alternatives can be attempted until a mutually satisfactory solution is finally determined.

Colleen and Warren seemed to be continually at odds over how to handle their expenses during the first six months they were living together. Colleen argued for a joint checking account, but Warren thought that this would be unworkable. He worried that if they were both writing checks from the same account their record keeping would get muddled and checks would start to bounce. He advocated a system where they would each pay for things separately, enter the expenses into a register, and total them at the end of each month, balancing the books. Colleen was against this method because she was afraid that she would lose receipts and forget to write down all of her expenses; she thought Warren's plan was too unwieldy and complicated, and too time-consuming as well.

After much discussion they finally decided to try a joint checking account for three months on a trial basis. After two months a few checks bounced and Warren called for an immediate change of plan. But Colleen wanted another month, as they had originally agreed, so that she could improve the system. She took the responsibility for entering the checks from

Warren's check register every few days and kept an accurate running balance on their account. The third month went virtually without a hitch and they have continued the practice of using a joint account ever since.

This is not to say that Colleen's method was the "correct" one or even the better one. If, instead, they had agreed to Warren's method, *he* might have assumed the major responsibility for reconciling their expenses at the end of each month and the process might have run just as smoothly. What *is* important in this example is that their problem-solving process was a cooperative one and both of their concerns were given due consideration.

Although some solutions may be inherently better than others, there are few, if any, absolute answers to any of life's dilemmas. Numerous good potential solutions usually can be found for every problem. In the end, therefore, what makes a solution most likely to work out for the best is the decision to get behind it and give it your all. The more you are able to take major responsibility when the idea is yours or else to embrace your partner's position when the idea is theirs, the more likely the outcome will be satisfying to *both* of you in the long run.

If you are open to an outlook in which each of you is free to rethink or refine a working solution, where the prevailing point of view is to work for what is best for the relationship, and where both people assume that their basic needs will ultimately be met, the end result may actually turn out to be both a constructive and pleasant surprise.

Carly was an endocrinologist in Wichita who was offered a six-month teaching position in Los Angeles. She was excited by the prospect of living there, but was concerned about Benjamin's reaction to the offer. She didn't want to go if he couldn't accompany her. Benjamin was quite impressed with the attractive opportunity Carly had been offered, and encouraged her to proceed with the paperwork while he considered how to arrange his life so that he could make a few week-long trips to visit her over the six months she would be gone.

Carly completed the application but was still not sure she would go through with the appointment if it meant being apart from Benjamin for so much of the time. In the process, however, Benjamin began to see that there were certain cultural and career advantages for himself in the Los Angeles area, so, with a new enthusiasm, he began to restructure his schedule in such a way that he was eventually able to spend more than half the time in Los Angeles with Carly. What had once been a problem was now something they each looked forward to with growing anticipation.

When both of you can shift your previously entrenched perspectives to new ones, when the glass is perceived as being half full rather than half empty, you can begin to accommodate to each other more easily without feeling resentful about any deprivation you may have to sustain along the way.

Going to the Wall

Occasionally an issue is of such supreme importance to a person that it is essentially not negotiable. On these *rare* occasions, there is little or no room for a trade-off or compromise, or even a temporary solution: we might say that at such times we are willing "to go to the wall" for the issue.

Chloe, for instance, said, "There are certain ecology issues that I'm unwilling to bend on. Even if it does inconvenience Derek to have to recycle the bottles, cans, and paper, I insist on it. I simply don't think it's okay to ignore certain environmental concerns. Derek was resistant at first, but he's less so now."

Beth's son, Alan, was six years old when she began dating Chris. And while Beth and Chris had become quite adept at negotiating their differences, Beth had recently found herself in a nonnegotiable position. Chris had brought a toy pistol home as a present for Alan. While she appreciated his generosity and his desire to form a relationship with her son, she felt very strongly that using guns and other forms of violent play were not consistent with the principles she believed in, and she did not want Alan to think she supported them in any form. She believed that if she allowed her son to accept this gift it implied her tacit approval. "Chris tried to convince me that boys will be boys," she said, "but it was no dice. I just felt too strongly about it."

A man we interviewed referred to such issues as "red couch arguments." He revealed that earlier in his relationship he had been talked into buying a red couch by his partner, against his better judgment. He ended up hating it. As a result, he refused ever again to capitulate entirely on an issue that he felt particularly strongly about. Instead, he would say, "This is not a red couch argument," meaning that there was no way he was going to yield on this one.

If we expect our partner to respect our nonnegotiable demands, we must express them judiciously and only after having given them due deliberation, or else we risk becoming like the boy who cried wolf: being dismissed or ignored when the issue is actually very important to us. As long as "red couch" arguments don't arise too often, partners in a good relationship should expect to accommodate willingly to feelings that are deeply held. Respecting and honoring our partner's strong feelings, and reasonably capitulating to them from time to time, is exactly what we would like our partner to do for us.

Making Lemonade

Howard Gossage, a former advertising executive, once said, "If all you have are lemons, make lemonade."

At those times when you must yield because your partner is "at the wall" with regard to a particular issue, the most constructive stance is one of gracious acceptance—at least, as much as you can muster—without behaving petulantly or being sullenly punitive in an attempt to make your partner pay for the dissatisfactions you are experiencing at the moment. The ability to be graceful under pressure is a genuine measure of character and of maturity.

Clearly, it is sometimes pretty difficult to move forward in the face of certain obstacles, but even a vacation at a beach resort where it rains every day can be salvaged once you shift expectations and goals: table tennis, good books, music, and lots of sex and sleep, perhaps, instead of the sunning and swimming you had anticipated.

ENLIGHTENED SELF-INTEREST

When you are generous-spirited and supportive, your partner will tend to feel appreciated and more fulfilled, which will encourage him or her to be more generous and supportive in return. This is what we mean by the term "enlightened self-interest": ultimately it is in your own best interest to see that your partner feels loved and fulfilled.

Enlightened self-interest may translate into such things as buying small gifts, preparing your partner's favorite meals, protecting their quiet so they can sleep in, easing some of their responsibilities in life. Enlightened self-interest may mean that you do all you can to help your partner get the piano they want even though you're a bit short of funds—because music makes them happy. It means helping a partner further certain aims, like going back to school, or exploring the creative arts, even if these pursuits are not going to be economically productive, because your partner really desires them for personal growth or contentment.

Enlightened self-interest can be the basis for extending yourself and accompanying your partner to the opera, a sporting event, or a family function you would rather not attend if you had only yourself to consider. It may mean going camping even though you would prefer to stay in a hotel, simply because it pleases your partner. Your motive in doing these things should not be to get something in return. If it is, you are likely to be disappointed. However, when you give to your partner willingly, with no ulterior motives, their general state of contentedness is likely to make them want to return the caring gestures.

In the process of being a donor, you also become a beneficiary of the good feelings generated when you add to the happiness or welfare of someone you love. Altruism enriches your spirit and your sense of self-worth. Often unexpectedly, you may find that you have benefited in other ways from having given to your partner: perhaps you enjoyed the soccer match despite yourself; the low, starry night may have been spectacular, despite the absence of a soft bed and a hot shower. And the memories you build together are riches you can tap into in the future.

Once you become aware of your partner's needs, you are in a better position to help satisfy them. For example, a common difference between people concerns their optimal need for emotional closeness or distance. One partner may have a greater need for time spent together, the other for time spent alone. Understanding that your partner's need to spend time apart or together is most likely a personality preference and not an attempt to abandon or to suffocate you should encourage you to be generous-spirited. Either person, of course, can make the first offer: "I know that you need comforting right now, and even though I need some time alone, let's spend some time together first. Then I'll go off and read." Or "I know that you need your space, so take that time for yourself first and then let's spend some time together later on." Either way could work, depending on whose need is more pressing at the moment. But the premise behind both actions is the same: when you support your partner's needs, you benefit in a number of ways—many of which are unforeseeable. Take the relationship of Chuck and Alana, for example, where conflict over the frequency of making love was of central concern.

Chuck's sexual need was far greater than Alana's. Rather than constantly wondering why Chuck rarely seemed to be sexually satisfied, Alana finally realized that none of that really mattered. What *did* matter was that he *was* sexually fulfilled.

Since she loved him, she felt that one way of expressing her love was to make herself more available sexually. Once she began giving to him sexually because she *chose* to rather than feeling she *had* to, she was surprised to find that *she* found sex more enjoyable as well. Chuck, in turn, began to take more time and give more thought to pleasing her—in and out of the bedroom.

Sometimes enlightened self-interest can look like a trade-off, but the attitude involved is quite different. Matthew was a football zealot, especially when it came to his home team. He had been following them since he was a boy and he knew everything about the team and its players. He either attended their games or watched them religiously on TV. Dana, no matter how hard she tried, could not get interested in the game; it bored her to tears. She found her religion in church and very much wanted Matthew to accompany her on Sundays, but Matthew felt about church the way Dana felt about football.

Dana knew that football was important to Matthew and she worked out their social schedule so that his games were always sacrosanct: she liked to see him happy. Matthew went to church from time to time, not because he was paying Dana back for letting him watch his football games uninterruptedly, and certainly not because he enjoyed church going. He went because he knew that a joint endeavor at spirituality was important to Dana and made her feel more fulfilled.

None of the people we have described here are martyrs. They are honoring their partner's needs out of love, and by doing so the loving spirit is reciprocated. In fact, enlightened self-interest is intertwined with love itself. It expresses the desire to have your partner fulfill their own destiny, to achieve their heart's desire and become all that they can be. It is no paradox that *you* will derive benefit from your partner's fulfillment, and it is not jaded to see things from this vantage point.

Enlightened self-interest as we are describing it, is not a form of cynical game playing, although on a superficial level it can sometimes appear that way. Haley reported that she was almost always the one who would lobby for a weekend getaway when it seemed that a bit of "freshening," as she called it, was needed for the relationship. Frederick preferred to relax at home, however, so whenever she wanted to present the idea of a weekend retreat she would first fix him a drink and then a special meal. When he was watered, fed, and relaxed, she found him to be in a far more receptive mind-set. But secretly, Haley felt uncomfortable about this carefully planned, purposive approach. When asked why she didn't simply present the idea at breakfast instead, she replied, "Because he's so grouchy in the morning that he'd never agree to *anything* then—even if it was the greatest idea in the world."

Haley's use of enlightened self-interest was not simply selfishly manipulative: it didn't falsify facts or compromise anyone's welfare. And in truth, Frederick never minded her approach. "I always know when she wants something from me," he said, "but her manner is so endearing, I can't refuse her. Besides, once we're on the road, I generally have a great time."

Choosing to present your point at the most propitious time or in the most effective way is more akin to lubricating the path to a desirable goal. Failing to appreciate this principle as being a vital part of healthy communication is an omission that is inevitably self-defeating.

Within a healthy relationship both people strive to satisfy their individual needs without endangering the structure of the relationship. This is most effectively accomplished by making decisions from the point of view of the relationship itself, discovering the third way whenever possible, or by making compromises, trade-offs, interim solutions, or "lemonade" when the need arises.

All of these approaches facilitate a couple's ability to make the innumerable critical decisions they will face as they go through life together, such as when they will choose to have children and how many they will have, how they will deal with such matters as aging parents and the possibility of relocating, buying a home, or starting a business.

None of these important life decisions can properly be one person's domain; they intimately affect both people and are immeasurably helped by their collective considerations. Creatively dealt with, they strengthen and solidify the union.

III

Commitment and Beyond

8

Perils Real and Imagined

The Decision to Commit

The greatest ordeal in life is marriage, it is the central focus for enlightenment and the natural therapeutic process in the culture.

—CARL WHITAKER, M.D.

Commitment. The very word seems to strike terror into the hearts of many men and women. Witness the following joke:

HENRY   I hear that you and Roxanne are in a committed relationship.
NATHAN   No way! We're deeply involved, but we're not committed.
HENRY   Deeply involved but not committed? What's the difference?

NATHAN   Well, it's a lot like bacon and eggs. The chicken is involved. The pig is committed!

A grim view indeed. And it is true that for many people commitment elicits images of stultification, confinement, relentless sameness and predictability, the loss of self, a form of imprisonment, the end of possibility: something to be avoided like the plague.

However, for many others the idea of commitment has very different associations. It can mean that a source of help will be there in times of sorrow and travail, an end to the nagging anxieties of loneliness, an expansion of choices for the future, with the opportunity to develop most fully by coming into a profound connection with the soul of another—the deepest possible companionship one can experience. For these people a committed relationship is a central part of the journey to discover what love—not mere infatuation—is all about. It is the birthplace of possibility and the beginning of one of life's greatest adventures.

Without some willingness to commit, a romantic relationship usually has a limited life span and curtailed possibilities for growth. We can enjoy quite an extended period of courtship but ultimately we each must put both of our feet on board if we are going to travel together. A relationship without commitment is like a house built with a weak foundation: the facade may be exquisite, the interior may be splendidly designed, but at some point a "quake" will occur, and the structure will too easily crumble.

As we see it, commitment is both an attitude as well as an ongoing decision. In a committed relationship there is an implicit acknowledgment of the long view of life, one that embraces our mate's imperfections—and our own as well—and which recognizes the inevitability of storms to come, of fallow times as well as fertile ones. People who are committed say things like this: "It means that I would do almost anything to try to make it work." "It means sticking together. If we have problems and feel like leaving or whatever, we just won't." "We are not in this for the short term, we are in this for our whole lives." "I don't want this relationship to fail, and if I work hard enough at it, it won't fail." "She's my swan. I'm mated for life with her."

Commitment involves both an investment and a promise: an investment of energies, thoughts, patience, feelings, and time, along with a promise to protect the relationship from harm and to remain in it to solve any issues that arise.

Making a commitment means that your *intention* is to *make* the relationship work; it does not mean waiting and seeing *if* it will work. It is an active, not a passive, stance, and it is exemplified by the willingness to continue working on problems until some satisfactory resolution can be reached, even if for a time there is no solution in sight.

A humorous but apt illustration of commitment is given in a familiar, though probably apocryphal, story of an actor who was being interviewed by a reporter: "Divorce is so rampant in Hollywood. People seem to think nothing of getting married four and five times, and yet you and your wife have been married nearly forty years. Haven't you ever wanted to divorce her?" "Divorce her?" the actor replied. "Never . . . but *murder* her?—yes, hundreds of times!"

The mental attitude of expecting to stay together forever has been pointed to by many couples as being directly responsible for their ability to work through the intermittent relationship difficulties, to enable them to keep going even when the going is rough. One woman told us, "As much as I disliked him at times, I didn't think about getting out of the relationship. Maybe it was because when I made the decision to marry him I was determined never to get divorced again. Besides, by then we had Hannah and nothing could deter me from making sure she grew up with two parents in a happy home. Whatever was broken, we were going to fix it somehow. And now, after two *very* rocky years, I can honestly say that we are quite happy together again."

Throughout life the most meaningful accomplishments are achieved over time and through tenacity, and this is particularly true if your goal is to work out a successful long-term relationship. In general, the longer both of you persist in striving to resolve problems and improve your communication, the more likely you are to succeed. The expectation of progress is positively correlated with the achievement of progress.

Obviously, this doesn't mean that committed couples never get divorced. But when divorce is a distant last on the list of possibilities for resolving problems, a creative pressure is exerted on the couple to discover other, less drastic, solutions to their dilemmas.

WHY COMMIT?

It seems that most people become aware of a growing desire to be in a committed relationship at some point in their lives. For certain of us it occurs early on, for others of us it may not occur until our middle years, when most of our friends have coupled or when we begin to feel the desire for children, or when we first come to grips with the idea that we are aging and, if we are lucky, we will indeed grow old.

We all must die some day, and clearly it is better to die having been deeply known and loved by another over many years than it is to die alone or in the presence of someone we have known only briefly, who has not touched our soul, with whom we have shared relatively few significant experiences. The profound comfort that is gained by having had a deep and long-term experience of this nature cannot be overestimated, and this is virtually unthinkable, unattainable without commitment.

A well-functioning committed relationship permits us to lay aside our defenses and be most truly ourselves. It involves a unity of mind and feelings. "All of a sudden," said one man, "I started to relax, and I realized that I hadn't really relaxed in fifteen years. Suddenly I was aware of having this feeling of 'coming home.' "

The security of knowing that when life presents obstacles that are greater than your talents or strength permit you to resolve on your own, your partner is there to help you, is a consolation of incalculable value, given life's unpredictability. "He knows that I'm there for him," said one woman, married twelve years, "and if there were any kind of emergency I'd immediately drop what I'm doing and be at his side. There are no two ways about it."

A committed relationship tends to liberate personal energy that previously may have been devoted to searching for, or trying to impress, a new partner, and allows it to be invested in other areas. After making a commitment it is not uncommon for a person to start a new business, go back to school, complete projects or actualize plans that have been waiting in the wings for years.

The Downside to Commitment

There is no upside without a downside, and commitment is no exception. When entering a committed relationship, most of us experience at least a quiet sorrow at the loss of a particular kind of freedom: the freedom to range openly with others, sexually and otherwise, freely satisfying our curiosity for diversity and a certain kind of personal adventure. And, of course, when we commit ourselves to another we must acknowledge that there is a certain loss of flexibility which arises from the need to attend to the concerns of our loved one, especially at decision-making times, when previously we had only ourselves to consider. We must also begin to hold our autocratic selves in check, and to do so graciously, as we learn to contend with the anxiety of dealing with a new set of unknowns, the by-products of binding our fate to another. We can never fully anticipate how our partner's health, financial state, work, or family relationships, for example, will affect our lives. All of these actual or potential downsides to commitment are among the issues which underlie many of the fears of commitment that we will address in greater depth later in this chapter.

THE DECISION TO COMMIT

Commitment is not an event, it is a process that grows and gains greater certainty as a healthy relationship evolves. Along the path of a relationship's development there are usually landmarks, notable moments when significant decisions are made, when feelings crystallize—for example, the decision to become engaged, or to live together, or to have a child. At such times, the commitment may deepen dramatically. As other more mundane issues are successfully negotiated the increase in commitment may be less perceptible. Only when looking back over time may we fully realize how our intimate connection has strengthened and grown.

A full commitment has not necessarily been made simply because we have elected to live together. In the beginning, for many people, living together is principally an opportunity to "test the waters" more thoroughly. While this is a reasonable approach to take, at some juncture a deeper, mutually agreed on commitment becomes imperative if the relationship is going to progress to a richer intimacy and go the distance.

Traditionally, commitment has been symbolized by the ceremony of marriage, the culturally sanctioned, legal, and public statement in which the couple solemnifies their relationship and announces their intention to stay together to the end of their days. One has merely to glance at the current divorce statistics to know that commitment is a lot more complex, more hard won, more profound than anything that can be conferred by a marriage certificate.

Like the symbolic act of getting married, no external event, even the decision to have a child together, necessarily results in commitment. A couple may have a child together merely because one person desperately wants to be a parent and the other is willing to cooperate, or, by contrast, they may decide in concert to enter the realm of one of life's greatest challenges and fulfillments. They may be buying a home as a sensible financial investment, or it may be intended as a nest that will house them into old age. Commitment is an internal stance, not an external one. It is not a symbol, something which stands for something else, it is the thing itself, the real thing.

In this regard, one woman said, "When I was married the first time, I had a back door painted right onto the set, so to speak, so if things didn't work out well, I could make my exit. This time I can picture us at seventy and eighty together."

A genuine and deep commitment is accompanied by a sense of calmness, completeness, and a lessening of doubt. As this maturation of the relationship occurs, long-standing unresolved issues may become resolved for the first time. A woman, married after six years of living together with her partner, commented, "Somehow, after we decided to get married, things started falling into place. It was like getting pregnant: nature just seemed to do something to turn us around. Some of our issues just disappeared. For example, I became more accepting of his children and he started to act more positively toward my son. We didn't talk about it any more than we had before; it just began to happen."

Since making a commitment is an ever deepening process, at what point do you decide to embark on this journey of a lifetime? While being infatuatedly in love is tremendously enthralling and exhilarating, the decision to move the relationship into the realm of a lifelong partnership requires a lot more than strong romantic and sexual feelings, more even than feelings of reliance, comfort and support. To some extent, the first step in deciding to commit involves a very practical decision: you must evaluate the relationship for its potential to survive, and even more importantly, to *thrive*, given that there is no way to know in advance what the future has in store. The decision to grow, and grow old in each other's presence, is not limited by a particular number of years, but limited only by the ultimate certainty of death.

MISGUIDED COMMITMENTS

The decision to commit cannot properly be determined by external circumstance: because the woman is pregnant, for example, or a parent is ill and it would mean a great deal to see their child married before they die. It cannot be arrived at simply because a job offer requires one person to move and the couple is not prepared to break up.

Giving your heart to another in a committed way is not an act to be taken lightly. While being open and emotionally vulnerable are attractive traits, being too open and inappropriately vulnerable with someone who does not reciprocate can lead to the kind of psychological injury that can inhibit trust from developing in future, more appropriate, relationships. (As if to lend emphasis to this point, one study suggests that people who have had their hearts "broken" repeatedly by grievous love affairs are more likely to suffer heart attacks, angina, and other serious heart conditions.[1])

While it is not always easy to tell for certain that a relationship has what it takes to make a fulfilling life partnership, there are some specific clues that can indicate when making a commitment is likely to be a mistake. For example, unless you are *both* ready, the commitment of only one of you will *not* be sufficient to make the relationship work. The decision to commit must be made *independently* by each partner, though both partners must be in accord in the decision.

Wisdom would have you listen very carefully to your partner to discover if he or she is less than ready to move forward to this level. You cannot force your partner, or yourself for that matter, to be ready to commit. Compliance is *not* commitment.

1. *San Francisco Chronicle*, April 8, 1987. Page 5.

Commitment must be arrived at freely, personally, and not under threat and duress.

Signs of Unreadiness to Commit

If your partner is unwilling to be in a monogamous relationship with you during your courtship, it is unquestionably true, of course, that she or he is not ready to be committed. This may seem so obvious that it doesn't bear mentioning. But surprisingly, many people manage to rationalize away this truth. If your partner has other ongoing relationships, or, perhaps, friendships of a suspiciously romantic nature, you will not be able to relax and develop trust as you warily await your partner's next sexual adventure. Even if your partner is willing to be monogamous, you may be uncomfortably aware that she or he has a substantial "wandering eye," and a particular "edge" to their flirting which suggests that the flirtation is not of an innocent variety. These actions may engender uncomfortable feelings of jealousy on your part that will ultimately get in the way of a loving relationship. In order to go the distance, both people must have a feeling of sacredness for what they have established together and do everything in their power to protect the relationship from being hurt by deceptions or diluted by outside forces.

Beware also of a partner who scrupulously avoids any future-oriented conversations, who diverts you from considering what the two of you will do next week or next month or next year. If your partner never talks about what would happen if and when you got more serious, where you might live, what plans you might make for your life together, it is a clear indication that his or her thoughts are not in that direction—at least not yet.

On the other hand, there are also those people who are only too delighted to talk about such things, who love the *fantasy* of it . . . but that's all. Unfortunately, these people can prove to be the greatest heartbreakers, leaving you to rely on what turns out to be only empty words.

In other ways, a partner who does not keep his or her word is sending out warning signals. Beware, for example, of lovers who tell you they are making plans for special events, but the plans never seem to materialize. And special alertness is necessary with those who tell you how much they love you and want to be with you but who never quite get around to filing the final divorce papers from their previous mate.

Another signal which indicates that a partner is not ready for commitment is their resistance to becoming involved with your family members or close friends, or their reluctance to introduce you to their own relatives and friends.

Needless to say, extreme wariness and concern must guide you when your lover is someone who has an alcohol, drug, or other substance abuse problem. Until the problem is resolved, your prospective mate is "mated" primarily to the substance being abused, and it is folly to suppose otherwise no matter what promises and protestations are made: trying to have a committed relationship with a substance abuser is buying a one-way ticket to misery.

Beware of someone who runs hot one day and cold the next while you remain responsible for generating and sustaining the good feelings. Certainly, if someone says that they do not want a serious relationship, that they are not available for the long term, *take them at their word*. Although there are some people who really desire an intimate relationship but make protestations to the contrary out of a fear of intimacy or guilt about letting their partner down, many more really mean what they say. Don't let your wishes distort or obscure the hard truth and assume, instead, that you can change your partner's mind. If you do, when you finally expect a serious commitment, you are apt to find yourself, instead, seriously alone.

Rebound Relationships

Far too often we rush headlong into a new relationship right on the heels of a previous relationship's demise. Usually, this "rebound relationship" is motivated either by a desire to take revenge on the previous partner who hurt us (by showing them how easily they can be replaced) or as a way of distracting ourselves from the pain and loss we have suffered. Often it's both.

Generally, the person chosen as the rebound partner will be diametrically different from the previous partner in the areas that were problematic. For example, if sex was a problem, the rebound relationship will be passionately sexual; if the prior partner was pessimistic or dependent, the new partner will be quite optimistic or independent; and, of course, if the old relationship's energy had flagged and it died with a whimper, the new relationship will take off with a bang and be filled with the delicious seductions of high intensity and excitement.

When the dominant motive of the rebound choice is one of revenge, the new partner will certainly have something over the previous one—more glamour, more power, more money—which is then made obvious to the previous partner as a way of injuring him or her, a way of flaunting one's newly acquired "superior status."

Without doubt, the motives underlying many rebound relationships are hollow and insufficient bases for a long-term satisfactory relationship to develop.

When one goes through the loss of a significant relationship, it produces psychic injury, requiring a reasonable period of mourning, time to work through the sadness and loss so that healing can occur. Having been recently rejected can leave you feeling very raw, wounded, and perhaps inadequate or unlovable. Although a new involvement can take your mind off the pain and sorrow of the previous relationship, this relief can encourage you to interpret what is essentially a distraction as "the real thing." In addition, if you do not allow a sufficient healing/mourning period between relationships, you run the risk of projecting your unresolved feelings from the previous relationship onto your new partner, a burden that can ultimately destroy the new relationship.

If there is any possibility that either you or your partner are on the rebound, you should definitely consider waiting an extended period of time before deciding to move forward toward commitment. As one woman told us, "I never should have married Cory when I did, because I hadn't completed my relationship with Jonah. So when I married Cory my heart was really with this other man. I don't know, maybe if I had waited longer, my marriage to Cory might have worked out . . . but it didn't."

Pressure-Driven Relationships

Another kind of relationship that requires especially serious and careful evaluation is a pressure-driven relationship, one in which you feel compelled to move forward toward commitment because of outside pressures rather than because of your own feelings toward your partner. For example, you may be approaching a particular symbolic age—say thirty or forty—and feel that somehow it is imperative to be married by that age. It may be the case that many of your friends are getting married or are having children and you don't want to be left out. You may feel that you would be perceived at work as being more substantial, with corresponding increases in pay and promotion if you were married, or one or both of you may feel that marriage is the only appropriate solution to an unintended pregnancy. Or, if you are a woman and fear that your biological clock is running out, or if you are a man who is concerned that you will be too old to be a good father, you may feel the pressure to make a precipitous decision about a relationship.

You may be feeling insecure, tired, afraid of being alone. The prevailing cultural climate still makes it a stigma to be uncoupled by a certain age, especially for women—as though it indicates failure or undesirability—so that moving into a relationship becomes an antidote to this form of painful oppression.

Perhaps pressure is being exerted because of the length of time that you have been together, and you are responding to the expectations of others rather than your own desires. Your parents or your partner's parents may be pushing you to make a further commitment. Maybe you have set the marriage plans in motion and now feel obligated to go through with them despite having serious reservations.

Some people move forward to commitment as a way to escape from their family. Women in particular have been made to feel that marriage is one of the few legitimate ways they can leave an unpleasant, confining, sad, or conflict-ridden home. As one woman confided, "Marriage seemed to be the only way out of a miserable household. I hated being there but it never occurred to me just to leave and go out on my own."

Some people marry because of the affection they feel for their partner's family rather than for their partner. As one man told us, "She had a wonderful family and my own was so critical and negative. I loved her parents, and they had two daughters and no sons, so they took to me very strongly. It was heartening to feel that much warmth and acceptance; I had never experienced that before."

Of course, for some young people, moving in with their lover or getting married is an act of self-assertion, an act of defiance *against* parents who may be opposed to their choice of partner or their independence, rather than a clear statement *in favor* of the person they have chosen and the union they have established.

Whatever the source of external pressure, relationships that are predicated on something other than your own genuine feelings for each other have a high probability of ending in failure. Once the outside pressures impelling you forward have receded, you may find that there is little else holding you together and that you have made a terrible mistake—one that may come to cause you far more pain than you ever imagined.

THE CRITERIA FOR COMMITMENT

For most people, the decision to make a commitment is preceded by a growing readiness to enter a more serious involvement. Having sown enough wild oats, the desire for freedom and total independence gradually becomes overshadowed by the desire for home and roots. However, the mere fact that you are ready to make a commitment does not necessarily mean that the person you are with is the right person to be your mate.

Deciding whether your prospective mate is truly the right one for you is a complex task. If your ultimate desire is to pick someone with whom you can establish lifelong love, making this most profound decision requires not only a consideration of your partner's qualities, but also an assessment of the way in which the two of you work as a unit.[2]

We have arrived at six major factors that, when taken together, provide a reasonable and quite comprehensive basis for guiding the practical aspect of this decision. These factors are chemistry, companionship, trust, respect, acceptance, and shared values. They represent the structural support of a healthy relationship, the essential underpinnings upon which a good relationship rests, as opposed to attributes that are more superficial or decorative. They are not to be confused with the lists published in popular magazines that pretend to describe "your perfect match." Quite often the person we may be best suited to spend our lives with has qualities which, in the abstract, we might not have considered to be particularly important and they may be missing others that we had erroneously believed to have been essential.

2. In the appendix of this book you will find a brief *Compatibility Questionnaire* which has been designed to help you assess how well you and your partner suit one another and what your prospects are for going the distance.

Chemistry

Broadly speaking, "chemistry" has to do with the degree or intensity of attraction between two people. Since we are animals, like many other species we are attracted by a partner's physical appearance—the look of their face, the configuration of their body, the way they carry themselves, the way they dress—as well as their mannerisms, the sound of their voice, the way their body feels and reacts to our own. We are also influenced in our attraction by pheromones: sexually stimulating hormonal aromas which each of us produces. These are very individualized, and while not always consciously noticeable, they can exert a powerful effect on whether we are drawn to or repelled by another.

But "chemistry" is not solely determined by your partner's physical characteristics, it is also revealed in your response to aspects of their personality. Your partner's sense of humor, for example, may have been the captivating force that first drew you together. Perhaps the initial allure was their passionate love of music, or the outdoors, or the way they interacted with children. Maybe you were enticed by their vitality, or the way they asserted themselves and handled their worldly affairs.

One woman, married eighteen years, reported, "I had this instant attraction to him, although I didn't define it as a sexual attraction at the time. I was fifteen years old and I was a little backward in that area. It was his sense of humor and just his kind of liveliness and intelligence that attracted me to him."

For many couples these nonsexual feelings of attraction develop over time into sexual feelings. For others, the frankly physical and sexual elements provide the major impetus for becoming involved. Regardless of the order, for many people an intense sexual connection is an extremely important element in evaluating a potential mate. As one woman said, "Without sexual chemistry it's just not enough. I've had long-term relationships based on intellect, companionship, philosophy, all kinds of things, but there's nothing like good sex."

Another woman recounted a story of the early days of her relationship: "Scott was always enormously physically exciting for me; our bodies were electric with one another. And once while I was trying to decide between the two men who wanted to marry me during my second year of graduate school, I saw a movie called *Tom, Dick and Harry*. The woman in the movie decides which one to marry according to whether or not the bells go off when she kisses him. When I kissed Scott back then, and even now, thirty years later, the bells still go off."

Beware, however, of placing too much importance on the sexual relationship. Far too many people make the serious error of becoming entranced with a sexually thrilling partner, mistake it for love, and then try to build a relationship around this core despite the existence of other serious deficiencies.

Although it is not necessary that the sexual relationship with your chosen one be at the very pinnacle of the sexual experiences of your lifetime, it must be sufficiently enjoyable to make you feel enthusiastic about your lovemaking. As a sixty-one-year-old man married thirty-seven years said, "Sex was never the number-one thing; neither of us ever had that blind, grand passion or sexual desire that sweeps everything before it, but still it has been very important. It's hard to imagine a marriage falling apart when the sex is going well."

Of course, there *are* some marriages that fall apart even though the sex is going well—but for most of us, lovemaking is a most powerful way of restoring intimacy, of opening our hearts to love, and of expressing our vulnerability and tenderness with our partner. Unguarded lovemaking strengthens our trust in each other. It is a pathway to the mystical union that develops between two people, and in a freely expressed orgasm we can experience a blissful state of safe and thorough abandon with our mate. One happily married woman told us, "We've always had a strong physical attraction to each other. I really think that has been a great help. If we had a fight or whatever, that sex drive was still there; it kind of helped us get back together and on track again."

In the beginning, even if the sexual attraction is not especially keen, or the lovemaking is not fully satisfying, there should be a clear indication that your sexual communication is deepening, and that your lovemaking is becoming more pleasurable before you decide to make the relationship a permanent one.

If, on the other hand, significant dissatisfaction exists in the sexual realm and you cannot rectify the problems, you may be witnessing a basic sexual incompatibility or evidence of an important lack in your ability to communicate and problem-solve together. One woman, married forty-four years, was quite honest about her situation: "What we had from the beginning was a strong regard for each other—real love, I think, but the sex wasn't very terrific, and that only got worse. I guess I didn't know how to relax and enjoy it enough. That was really the main problem. We both knew it, I suppose, but we just kind of muddled through. By the time I decided we should get some help and I mentioned it to Morgan, he wasn't interested. That was when I first began to realize that he had something else going on."

Above all, beware of convincing yourself that if you just get married the sexual problems will work themselves out. Although it is true that occasionally sexual difficulties spontaneously resolve themselves, it is a rare event when they do. And while sex may have a lower priority at certain points in a couple's life, most couples find that if their sexuality is pallid or absent their intimacy falters as well. For most people, problems in the bedroom will deeply curtail intimacy, and as sex continues to be unsatisfactory, the relationship will grow more distant and diluted.

Companionship

In the most fulfilling relationships, one's partner is one's best friend, or at least, an excellent friend. The person you commit yourself to is going to be someone with whom you will be spending a tremendous amount of time, therefore you need to carefully consider and evaluate your ability to be pleasantly and comfortably in each other's company. The ability to play, to have fun, to work and relax together, are all important considerations in making this evaluation.

Being good friends and companions also means that you and your partner have a trusting confidence in each other and that you treat each other with care and respect. It is all too common for people to treat their mates more rudely or thoughtlessly than they would a neighbor, as though mateship confers the perverse privilege of being able to express nasty or inconsiderate behaviors that would certainly mark the end of any other friendship. Being comfortable in a relationship doesn't give you license to be insensitive and disrespectful, and if the caring, consideration, and sensitivity you would expect from a longtime good friend are not present in your relationship during the courtship stage, the situation is likely to worsen as time passes.

Before making a commitment, you ought to have had ample evidence that your communication is improving, that it is becoming increasingly possible to resolve conflicts with few or no lingering negative feelings. Taking the time to develop this aspect of any good friendship will save you grief later on: if you have serious problems *before* making a commitment, they are only likely to intensify afterward. It is fair to say that a relationship which is *characterized* by frequent and unresolved struggle during the courtship period is in serious trouble and has a high likelihood of not surviving for very long.

Another hallmark of friendship is the sharing of certain interests and enthusiasms. One woman, married over forty years, said in this regard, "We enjoy each other as friends more than anybody else we know. We have good conversations, we like music, art, we like to walk and hike together, and when we travel we have a terrific time. In fact, we spend a great deal of pleasurable time together."

It should be obvious that you are not going to have a successful relationship simply because your interests are compatible, and while having many activities in common can enhance a relationship, it is by no means a necessity. What *is* essential is that you share *some* important interests, and if you have only a few interests in common, that you have a real ease in doing things separately. One woman in a long, successful relationship told us, "We actually don't share many activities. He does sculpture and I read a lot. We both like to go on trips to nice places, we like dinners out and going to the movies, so those kind of things we have in common, but in terms of how we like to spend our free time, there isn't much overlap. I really like to get together with my friends and talk. He's more of a loner, though he enjoys playing chess competitively and I have no interest in that. Even when we're on a vacation together we'll do totally different things a lot of the time. He'll get up early and I'll sleep in. He'll jog on the beach while I read a book. But we have real good times together being separate." Indeed, some people seem to require a fair amount of time spent apart. For them, too many shared interests feel somewhat suffocating—an unpleasant restriction of their individual autonomy. However, when they do get together, after spending time alone, they are all the more pleased to be in each other's company.

Trust

Trust is the keystone of any relationship. There can be no friendship worth very much without mutual trust. Trust is the outgrowth of having exposed your feelings to another without being injured for having done so: ultimately, trust has to do with feeling safe. The safer you feel with a person and the more you can relax your defenses and allow the person to share your innermost private self, the less alone in the world you will feel. Feeling safe while being vulnerable allows you the freedom to grow, to heal.

Trust also develops in direct proportion to your partner's reliability and integrity. There must be an excellent correlation between their words and deeds. If your partner is unreliable, breaks promises, makes excuses time after time for being unable to come through for you when you have good reason to expect they should, you will inevitably discover yourself growing distant and guarded, retreating into a private inner space where you will be safe from painful disappointment, and the possibility of achieving intimacy will be dramatically reduced.

During courtship you have the privilege of being able to observe your partner in many different circumstances. This provides you with ample opportunity to assess their character. Do they keep their word or does their relationship to the truth come and go depending on which way the wind is blowing? Do they handle themselves ethically in business and in social situations? Do they cheat or lie when it appears they can get away with it? You may reasonably suppose that dishonest habits expressed in other settings will eventually be expressed in your relationship as well.

Unless you are comfortable with your partner's trustworthiness and, in general, you are positively impressed with other dimensions of their character, you have no basis upon which to move forward in the relationship.

Respect

It is difficult to see how a relationship can hope to be successful in the long run unless each partner respects and admires his or her counterpart. Significant aspects of your partner's being must meet with your sincere esteem, or the lack of this esteem will, on balance, erode the relationship in the days to come.

Pride in your partner's concern for others, or career, or accomplishments, or esthetics, or talents, or ethics, or capacity to earn an income, or courage, or warmth, or intelligence is a part of what defines healthy love. In every marriage or other long-term committed relationship you will surely come to see all of your partner's frailties, imperfections, and vulnerabilities. None of us are without our faults, and these easily become magnified in times of stress or conflict. Faults and failings also loom larger without the balancing influence of significant feelings of respect and admiration.

When we have these feelings of respect, our own growth and development is abetted as our partner acts as a positive role model for us in certain areas. The admiration we have for someone encourages our desire to learn from them, and when we learn from one another, the relationship as a whole benefits from the generativity produced, a generativity that counteracts staleness and boredom.

Acceptance

When you respect your partner, you can more easily accept their faults or downsides. This sense of being accepted for who you are is an important component of any relationship that expects to thrive over time. Feeling "supported," and "understood" are descriptive terms used over and over again by couples in loving, committed relationships. In essence, the quality of acceptance that we are referring to means that each person feels loved for who he or she *is*, not just for what he or she *does*.

When the feeling of acceptance is present in a relationship, the partners are able to enjoy themselves together without worrying about making occasional mistakes or about having to produce, achieve, or entertain one another. If love and affection is principally contingent on momentary actions, you can never let down your guard and truly relax. This heightened state of vigilance is actually a form of stress, and may soon lead to a desire to avoid your partner in order to be free and at peace with yourself.

Some people worry that if they accept their partner as is, their partner will never grow, develop or correct their bad habits. The truth, however, is quite the contrary. A healthy level of acceptance frees us from constantly having to look over our shoulder for our mate's approval. This sense of freedom can then augment our own desire to pursue constructive change.

There is an obvious connection between the feeling of being accepted and the capacity to be emotionally accessible, and clearly, emotional accessibility is a central component of true intimacy. This is exemplified by what one woman told us: "He's been willing to share with me his deepest feelings, his insecurities and vulnerabilities, his dreams, his hopes, his doubts, his failures and his successes. This gives me a real sense of emotional connection with him. It's almost as if a physical bond exists between us which makes me feel safe in the world, protected and not alone." Without this feeling of acceptance we can end up feeling alone in a relationship: two ships in the same sea, parallel to each other, passing in the night.

Shared Values

The greater the range of basic values you share with your partner the fewer big issues you will have to reconcile and the greater harmony you are likely to experience.

By basic values we are referring to similarities in outlook, in what one deems important in life, in the fundamentals: one's philosophical stance, ethical system, political persuasions, one's larger relationship to matters of the spiritual and material world, to general life goals.

To a significant extent it is true that people who are successfully mated develop more closely shared values as the years pass; however, it helps immeasurably when many of these shared values are present at the start of the relationship. A distinct comfort results from this shared territory of values, and when this component is present we don't feel the need constantly to explain ourselves.

It is possible for two people to have very different backgrounds yet have many essential values in common: different ethnic, religious, racial, or national origins do not preclude agreement about how people should be treated or what is deemed to be important in life.

How you want to live (your lifestyle) and where (city, country, or suburb); what your idea of family is (if, when, and how many children); your ideas about work, money, and leisure are some of the most significant values that should be in accord. Clearly, it is rare when two people have the same values across the board, but where there are discrepancies it is helpful that they occur in areas of lesser importance to both of them. For example, even though politics is everywhere—in your local community, in how you feel about the issue of abortion, in how your tax dollars are spent, and so on—differences in political ideology may be relatively inconsequential if neither of you is particularly active in political work. If, however, one or both of you are strongly involved politically, disparities in outlook may create serious difficulties. The same holds true for religious or spiritual values. While sharing a common religion or spiritual orientation can greatly enhance a relationship, a disparity in belief between two people assumes far less importance if spiritual or religious practice is not a high priority. For example, the marriage of someone who is Catholic to someone who is Jewish is less likely to be problematic when neither is orthodox in belief and neither insists on one religious practice to the exclusion of the other or on a particular religious education for the children.

When fundamental values conflict, the possibility that the relationship will eventually be torn asunder by irreconcilable differences must be considered very carefully. This possibility underscores the overriding importance of spending sufficient time during courtship getting to know one another well. Consequently, we strongly recommend that extensive exploratory conversations concerning fundamental values occur *before* any decision is made to link your fates together permanently.

EVALUATING THE FIT

While these six categories of evaluation are of unquestionable importance, a commitment is never made as a result of a mere statistical assessment. Our intuition and heartfelt feelings form the basis for the desire to make a commitment. Still, assessing the qualities we have described provides you with a way to double-check your feelings and may help you to clarify any gnawing reservations you may be experiencing.

The truth of the matter is that every relationship has its imperfections, its limitations within some of the categories we have discussed. The question to be addressed, therefore, is whether the insufficiencies are of such magnitude that you think they jeopardize the viability of your relationship. If an essential quality is entirely absent or if a number of those we have described are only present to a meager degree, you are probably treading on thin ice, and the deficit may prove to be the fatal flaw in your relationship.

Therefore, take stock to determine what you deem to be your most important needs, in order to make certain that these, at least, are significantly being met within the relationship. For example, one woman said: "I was clear about what I simply couldn't tolerate and what I could. What I couldn't tolerate ever again was an ambivalent man or a man who flew off the handle whenever things didn't go his way. Winston was different. He was neither wishy-washy nor crazy. He was totally committed to me and loyal, and it didn't hurt that he was also gorgeous and successful. His incredibly corny sense of humor gave me problems, and the fact that he was a minister gave me *real* problems, but since I respected him and we had a lot in common, I felt secure in marrying him, despite the deficiencies."

Alexis had grown up in a financially secure family and had never been concerned about money. Both she and Preston recognized that his chosen work in the nonprofit field meant that he would never earn a sizable income. Alexis struggled with this issue, particularly since she was close to her parents and they had openly expressed their reservations about Preston's ability to be an adequate provider. Finally, after considerable internal debate, Alexis decided that her admiration for his commitment to righting societal wrongs offset the fact that their pocketbook might be a bit pinched. She thought that she could accommodate to a shift in material comfort and that the problem would prove to be a fairly minor one, since they were so compatible in other areas. Besides, she had never put the same premium on material values that her parents had.

Had Alexis instead harbored secret fantasies of influencing Preston to move his career in a more lucrative direction, her basic lack of respect for him as a wage earner might have led her to undermine his sense of self-worth, making him feel inadequate and defensive. Eventually, if neither of them could adapt to the other's values, this issue might have proven to be an insurmountable obstacle, a toxin that would poison their relationship.

It is also possible that had Alexis come to discover that having considerable material worth *was* of great significance to her and of central importance for her happiness, she might have determined whether she could earn the additional income on her own. If she felt that she could not, she might have been better off deciding to end the relationship with Preston, seeking someone else with whom she was more *simpatico* in this regard. In fact, we interviewed one woman who was involved in this very scenario. She said, "I wanted assurance that the man I married would make it possible for me to have a bit of the life my mother had; maybe not quite as privileged, but at least some luxury without having to think that he was looking down at me and making me feel guilty about it. Brad certainly would not have been comfortable with that kind of life, so I just couldn't go through with it. Three years later I met Rick. Having a good deal of money was important to him, too. We have other problems, to be sure, but I don't find them as personally painful as the money issue would have been."

One man was concerned about his partner's lack of knowledge and sophistication in the arts. As a composer, he had no desire to compromise this value, and intellectual companionship with his mate was of paramount importance. "That's why I waited two years before marrying Nadia," he said. "During our courtship she began reading widely, and when I took her to lectures and concerts she reacted with great enthusiasm, so even though she was rather unschooled when we met, I had no doubt of her genuine interest in the areas that mattered so much to me. Her interest was keen from the start, and it has continued to this day. In fact, now she recommends books for *me* to read."

For one man, having a sense of freedom, not feeling hemmed in, was at the very top of his list of relationship necessities. He met a woman who was in her late thirties, who had a career and full life of her own. However, she felt the same way about having a family as he did about his sense of freedom: it was ironclad. Since he already had grown children, he did not want to begin full-time fatherhood again, particularly because of the constraints it would impose upon him. Consequently, the two of them went through an agony of soul-searching until they finally and sadly agreed to end their relationship.

Do not fool yourself into believing that getting married will change ongoing basic problems in the relationship: that suddenly he will settle down and stop spending so much time partying with the guys; that she will stop talking endlessly on the phone to her mother, seeking advice on every detail of her life; that he will be more interested in sex; that she will keep her promises and appointments . . . In fact, once a commitment has been made, the area that was unsatisfying *before* the commitment—her drinking, his weight, their lack of money— is likely to become even *more* intolerable. Marriage will *not* make major conflicting issues disappear. Quite the contrary: marriage or living together will generally highlight and exacerbate them. In some fashion, marriage or its equivalent shifts our perception of a problem. When a relationship is temporary, the problem is seen as temporary, however, it tends to grow in magnitude as we imagine living with it for the rest of our lives. Consequently, if you are aware of a decisive problem in your relationship, ask yourself whether the commitment you are about to make is actually contingent on your partner changing, or if you can live with it " 'til death do you part."

It is possible that your partner will change for the better as a result of making a commitment, but the safer bet is that he or she will probably change only slightly. This means that if there are areas which must be resolved before you can be satisfied in the relationship, you are much wiser to extend the courtship and attempt to reconcile the problems *before* making the relationship a permanent one.

Love

In all of this rational categorization and evaluation you may wonder what has happened to "love." Why is the word or concept of "love" absent from our list of essential qualities? We believe that love is too often confused with infatuation, a narrower, more sexually focused and ephemeral state, which, because of its intensity, is very persuasive and captivating. Infatuation is wonderful and exhilaratingly delicious, to be sure, but it is not the same as love.

True love emerges and ripens over time. It is the amalgamation of chemistry, friendship, trust, respect, acceptance, and shared values. Unlike infatuation, there is nothing that limits love from lasting a lifetime—it is not predicated on novelty—and indeed, properly nurtured and cared for, it becomes richer, more spiritually fulfilling, more powerful, as the years pass.

FEARS OF COMMITMENT

"Fear of commitment" is a rather ambiguous and hackneyed term used to "explain" why someone is hesitant to move forward into a serious, monogamous relationship, to throw his or her hat in the ring. Almost everyone has experienced a fear of commitment in one form or another. Sometimes these fears are fleeting and cause no problems. At other times they can paralyze a relationship and prevent it from moving forward.

Although by no means exhaustive, the discussion that follows illuminates the more common fears of commitment. For some people, more than one of these fears may be operating simultaneously. However, by understanding their sources, you may be better able to resolve them, or at least cope with them somewhat more effectively if they are blocking either you or your partner's path to greater intimacy.

Fear of the Unknown

Ambiguity (or uncertainty) and anxiety are bedfellows. Generally speaking, the unpredictable is met with a degree of hesitation by most of us, but by some more than others. Security, predictability, and control are also linked to one another. When we make a major life change, such as beginning a committed relationship, we necessarily embark on a less predictable course, one that is often accompanied by the loss of a certain amount of control and an attendant increase in anxiety.

Many people are frightened by the prospect of these imminent changes in their lives: a lot more could go wrong in ways that are unforeseeable. They worry about their ability to adapt to the numerous accommodations that are a part of the picture of living with someone else. In particular, people who have been single and on their own for a long while, "calling their own shots," may experience this fear more intensely, especially if they are older and more set in their ways.

Fear of Responsibility

Certain people veer away from committed relationships predominantly because they are troubled about assuming the responsibilities entailed. Generally, these fears of responsibility are sex-role scripted, with men being more concerned with the financial aspects of supporting a family and with the ultimate role of fatherhood, and women more worried about taking on added household responsibilities, and the role of motherhood while maintaining their careers. In addition, as women are feeling increasingly oppressed by their dual obligations, they are placing greater pressure on men to do more domestically than they have had to do in the past.

Other fears enter into this picture as well, those that relate to having partial responsibility for the fate and welfare of one's partner: taking on a partner with large debts, medical problems, difficult children, or other current or future life difficulties.

Fear of Failure

If you don't commit, you can't fail: it is the ultimate protection. If you do commit and it doesn't work out, you might fear the embarrassment—particularly if others have expressed serious reservations about the wisdom of your choice.

The fear of failure can be especially acute for someone who has already been divorced, but you needn't be divorced yourself to dread the pain and loss inherent in the dissolution process. Those who have experienced divorce secondhand through the dissolution of their parents' or close friends' marriages know only too well of the emotional turmoil, bitterness, and financial cost that results from breaking such bonds. The fact that it is more difficult to end a committed relationship—especially a legal marriage—should it not work out, along with the fear of getting trapped in a prolongedly unhappy or stultifying connection, can be sufficient motivation to keep some people as far from commitment as possible.

Fear of Abandonment

In addition to having had past experiences of feeling abandoned, the fear of abandonment may also result from the tendency to place too many of one's dependency needs in a single basket, relying rather exclusively on someone who could suddenly leave you high, dry, and devastated. There is probably a biological basis for the greater prevalence of this fear among women because of their unique vulnerability during advanced stages of pregnancy or when nursing a newborn. But certainly the social, cultural, and familial conditioning that many women have received while growing up, about needing a man in order to make their way in the world and be complete, is likely to be even more influential in promoting this fear.

It must be emphasized, however, that a substantial number of men dread a possible abandonment as well, since the pain of loss is not limited to one gender.

Fear of Entrapment

The counterpart to the fear of abandonment is the fear of entrapment. When a partner is extremely controlling, of course, this is not an unreasonable fear. Usually, however, this fear has more to do with the loss of autonomy and freedom that are seen by some as the inevitable sacrifices demanded by a committed relationship. Concerns about the reduced possibility for adventure, especially sexual adventure, and the frightening possibility of a life of boredom if limited to one partner are frequently central to this fear, which appears to be more prevalent among men. This, too, may have a basis in biology as well as social conditioning. Earlier in our evolutionary history men were the hunters, requiring freedom to roam in order to catch game and provide food for the family. Even today, men are encouraged to wander more in the world at large and clearly are given more license to enjoy sexual adventure than their female counterparts. In this case, biology and culture may combine, creating greater resistance to the limitations and confines posed by monogamy. One man put it this way, "I felt that committing myself to marriage was like committing myself to a monastic order. It was that scary."

Although men more frequently tend to fear entrapment, women, especially those who have developed their own sense of power and possibility, can easily feel the keen edge of this fear as well.

The "Grass Is Always Greener" Syndrome

Obviously, any decision that a person makes necessarily excludes other possibilities, and these other alternatives have an odd way of becoming mysteriously more attractive when they must be given up. No matter which side of the fence you are on, the grass always seems greener on the other side. You can straddle the fence or jump from side to side, from noncommitment to commitment and back again, but sooner or later you will become exhausted by the exercise and you will feel at home nowhere. The "grass is always greener" syndrome quite commonly arises shortly after you have made a commitment or just as you are about to make one. Alas, poor humans, all we want is everything!

RESOLVING COMMITMENT PHOBIAS

To a certain extent, at the outset of a committed relationship almost everyone experiences one or more of these fears. Consequently, such fears need not prevent the possibility of enjoying a fulfilling and enduring relationship. If they did, very few committed relationships would exist. Resolving these commitment phobias is generally a natural by-product of the process of deepening intimacy. In fact, for some people, these fears are not fully resolved until some years *after* the actual commitment has been made.

Despite the numerous guises of these fears, they are most often, though not always, based *within* our psyches, and not in the particular realities of our partner and the relationship *per se.* Nevertheless, it is sometimes difficult to ascertain the difference. Are they advance warnings of impending doom? Or are they instead an expression of some neurotic fear that, regardless of the particular relationship, must be overcome if intimacy and happiness is ever to be attained? To help make this determination, take the time to evaluate your partner on the six categories of chemistry, friendship, trust, respect, acceptance, and shared values. When we spoke with couples who were quite satisfied with their long-term relationships, we discovered that although they may have experienced other uncertainties and fears at the time they began their commitment they rarely doubted that their partner was the right person for them. Instead, they said such things as:

"The night before my wedding I was very anxious—I kept thinking about losing my freedom. I had no doubt that he was the right person, but the idea of getting married frightened me."

"I started thinking that I hadn't been to Europe yet. I was only twenty-three; I had only slept with one other person. I thought that I must be crazy to do it, but I knew that I loved her."

On the other hand, people who ultimately divorced talked of having basic concerns about their *partner* right from the beginning:

"I don't think it was anything he did or said, it was just the way he was. He wasn't smart enough for me. I didn't like his humor—it just wasn't funny. And when I tried to have a conversation about something, he didn't hold up his end of it enough to satisfy me. These may have been small things, but they kept nagging at me."

"I had doubts even when we were going together, even when

we were engaged. I would think, I don't know if I really love her. I don't know if I want to be married to her or if I even like her very much. But I pushed those feelings down and kept moving forward."

"He felt more like a brother to me than my lover. Something about it didn't feel quite right but somehow I couldn't put my finger on it—it seemed so right 'on paper.' A week before we got married I told him that I wasn't sure that I could be committed to him for more than a couple of years. We got married anyway."

Intuition

The three examples just quoted illustrate the consequences of a common and unfortunate tendency: *the dismissal of intuition*.

An intuition is a way of knowing something that is instinctual; it is *pre*-cognitive, which is to say that it is not the product of careful, deliberated thinking. It is, strictly speaking, neither a thought nor a feeling, but somehow a blending of the two. An intuition is distinguished by a few significant characteristics: it comes as the *first*, rather instantaneous "take" or impression you have in your considerations; it is *fleeting* or evanescent, and is easily and commonly blanketed out by secondary considerations: thoughts, rationalizations, other feelings, and the like.

We all have intuitions, although we often ignore them in favor of more strictly rational or reflexive emotional responses. As with all skills, if we do not use our intuitive faculties we lose them, at least temporarily. With practice, we can almost always resurrect them.

Along with many other instincts, intuitions are related to the universal and most fundamental need: self-preservation. Therefore, not having well-honed intuitive skills compromises the excellence of our survival. In addition, having a well-developed, well-practiced connection with our intuition is a powerful, primordial way to stay in touch with our deepest, most personal selves.

For these reasons we emphasize that in addition to a rational, conscious assessment, it is of great importance that you also consult your intuition in regard to your potential mate. Remember, an intuition is located neither in your head nor in your heart but somewhere in between. In order to get to it, you must go back to a time in your experience with your partner before other persuasions or emotional pressures exerted their influence upon you. Try going to a peaceful place to meditate, or in some other way try to quiet the "noise" of other messages, so that you may more clearly contact your intuition.

An intuition can present itself as a peaceful certitude that this is the right relationship for you, or a gnawing feeling inside you that something just isn't right, though you may not be able to put your finger on exactly what the problem is.

A few weeks before getting married, Sophia recalls having written a confidential letter to her father saying that while she loved her fiancé, Rasheed, who was wonderful in many ways, she wasn't happy. "But my father just wrote back telling me to calm down," said Sophia. "He made me feel that there was something wrong with me for feeling the way I did, as if I were crazy or something. He warned me that if I gave Rasheed up I'd regret it the rest of my life and never find another man as good as he was. So I kept sitting on my feelings and thinking that the problem was entirely with me. It took me years to learn that there *were* problems and I wasn't stupid or crazy for feeling the way I did."

Intuition can take many forms. Some people experience intuition as a palpable or "gut" feeling that they can't quite explain rationally; others hear intuition as a "voice" inside their heads. Sometimes a vague "knowing" may be your intuition trying to tell you something that you have not yet been able to fully understand or articulate.

One man told us of a relationship he had with a woman he intended to marry. She was beautiful, intelligent, and wealthy, and their sex life was terrific: she was the "perfect package," by any rational assessment. Even though they fought a good deal, he felt they could work out their problems. Yet, for months, each time he went out alone on a run, which he did several times a week, he would hear a voice inside himself reciting a litany, keeping pace with his footfalls: "You don't love her, you don't love her, you don't love her . . ." He decided that this voice was really a sign of his own neurosis and his general fear of getting involved in an intimate relationship. He tried his best to ignore it, dismiss it, override it, because on the surface everything looked so good, and he was beginning to fear that he would never meet anyone he could love lastingly. Eventually, however, the repetitive bickering between him and his fiancée caused him to delay formalizing the marriage plans. After a number of months they terminated their engagement, painfully and with great difficulty and sorrow. Yet after a short while he felt a tremendous sense of relief: he would not have been happily married to her. The voice inside him was right after all; his self-preserving intuition had expressed itself in a form that he had not initially recognized.

If you notice that you are making elaborate rationalizations in an attempt to minimize or dismiss existing problems, your intuition is probably trying to tell you something. When the relationship is right, you don't have to twist yourself into a pretzel in order to make it work. For one woman, a dream conveyed her intuition and *confirmed* her feeling that her partner was the right man to marry: "When I was considering whether or not to marry him, I had a dream that there was an enormous mess on my kitchen floor: coffee grounds, broken crystal, just a horrible mess. Underneath the sink there was this box of cleanser called 'Faith,' and I poured the cleanser on the floor and mopped up the mess. I think I had come to the point in my life that I really had faith in myself and had the faith that we could work out whatever messes we would get into."

No way of knowing is perfect, of course, but your intuition offers the best advice that your inner life can provide. However, if you are particularly good at fooling yourself, how can you be sure that your neurotic fears aren't really masquerading as intuition?

To help clarify the distinction, again review the six categories. Do your intuitions coincide with a particular deficit in one of the categories? If everything looks good on paper, next analyze your past relationship patterns. Do you have the habit of regularly getting cold feet just as you become more intimate, or as soon as your partner becomes more invested in the relationship? When you *have* been able to feel committed, were you in a relationship where, paradoxically, your partner had one foot out the door, or was in some other way not fully available?

If your history shows an inability to be committed whenever your partner *is*, and vice versa, your fear rather than your intuition may be speaking, and you might do well to stay in the relationship and address the fear. However, if you have had a fulfilling, intimate, long-term relationship in the past, one in which the two of you felt equally committed, you should pay special attention to these intuitive doubts. While it is possible that you have been so severely traumatized in a previous relationship that you have been rendered phobic, it is also possible that your little voice inside is telling you an important truth that should not be ignored no matter how eager you are to be part of a couple.

In order to contend with these fears most effectively, begin talking with your partner about them. Do not suppress them and try to deal with them secretly on your own. Forthright conversation can help bring the two of you closer, and your partner's way of dealing with your reservations and anxieties will provide you with even more data to help you further appraise and evaluate the prospects of the relationship.

The Slowest Common Denominator

The fear to commit, like other fears and anxieties, is most often the result of past injuries. Whether the injury is real or imagined, the wound it produces is indisputably real. As we

have indicated, these wounds, in turn, lead to the development
of protective mechanisms which attempt to prevent the injuries from being repeated. If you are truly fearful, then obviously it makes no sense to bully yourself bluntly through the
fears. Such bullying will usually cause the fears to be *increased*,
leading to even stronger protective defenses.

If you want these defenses to recede and resolve most rapidly
and most favorably, you must find a way to *heal* the wounds
they are protecting. Unquestionably, healing occurs best when
there is a safe atmosphere, one that is free of the pressure to
make a decision by a particular date, regardless of whether this
pressure is coming from within you, from your partner, or
from some other source.

It must be remembered that healing takes time. This means,
among other things, that the pace of the relationship's development is usually determined for the most part by the person
who has the greatest fear, the one who wants to proceed most
slowly. This is the principle we term the "Slowest Common
Denominator."

The Trial Separation

If, after a period of time with no pressure and a "vacation"
from scrutiny and analysis, you are still at a loss as to whether
or not your hesitation to move forward is based on an irrational
fear, it would be wisest to ask your partner's indulgence for a
month or so as you mutually agree to have a nonpunitive trial
separation. Do this while you are still feeling good about each
other, before too much anger and hurt have accumulated.

During this time you may talk together occasionally, but in
general the *less* contact you have, the better; and sexual contact
is especially inadvisable. Since you are sincerely trying to resolve an important life decision, it is also inadvisable during
this separation for either partner to date anyone else romanti-
cally and/or sexually. To do so will only add to the confusion
and create a threat during a particularly sensitive time.

Ross and Christine had been good friends for almost three years before they became lovers. At first it was just a casual, sexual relationship, but a few months later Ross began wanting to spend more time with Christine. To his surprise he was falling in love with her. Christine, however, had been divorced a little more than a year before and she was wary of making a commitment again. Finally, the issue of children came between them: Ross had two grown children and didn't want any more, while Christine desperately wanted a family of her own. She also felt more like a sister than a lover to Ross at times and this confused her. And while they openly discussed these subjects, they felt no pressure to decide about the relationship one way or the other.

After more time had passed, Ross rather tentatively began to change his mind about having another child. Even though he was looking forward to his retirement in the not too distant future, his deepening knowledge of Christine and his trust of her alleviated his fear of becoming a father once again and assuming the many responsibilities it entailed. But Christine was still unconvinced and afraid it wouldn't work. She didn't want Ross to discover several years hence that he was actually quite resentful at having compromised his freedom; her fearful uncertainty and her deep caring for Ross led her to propose breaking up before the relationship grew even more serious. Finally, she told Ross of her decision. Because she seemed resolute and could not be persuaded to reconsider, Ross had no choice but to agree, however reluctantly.

This time it was Christine who surprised herself: after their painful phone conversation she spent the entire night in tears. She was aware of a longing feeling, a loneliness and an emptiness she had not felt when she had ended previous relationships. Her intuition was telling her that she might be making the biggest mistake of her life. In the morning she called Ross, described her experience the previous evening, and resurrected the relationship. It took a few months before her platonic feelings gave way to more romantic ones, but they did, and the three of them, Ross, Christine, and their now eleven-year-old son are still happily together.

If you feel increasingly relieved during the experimental hiatus we've suggested, if you find that you are thinking relatively little about the relationship, have few regrets, and if these reactions don't change significantly over the month, the experiment has given you a clear answer to your relationship dilemma: do not go forward with it. If, however, you feel much more upset than you expected, find that you are pining for the person (as distinguished from just being lonely in general), frequently have a hard time resisting calling them, and discover that you are focusing on all the good qualities about the relationship while the negative ones seem to drop from sight, your reaction may be telling you that your fears of commitment may be the problem. In this case, you may find that the time and space you took to evaluate the relationship have prepared you to move forward more easily to the next level of intimacy.

When it is your partner who is considerably more ambivalent than you are, the process remains the same, but now *you* must resist the temptation to brush aside your partner's fears, attempting to convince her or him to make a commitment under the premise that everything will work out for the best. Even if this turns out to be true in the end, the process of how you get there is all important. Each person must freely and independently *choose* to be part of a relationship if it is to start off on the right foot.

After dating Lauren exclusively for two years, Sean was happy with the way things were, but Lauren, feeling a need for greater security, wanted to get married. Sean really didn't feel ready to take such a big step but he didn't want to break up, either. He finally succumbed to Lauren's pressure, but the resentment he felt expressed itself as a change in his attitude and feelings toward her. Almost immediately after their wedding he became strangely unavailable emotionally. Within two years they were divorced.

Had Lauren encouraged Sean to test life without her, rather

than pressing him to make a commitment against his own wishes, he might have experienced his *own* feelings of abandonment and loss. If these feelings had persuaded him to marry Lauren because he truly loved her and didn't want to lose her, this would have resulted in his having had a greater investment in the marriage. On the other hand, had he decided instead *not* to move forward, Lauren could then have assumed that a successful marriage to Sean was out of the question, and she either could have chosen to remain in an unmarried relationship with him or to look elsewhere for her life mate. In any event, opting for a trial separation rather than succumbing to the pressure to commit would have enabled Sean and Lauren to arrive at the best decision.

César and Juana had been dating for nine months. César wanted to be married and have a family, but Juana kept feeling that this was not the right relationship for her. Since her father had died when she was three and her first husband had died only a year after their marriage, Juana couldn't tell whether these traumas and the resulting fears of loss were affecting her ability to make a commitment or if her concerns about not feeling emotionally close enough to César reflected a real limitation in their relationship.

César was certain he could show Juana that their love was true and deep if only Juana would relax and trust him, but she was like a rubber band: he could pull her close to him momentarily, but she would bounce back out again after a brief moment of intimacy. Finally, exhausted and impatient, he told her that if they were ever to get together again *she* would have to be the one to initiate things. He was prepared to let the relationship go if she did not take primary responsibility for making arrangements to get together. At the end of ten days Juana had not called, and César finally realized that whether her fears were real or imagined, she was simply not available for the kind of relationship he wanted, and he was then able to let her go and get on with his life.

It should be noted that there are a few situations in which

the results of a creative trial separation may be misleading. The first concerns relationships in which you feel powerfully drawn to a partner who abuses you physically or emotionally. In this situation, you may find yourself longing for your partner during a trial separation—even feeling as if you cannot make it on your own. When you reunite, your partner treats you royally—at least for a while. But beware, if your partner has not begun serious psychological treatment in the interim, the new behavior is unlikely to last, and when your partner returns to feeling secure in the relationship, you are likely to find yourself physically or emotionally scarred once again. Your desire to return to an abusive situation means that you, too, need professional help, and you should seek it without delay.

The second situation that can be misleading involves a partner who significantly abuses a substance. You may find that during the separation he or she abstains from abusing the substance in question—a demonstration of control that persuades you to try the relationship again. Once again, however, if neither of you has sought treatment in the interim, the abuse is very likely to be resumed.

Ending a relationship that involves any form of abuse requires a firm, rational decision as well as a lot of support from family, friends, self-help support groups, or professionals, in order to counteract the false hope that your love will be powerful enough to change your partner's well-entrenched habits. Most often such a relationship continues as is until the abused, co-dependent partner finally bails out, exhausted, damaged, angry, and very wary of relationships in the future.

One Step at a Time

If you feel relieved *every* time you pull back from a relationship, *regardless of its potential,* then a trial separation is *not* an appropriate solution because it will tend to solidify your resistance to going forward to intimacy. In this instance, if you would like to move beyond your fears and have no solid reasons to doubt the suitability of your partner, you should probably stay in the relationship and work on your resistance. Mutually decide on a small step that would be tolerable for you yet would still represent an advance toward greater intimacy—for example, dating exclusively, getting engaged, deciding on a future date to move in together. Then try on this new behavior as if it were a robe, to see how it fits. Allow yourself a couple of months to adjust to it. During this period your anxieties should dissipate enough for you to evaluate whether or not you are comfortable with this new level of intimacy.

In fact, many people who fear commitment nevertheless "take the plunge" in exactly this way and actually find themselves quite content with their decision, often wondering, months or years afterward, what they were so frightened about. As one man, married thirty-seven years, said, "For me it was a fear of losing my freedom. In all honesty, I saw it as the sort of commitment that would deplete my energy or attention for other things. I was very ambitious about my career. I had extremely romantic and high-flung notions about what a great musician I was going to be and how I was going to set the world on fire. I imagined myself working twelve to fifteen hours a day and I couldn't fathom how a married person could do that. But once I made the commitment, I didn't feel restless. I never felt I was denied anything. Far from it. My wife was totally supportive of my career."

A reasonably protracted courtship provides you with an opportunity to get a good overview of the relationship. It gives you a chance to see if you are making progress, just treading water, or backsliding. Rather than speed, focus on moving forward. The object is to continue to move ahead even if the pace is slower than you would wish for, or if the periods between each significant advance are longer than you would like. As long as there continues to be positive growth and change, you can assume you are on a path that is worth further exploration.

If you find that you keep going round and round the same

issues with no resolution and that the love and pleasure in the relationship is being exhausted and eroded, it is probably time to get help from a competent therapist who specializes in counseling couples.

Justin wanted Molly to marry him but she was having difficulty making that commitment even though she loved him. They had lived together for over three years but had briefly separated many times during that period. In Molly's words, "The last time we separated for a week I was sure I wasn't going back, but Justin began courting me all over again and saying how he couldn't live without me. So I told him that I wouldn't come back again unless we went to counseling together, and for the first time he finally agreed. Well, we went for about six sessions and things were going great, but they usually did go very well for a while after one of our breakups so I was still skeptical. Sure enough, the same old pattern began: Justin thought we had had enough therapy, his work pressures gave him an excuse to cancel a few of our appointments and before I knew it he was back into drugs and watching TV all the time. Finally I was clear about the situation in a way that I had never been before. I ended the relationship and never looked back."

There are times when several sessions with a good therapist who specializes in working with couples can bring into clear focus the nature of the difficulties in the relationship so that you can extricate yourself from it, if that proves to be the healthiest option. At other times a therapist may be able to give you a fresh insight into your problems and suggest some more effective ways of dealing with them. It is important to emphasize that therapy should be sought as soon as possible after you realize the significance of your problem, *before* you pass the point of no return where the negative feelings that have accrued have dashed any possibility that love can survive. A partner who refuses to seek counseling when you are at a serious and unresolvable impasse in the relationship is, in essence, telling you that he or she is not interested in investigating the feelings and issues necessary to make the relationship work, and is expressing an unwillingness to progress to a level of greater intimacy.

Making a decision that will profoundly influence the rest of your life is not to be taken lightly. Yet, no matter how cautiously and carefully you evaluate your relationship, you cannot fully eliminate risk. If deep intimacy and a shared life is what you want, the rewards of a committed relationship make the risks worthwhile.

As one man in his mid-forties, married six years, told us, "It's such a Catch-22 paradox: when you're out of a relationship you're thinking about how much fun it would be to be in one and when you're in one there are problems to deal with that sometimes make you think about how nice it would be to be playing the field again. But, for me, it boils down to having made a decision to work it out in the relationship I'm in. The grass is not really greener on the other side—it just looks that way sometimes: it's a deception, and dating new people gets tiresome after a while. It definitely requires some work to stay in a relationship, but as far as I'm concerned it's worth it because of all it gives back to you."

Being in a relationship that goes the distance lovingly and well requires a fair share of tenacity, forbearance, and ongoing rededication, especially in light of the kinds of stresses and transitional adjustments that are part of all relationships.

Managing the stresses and transitions and keeping love alive while you do so is the focus of the following chapters.

9

Stormy Weather

Stress and the Relationship

For one human being to love another: that is perhaps the most difficult of all our tasks, the ultimate, the last test and proof, the work for which all other work is but preparation.

—RAINER MARIA RILKE,
Letters to a Young Poet

On a serene and verdant mountain, high in the Himalayas, far away from the hubbub and demands of the industrialized world, a place where there are no newspapers, no telephones, no radio or TV, perhaps there is a group of people who are living blissful stress-free lives. Perhaps . . . but don't bet on it. As we poor mortals eke out our daily existence, there appears to be no place to hide for very long from the impact of stress, whether it is the stress of illness, economics, interpersonal conflict, whether it is only occasional and mild, or whether it is constantly bombarding and besieging us.

In addition to the stress that results from dealing with the shifting needs of two people and in working through the occasional conflicts that are the natural by-product of differences between partners, there is a wide array of stressors which impinge upon us from outside sources. These externally produced stresses can have a very disruptive impact on the delicate balance of any relationship, especially a relatively new one. Many of them are, of course, unavoidable, and have always been so— they flow, for instance, from the demands of one's work, from maintaining the household, from raising children—and they are likely to be exaggerated at this time in history when dual-career couples are becoming the norm and where the pace of life is more rapid than ever before.

The list of potential stressors is virtually endless. Serious stress may be imposed by real financial privations, or simply by living in a society that evaluates personal worth by an ability to keep up with the Joneses; considerable stress is the usual consequence of moving to a new residence or renovating an existing one, a visit from parents or in-laws or other major disruptions in established routine. Enormous stress may result from the serious illness or death of a loved one, even from global political conflict or crime in the streets. Since stress is so ubiquitous and unavoidable, to be forewarned permits us to be forearmed. In preparation for its advent, we can learn coping strategies that will enable us to deal with stressful situations swiftly, creatively and resiliently so that its negative impact on ourselves and our relationships can be minimized.

PSYCHOECONOMICS

When we talk about stress, what we are referring to is a state of imbalance in our equilibrium, of either brief or of longer duration. Individuals as well as relationships each have their private "economy" based upon the way their "output" compares with their "input." Every demand on the relationship, or the individuals in it, that involves a degree of work or effort, whether emotional, intellectual or physical, may be considered output. And everything which comes into the system that nourishes, supports, sustains, relaxes or gives delight may be considered input. Obviously, a harmonious relationship can result only when there is a proper balance of inputs and outputs.

When this balance is thrown off kilter, the resulting stress may be reduced and the equilibrium restored either by *lessening* the *output*, or by *adding* sufficient *input* (rest, supportive communication, play, affection), or, most rapidly, by doing both. If equilibrium is not restored, the relationship eventually moves into a state of distress, or, in economic terms, a state of deficit. The couple begins to show symptoms: boredom, quarreling, anxiety, alienation, depression, sexual apathy, insomnia, disturbances in eating, increases in drinking or smoking, psychosomatic or physical illness, and other hallmarks of trouble. The longer this psychoeconomic imbalance persists, the more likely the symptoms are to increase in number and severity.

Within limits, stress does not have to be destructive, but if the couple's system is already in a weakened or imbalanced state or the stress is particularly intense or chronic, some degree of damage is a virtual certainty.

Clearly, no relationship can go from beginning to end without confronting times of great difficulty. In fact, the realization that some dark times are bound to lurk over the horizon can help you better appreciate and enjoy the good times while you are having them, and help prepare you to handle the stressful times when they descend.

TRANSITIONAL STRESSES

In addition to the unforeseeable stresses that are an unavoidable part of a life well lived, there are a number of predictable transitional periods within every relationship—highly sensitive times that are virtually guaranteed to be problematic.

In the stage of early growth every living organism is most easily damaged. Just as the newest leaf opening up on a plant is the one most susceptible to injury from the effects of reduced watering, sunlight or nutrients, the newly formed relationship is similarly vulnerable.

Vulnerability, however, is also heightened at times when change is taking place most rapidly from one stage or form to another. While the potential for growth is probably greatest during these transitional periods, the stability and cohesiveness of a relationship is also at its greatest risk. Since it is our premise that being forewarned permits us to be forearmed, we will describe the most important transitions, periods when the risk of disruption by stress is particularly high. We hope this will increase your understanding and preparedness, and improve your chances of successfully coping with the difficulties associated with these critical times, nipping potential problems in the bud.

Career Development

One's job or career can place considerable demands on a relationship, especially when the work is wearisome, takes place in an unpleasant setting, with unpleasant people, or extends considerably beyond the typical forty-hour workweek. An alienating, pressured, or tedious job can take a great deal out of a person's spirit or energy, compromising the enthusiasm they bring back to their relationship. No relationship can thrive when one or both partners grow so dulled or robbed of energy that passivity, sleep, and other forms of rest become the predominant (non)activity when they are at home.

As one or both members of a couple attempt to better their financial position, whether it be through returning to school, starting their own business, taking on additional work, or climbing the corporate ladder, their relationship may suffer further deprivation. The time and attention that previously was devoted to their partner is apt to be refocused onto work.

Many people mistakenly consider their *relationship* to be endlessly flexible and accommodating, and the time devoted to it to be *elective*, whereas, by contrast, a *career's* demands are seen as *fixed*, stringent, beyond one's control, if one is to become successful. The boss, deadlines, competition, all seem to insist on a career-first attitude, and the relationship becomes a fading priority. The erroneous assumption that a relationship can sustain considerably greater deprivation than one's career can be very destructive, and is unfortunately all too common.

When both members of a couple work outside the home, their schedules often differ. This can make it difficult to have dinner or breakfast together, to have a decent conversation, make love, and restore their friendship. When one's career requires work to be brought home in the evening and on weekends, the relationship is even further compromised. After a while, it is predictable that the deprioritized relationship will suffer and begin to atrophy.

Family

In addition to the obvious joys that children can bring to a relationship, there are also the attendant drawbacks. During pregnancy, when each person's individual preoccupations are diverted—toward concerns for the well-being of the growing fetus, the impending birth, being an adequate parent, providing for the child economically—the focus is shifted away from meeting the intimacy needs of the couple.

Once the child is born the couple contends with sleepless nights, exhaustion, and endless talk about the new baby. These, in combination with the probable reduction in their sex life during the time immediately preceding and following the birth, all combine to take their toll on the couple's intimate relationship. Each partner may be jealous of the other's attention toward the baby and feel deprived of certain needs her or his partner fulfilled before the child arrived on the scene. Of course, when there is more than one child the complications expand geometrically, with even more people contending for the limited supply of attention and time available.

Unlike other life stages, the family stage is extensively prolonged and comprises within it a number of subtransitional periods. In addition to pregnancy and birth, as children grow, they encounter numerous developmental hurdles that may require a good deal of parental attention. Differences in regard to child-rearing methods may cause conflict between parents at varying stages of a child's development. And it is impossible to overlook the long and trying test that adolescence imposes on almost every parent, or the unique problems posed by integrating stepchildren into a new, blended family.

Overall, contending with the challenges of raising children can divert the parents from attending to each other's needs. This is precisely why many couples report that their personal relationship was best before the first child was born and then again after the last child left the roost.

Midlife

At some point during the midlife years—in our forties or fifties—most of us confront our own mortality and the finitude of life in a powerful, emotional way. The realization that our life is about half over presses us to reconsider our priorities and to question how we want to live during the remaining years.

Midlife is a time to reflect more deeply on the fulfillment of latent desires and other aspects of our individual destinies that have taken a back seat to the worldly exigencies that have long occupied us. Perhaps we would like to devote more time to a hobby, an artistic enthusiasm, a new career, travel, living a life fettered by fewer responsibilities, dedicating ourselves to service in the community, to a favorite charity, to our family . . .

For some of us this reevaluation means a change in our life's work, a second career in a field that now feels more meaningful. For others of us the dissatisfaction is felt to be in our intimate relationship, and another partner—younger, more exciting—is pursued.

With the inexorable waning of our youth we are increasingly drawn to methods of perpetuating it—an invigorating romance, immersion into a fitness program, even plastic surgery, become attractive. The dramatic hormonal changes of menopause can result in a mercurial emotional climate that can provoke serious conflict within our intimate relationships.

Regardless of the form it takes, a midlife crisis can shake us at our very foundation, and if this transitional period is not approached with a good measure of self-awareness and some deeper understanding of the meaning of this stage of life, it can seriously threaten the viability of an intimate relationship.

The Empty Nest

When the children have grown and left home, a kind of vacuum is created. For the woman whose career has primarily been that of mother and homemaker, this change of role may lead to a period of considerable insecurity as she comes to terms with the meaning and direction of the remainder of her life.

Even when both partners work outside the home, the empty nest syndrome can create an unexpected awkwardness as the two partners face each other across an otherwise unpopulated dinner table. When children in a family have acted as buffers, go-betweens, or even as primary emotional resources for one or both parents, when too much attention over the years has been diverted to the children and too little energy has been invested in sustaining and nurturing their private, intimate relationship, a couple may need to spend considerable time restructuring their connection to one another and restoring the meaning and vitality to their relationship.

Retirement

After retirement there is a significant opportunity to enjoy a time of renewed intimacy. The children have left, the demands of regular employment are gone, potentially more free time is available for play and creative diversion and for projects that were put aside during the work years. Although many couples face economic hardship or the duress of illness during these years, these potential stressors may in fact lead to a feeling of greater togetherness if the couple is able to unite in dealing with them. However, if the couple did not properly care for their relationship during the many years *prior* to retirement, they may feel more alienated, even torn asunder by the struggles common to this life phase.

For those couples who do not have to deal with economic privation or declining health, the most common stress during the retirement years, especially at the beginning, is that of making the transition from one set of role expectations to another.

Those who have been gainfully employed outside the home for decades may feel lost, bored, or even depressed by the dramatic shift in their routine. For most people, employment provides a major source of self-worth. Without a job to go to, they may feel useless, and in an attempt to occupy themselves, may get underfoot, interfering with the established routine of the other partner. This shift may then become a source of irritation to both of them until the challenge of establishing a new equilibrium is met successfully.

Given that most women are younger than their partners, those who have careers outside the home may still be working long after their husbands have retired. If the husband is slow to pick up the slack of household maintenance or is uninterested in learning new domestic skills, friction and tension can undermine the relationship.

The happiest couples during the retirement years are those who have paid attention to the quality of their relationship all during its course and who each have developed continuing interests to keep aglow the spark of their enthusiasm for life.

THE IMPACT OF STRESS

Unfortunately, the tendency of many of us when we feel really stressed is not to use our relationship as a resource, but rather to do just the opposite: to withdraw into ourselves for comfort and safety, thereby creating an emotional chasm between us and our mates. Most often the motives for this form of withdrawal are protective and benign. Many of us are genuinely worried about being a burden to our partner. Wanting to avoid imposing our problems on the one we love, or concerned about appearing weak or incompetent, we may then withdraw to our own inner sanctuaries, sanctuaries that can turn out to be our prisons. And our partner may feel punished by the emotional distance that has been created.

At other times we unintentionally isolate ourselves through chronic overwork or through the abuse of drugs and alcohol, all of which put an unbreachable barrier between our partners and ourselves. The abuse of food, too, may be one of the most powerful and frequently used distancing mechanisms, since the consequences of overeating are soon likely to make the overeater feel unattractive and the other partner feel less attracted to them. Excessive television watching—or *non*watching, when the TV set is perpetually on, inserting its distracting presence into the atmosphere of the home—is another common method of blunting the emotional connection between partners.

There are many other distancing mechanisms—too numerous to describe here—but the most radical and destructive distancing technique of all may be that of having an affair. Certainly, an affair can provide a momentary diversion from current sorrows or temporarily alleviate a sense of fractured self-esteem, but it will probably throw the primary relationship into a crisis, one from which it may never fully recover.

RELATIONSHIP AS HEALER

Dealing with an illness, facing a midlife crisis, starting a new job, or any of the other disruptive dramas that punctuate each person's life from time to time, are generally more stress-inducing when they are dealt with alone than when they are managed within a healing relationship. As we distance ourselves, we limit the opportunity for our partner to give to us nonmaterially, to provide us with the alternative viewpoints and solace that we may need. We deprive our partner of one of the great purposes and pleasures of being in a relationship: the sense of personal worth and usefulness that comes when we are *needed* for who we are. When we create distance instead of reaching out in times of need and vulnerability, a major gateway to intimacy is blocked. A relationship needs to be needed, or it loses its purpose and becomes a hollow, lifeless shell.

Communication

During periods of increased stress, fairly constant communication becomes all the more critical to a couple's welfare. As one woman married thirteen years said, "I want Pat to let me know what's going on inside him, to be open with me. I think he knows that if he's having a rough time, he doesn't have to go it alone, that I'll be there for him. I don't expect him to be perfect or strong all the time, by any means, and I love him even when he feels frightened, or miserable, or like a failure. And when he can open up to me, I can just see the pressure lifting off of him."

No person is an island; anything that strongly affects one person in a relationship will automatically affect the other, altering the mood, the level of energy, the quality of the connection between them. When stress is dealt with from the point of view of the relationship, when the *couple* bands together against the stress as if it were an outside invader, preventing it from pitting them against each other, the relationship can actually be strengthened.

Brooke and Taylor described a difficult five-year period early in their marriage. They had just bought a new house when Taylor's business went into a nose-dive. The going was very tough, and the strain was made more severe by the colic of their infant daughter, whose crying interfered with their ability to get a good night's sleep for many months. Their tempers had worn thin with stress and exhaustion. "It was a mess," Brooke said. "We were both at the edge much of the time, needy and feeling desperate. We couldn't say we loved each other, we couldn't even say we *liked* each other or that we wanted to stay together. At first I blamed him because I always saw him as the one with all the answers. Finally, one day after we had been doing our usual share of petty bickering, I just started to cry, and before you knew it he started to cry too. I had never seen him cry like that. We felt wretched, but we held each other and realized that although neither of us could solve it for the other, we would muddle through somehow. Just how, of course, we didn't know. We reassured each other—reassurance was all we had, I think—and we kept it together until things began to change for the better. It's funny, but it really helped just to share our private misery."

Mistakes will be made by both of you, but they will probably be inadvertent; each person usually attempts to do their best under adverse circumstances. As long as each of you maintains an attitude of "We're in this together," and as long as neither of you is casting blame, you can utilize your partnership productively in order to vent some of your frustrations. Initiating the discussion with a prefatory remark such as "I'm really upset about something. It's not about you, but I'd like to talk to you about it," will help your partner to relax and be more receptive to what you have to say without feeling accused. If occasions arise in which you believe your partner has been taking out his or her frustrations on you by being curt, sarcastic, dismissive, or fault-finding, try to avoid responding in kind, no matter how tempted you might be to strike back. Ask your partner directly whether the anger is due to the set of circumstances you both are in or really in reaction to something you've done. Even when your partner is in a foul mood you can be far more supportive, without condoning the behavior, when you are clear that you are not being blamed. Your nondefensive reaction will help prevent the situation from deteriorating.

At other times, when an external problem has become repetitive, or chronic, and you and your partner have virtually talked it to death and are bored by endless conversations that seem to go nowhere, a sense of humor can provide an effective way out. Glen was really tired of talking to Dorothy about his business anxieties every time his company couldn't make the payroll. The fact that it had occurred a half dozen times, even though each time he had managed to find a solution at the last minute, didn't make the experience any less stressful for him. He experienced each occurrence as if it were the dreaded one that would finally put him under. When he arrived home on those occasions, looking glum and tense, Dorothy would ask him what was wrong. He would simply reply, "Code forty-three," his shorthand way of saying "Couldn't meet payroll." He would feel relieved at not having to go into all the details and Dorothy would then give him the support or space he needed. The atmosphere in the home, even in the face of the crisis, was a bit lighter, each of them presuming that somehow they would get through this tough time as they had other such times in the past.

Problem Solving

Sharing personal problems with your partner permits you to take advantage of the fact that two heads can be better than one: your partner may provide you with an alternative approach or solution that you hadn't considered. In fact, merely engaging in a dialogue about a particular problem is itself likely to be stress-reducing, whether or not you arrive at a thorough resolution.

As a result of serious conversation with your partner, it is also possible that in certain instances an impasse may be overcome by a joint decision to make a significant life change: in your career, where you live, how you live. The recognition that you do not have to go it alone, and that there will be support along life's new path, makes room for many more imaginative possibilities.

Anya and Rod, for example, had recently had their third child. Anya was working part-time as well as being the primary caretaker for the children. Rod was commissioner of the Little League and in charge of a major church fundraiser in addition to his job as sales manager for a large office supply company. Their schedules were so compacted that they had very little time or energy available for each other. Their lovemaking, for example, had gone from about twice a week to once a month, and their conversation had slowly deteriorated to being almost exclusively about their endless mundane problems.

After his father suddenly died, Rod and Anya assumed responsibility for helping his mother move. In the moving process, Rod's back went out. He was in a great deal of pain, and because he was immobilized for a time Anya tried to pick up the slack. Given the other demands upon her, the strain was enormous. She found herself in tears at various times during the day, becoming a harsh disciplinarian with the children and feeling annoyed with Rod for being physically out of commission.

Clearly, things couldn't continue this way, and one evening after a long, emotionally charged conversation, Rod and Anya began to think about restructuring their lives. They agreed to reduce a number of their outside commitments in favor of spending more time taking care of their immediate family's needs, and this included a new emphasis on finding ways to have more fun and pleasure. "Actually," said Anya later, "it all led to a refreshing and necessary change for us. It was too bad that it took Rod's father's death to bring us to this realization, but our family and our relationship had been getting lost in the shuffle of our too busy lives."

The feelings of anxiety and helplessness that accompany periods of high stress are, of course, most unwelcome additions to the difficulties already being faced. Having discussions with your partner in which you work together to set *specific* priorities for addressing the problems you are confronting, as well as a schedule for their accomplishment, provides a useful antidote to the unpleasant state of uncertainty that accompanies such moments. This sense of greater control is quite stress-reducing in itself.

For example, if a health problem arises, sit down together and plan precisely how you will proceed: which doctor you will consult, whether you will need a second opinion, who will make the appointment and when, and whether you will go to it together.

It can be a useful part of any problem-solving endeavor to discuss a worst-case scenario. For example, suppose you're in a court battle and are feeling immobilized by the possibility that you might lose the case. In this instance, the worst possible outcome might be that having lost and being unable to pay the costs, you are forced to declare bankruptcy. An awful eventuality to be sure, but what would you do then? Perhaps you might have to sell your home to pay off your bills and then move back with your parents, or get an extra job on weekends to earn more money. Although a worst-case scenario is unlikely to come to pass, by discussing particular ways of coping with the direst possible circumstances you make anything short of this outcome feel more manageable. It also helps to keep the actual situation in perspective.

Prioritizing the Relationship

Regardless of how well you go about addressing the problems that are distressing you, in your lifetime you will probably encounter some difficulties that are beyond your control and that you are essentially powerless to resolve. Despite the most heroic efforts, certain solutions occur only with the passage of time, as when a child moves through a particular developmental stage or when a parent, gravely ill, finally dies.

Even the best communication has its limits. When problem-solving discussions have become dispiriting and energy-draining, when they have reached a point of diminishing returns and no new light is being shed on the subject, it is more prudent to shelve the issue for the time being and allow yourself diversions: activities that are entertaining, relaxing, and healthily restorative. Shift gears and go out on the town or for a hike in the country; cuddle up together in front of the fire and talk —but about something else.

When finances are the cause of the stress, you may find it difficult to justify even minor expenditures, yet spending a few dollars having a pleasant day and nurturing the relationship by going to a film, visiting a museum or park, or having a modest dinner out can have a far-reaching payoff. It doesn't really take a lot of money, or time, for that matter, to nurture an intimate relationship.

Making certain that you have arranged for private time together is particularly important when visitors and houseguests are around. Even a welcomed guest can create stress and dilute your intimate relationship when their stay is prolonged. Although it may be somewhat difficult to say "Sorry we can't be with you this evening because Wednesday is our traditional night out together," most friends will not take offense if you do so.

June and Kirk had been married for only a year when they moved back to Kirk's hometown, but the move nearly devastated their relationship. "June had really been very happy in her job and we had developed a close group of friends in Ohio," Kirk told us. "Coming back here made us miserable. She hated her new job, and my old friends seemed to be around all the time. There frequently were people in the house when she got home from work and they didn't leave until she went to sleep. We talked about it and finally decided that things would have to change or we were in danger of splitting up. I loved June, and that was the last thing I wanted to happen, so for starters we decided that she would quit her job: a big financial strain but a major emotional gain. We moved to a smaller apartment, stopped associating with my old friends as much as we used to, and started spending more time doing things with just the two of us. We really focused on our relationship, and I don't think we'd be together today if we hadn't made those changes."

Another instance in which particular attention must be paid to prioritizing the relationship occurs when you are experiencing stress caused by children, especially young children. Their needs and demands for time and attention are often extensive and cannot be ignored. For example, in order to get what they want children may pit one parent against the other. Stepchildren, in particular, may attempt to break up a new relationship this way, all the more so if they feel displaced by the new parent—as they often do at first, and, in truth, often are.

The best way of dealing effectively with a child's attempt to divide and conquer is to maintain a united front, while at the same time giving the child ample reassurance and a reasonable amount of personal attention. The most satisfying child-parent relationships occur when respect is mutual, when rules are reasonable, consistent, and democratically applied, and when boundaries are clear. We should not be forced to choose between having a good relationship with our child or having one with our mate. We can and should have both. To reduce the frequency of a child's challenges and the interference created by them, the couple needs to privately stake out the dimensions of their united position: the rules for bedtime, snacks, gifts, activities, and the like. These rules must, of course, take into account the needs of the couple as well as those of the child.

This, Too, Shall Pass

Remember that most stress is time-limited. All difficulties will eventually draw to a close, and more rapidly so if they can be helped along by a specific game plan for their resolution. Even the prolonged stress of having children who are passing through adolescence comes to an end—though at the time it may seem interminable.

We are all aware, however, that not every stressful circumstance ends successfully; despite our best efforts, some conclude disastrously. Yet, even when something works out for the worst, the stress ultimately lifts. A chronically ill loved one may die; you may lose all your savings; the creative project you are working on may turn out to be a flop; your business may go belly-up. But then, at long last, the time comes when it is over and you can begin to heal and get on with life again. Though life may be quite difficult, at least there is possibility and hope to keep you going, and if you are fortunate, you may have learned something that will enable you to steer a better course during the next part of the journey.

Jules and Lillian will never forget the fourth year of their marriage—it was hell on earth. Just when they thought nothing more could go wrong, something did. First, Jules's mother had a heart attack and underwent open heart surgery; then six months later his father had a stroke and while he was recuperating Lillian had an ectopic pregnancy and lost the child. They had been trying to get pregnant with no success for two years and they were devastated by this tragic turn of events. There were days when they couldn't get out of bed in the morning, or wandered around as if lost in a bad dream.

Yet now, two years later, they have a healthy baby boy, even though a *placenta previa* required Lillian to be bedridden for three months. Both of Jules's parents are doing reasonably well, and Jules was awarded a book contract. Things aren't perfect: following maternity leave Lillian had to return to a job she disliked when she would have preferred to continue being a full-time mother. But after all they'd been through earlier, she could bear this comparatively minor unpleasantness until Jules's book was finished and their financial circumstances changed.

When stress is bombarding you, it can be useful to take a step back and reflect on the positive aspects of your life. This not only serves to keep the stress in perspective, but it helps to remind you that the current misery will eventually pass into a fading memory and life will go on.

Caretaking

Even as you are being tossed about on the waves of stress there are things you can do to make day-to-day living more tolerable. Taking good care of yourself is probably the most important of them. Eating properly, taking vitamin supplements, and getting ample rest should be given the highest priority during stressful periods. Aerobic exercise, especially, has been shown to counteract anxiety, depression, and fatigue.

Make sure to take time for yourself on a daily basis: music, religion, movies, sports, reading, naps, nature, and other positive experiences will help to keep your stressed system in better balance. But taking time for yourself requires being able to ask for it, giving yourself permission to be a bit selfish. For some people, asking for time for themselves or saying no to the needs of others is a very difficult task. Unfortunately, it can take some people years before they learn to give to themselves in this way without feeling guilty.

Michelle and Owen fought every time Michelle's parents came from France for one of their long visits. "I was such a dutiful daughter," said Michelle, "that it took me almost twenty years of being married before I could say, 'No, Mother, it won't be possible for you to stay with us for two months.'

I'm sorry it took me so long to be able to do it because I put both Owen and myself through a lot of unnecessary misery before I did."

A reasonable amount of self-indulgence at times of high stress can even include a bit of shopping—the purchase of a small gift for yourself can cheer you up for the moment. Hiring people to help you with your chores is a good idea if you can afford it. Finally, friends can provide a very important source of sustenance, as well as a fresh perspective, as you discuss matters with them. If you can get support from a number of your friends, it will relieve your partner from some of the pressure she or he may feel and help preserve the balance of your relationship.

When it is your partner who is the one predominantly affected by the stress, it becomes important to find ways to temporarily subordinate certain of your own needs. Take less; give more. To whatever extent you can, rearrange schedules and plans, daily tasks and domestic conventions, so that your partner can have more time to rest or attend to resolving the causes of the elevated stress. Your partner may require a fair amount of encouragement to accept your help. If there are feelings of guilt, they can be assuaged by the certain knowledge that the shoe will inevitably be on the other foot some day and the favor can be returned.

In these circumstances, it makes sense to ask your partner what he or she needs most from you, rather than making this decision on your own, perhaps incorrectly. They might want you to lighten their load by carrying out some tasks that would normally be their responsibility: child care duties, errands, bill paying and the like. They might simply appreciate a massage or a special home-cooked meal. One woman was most grateful that when the children were young, her husband would read to her in the evening as she did the family's laundry and ironing.

Often enough, the most important offering you can give your partner in difficult times is a sympathetic ear, resisting the temptation to advise, warn, instruct, or attempt to solve their problems. And sometimes the best thing you can do is to leave them alone. One woman told us, "I've learned that when he is pushed out of shape there is really nothing I can do to soothe him or make him feel better. In fact, since his stress stresses *me* out, I'm happy just to give him room to work things out on his own. When we go to sleep we snuggle a little bit, but I can't say there is any real closeness. I just leave him to his own devices and within a couple of days he comes around."

Supporting the Supporter

As stress continues it tends to invade all members of the household; the "supporters" of the person originally affected by the stress begin to grow weary and tense as well. Obviously, this means that if your role is that of supporter, you must be certain to attend to your own care or you will soon be of no use to your partner. When your partner is not available to help you, you must look to other sources—spending time with friends and getting involved in activities that recharge your own emotional batteries, just as you would if you were being directly rather than indirectly affected by the stress.

Whenever possible, preparations should be made in advance for periods of stress that can be foreseen. Some stressful situations are cyclical. They occur, for instance, each time a final report is scheduled, the children's school is closed for vacation, visits from family are imminent, or taxes are due. Compensations can be arranged in advance to dilute the impact of the stress when it arrives on the scene—once again, forewarned is forearmed.

For example, Alberto would warn Flora a few months in advance about the dates of the annual meetings of the foundation which he directed. Even though Flora would still feel the absence of Alberto's attention and physical presence during that week, she would have planned a few special projects and made dinner dates with her friends, both to help stave off her feelings of deprivation and to take pleasant advantage of his brief absence.

In the Wake of Stress

The aftermath of stress is usually marked by a period of exhaustion and depletion. Once the storm is over—the lawsuit is concluded, the last exam has been taken, the medical treatment completed, the houseguests gone—time should be spent reuniting with your partner and rebuilding your energy reserves and the spirit of your relationship. Get a babysitter for the children and take a day off and spend it together. If you have been through an unusually traumatic period, take a weekend off together, or a week, if possible. Since stress tends to create emotional distance between partners, reconnecting with your mate is a necessary first step once it has passed.

Remember, unexpressed feelings will inevitably find their way into expression, so if negative emotions have accumulated during the stressful episode and have not been dealt with directly and resolved, they are likely to contaminate the relationship before too long. Consequently, take the time to "debrief" each other and air your feelings. Attend to any matters that were put on hold temporarily while more pressing issues demanded your attention.

Once stress has been put behind you, you are likely to find yourselves closer to one another than you were before. A common "enemy" *does* promote increased cohesiveness.

Steven and Kay had been married for sixteen years when they learned that Steven had cancer. Ironically, the discovery of his disease changed their relationship dramatically for the better. Before the diagnosis their lives had revolved excessively around their business: they owned and operated a small chain of clothing stores. According to Steven, "The crisis made us realize how much we meant to each other and how we had been taking the relationship for granted. We made some immediate changes, putting less emphasis on the business and more on our relationship. It's ironic, but we both agree that this has probably been the best year of our married life."

After eleven years of marriage Neil and Adrienne decided to adopt a child. Marshall was a challenge from the day he arrived. "Because Marshall was such a difficult child, he pushed us to expose our vulnerabilities to each other," said Adrienne. "I know more about the depths of Neil's pain about his own upbringing than I ever would have known if Marshall hadn't been such a trial. And he knows more about my own stuff, too. There are things we've shared with each other that I don't think would have ever come to the surface without Marshall's impetus, and our marriage has become significantly deeper as a result of that."

Each of us will certainly encounter adversity in our lives, and in its presence our mission must be to find the strength, courage, wisdom, and love to stand by our partner, to heal each other and thereby to renew and deepen our intimacy.

10

The Journey to Forever

Keeping Love Alive

It is love in old age, no longer blind, that is true love. For love's highest intensity doesn't necessarily mean it's highest quality.

—BOOTH TARKINGTON

It's not that the two of you are having serious problems—at least not yet—but it may have been quite a while since you've had a good talk, like the ones you used to have, and maybe you've had less enthusiasm for lovemaking. Perhaps you've noticed that you don't really look forward to getting together at the end of the day, or that you've been bickering more frequently.

No doubt about it, something has changed: the honeymoon is

over, the bloom is off the rose. It just may have seemed to slip away, imperceptibly. Perhaps you thought this time would never come, not in *your* relationship anyway. Perhaps you dreaded its arrival. You may find yourself wondering: "What went wrong? Have I chosen the right mate? Is that all there is?"

ENTROPY: THE DOWNHILL SLIDE

The answer to these questions may have more to do with the process of entropy, another of the immutable laws of physics, than anything else. According to this law, *all systems*, biological, mechanical, or other—including relationship systems—wind down into lower energy states and into states of greater disarray when left to their own devices. In the words of the poet W. B. Yeats, "Things fall apart; the centre cannot hold."

Entropy is the opposite of energy: within any system, as energy decreases, entropy increases. As energy increases, entropy decreases. Obviously, therefore, entropy is preventable *only* by infusing a system with regular supplies of energy.

As time goes by it is easy to become complacent, to take the relationship for granted, especially as other exigencies demand attention. Far too many couples seem to assume that the energy and intensity that characterized their courtship should fuel the relationship for the rest of its days, and they are disappointed and disheartened when the relationship seems to have run out of steam. We would never consider investing our time and energy into a business for its first few years and then, once it has become established, sit back and expect it to support us for the rest of our lives. We know that a business always needs attention, guidance, and other forms of energy to thrive. So it is with relationships.

Brittany and Michael provide a good example of the "creeping entropy" we are talking about. They are both professionals in the same field and have been married for six years. In the four years since their child was born they have taken only two weekends away together. Being absorbed in work and child rearing, they devote very little thought to ways of refreshing their intimate relationship. Sometimes they manage to take a day or two off when they go away to a scientific convention, but then business is mixed with pleasure, and they always take their son with them. Brittany and Michael are comfortably well off financially. They seem to be getting along quite harmoniously with no obvious outward conflict. But they haven't made love more than a dozen times during the past year, and although there is a nagging feeling between them that something is not quite right, they have "adjusted," and no longer really miss sex all that much.

Entropy is sometimes difficult to identify because its onset is subtle and its growth is insidious. Early warning signs that should cause you to take notice include a decisive lessening of verbal and physical affection, of time spent in personal conversation, of playfulness and humor, of caring about how you look, and about meeting your partner's needs. Because the human mind is expert at rationalizing difficulties that arise, it is all too easy to dismiss these important indicators.

If no care is taken to keep entropy in check, additional harbingers of trouble begin to appear: you start to feel tense and awkward around each other; there are long silent periods where once there was conversation; disturbances in sleeping and eating begin to crop up; feelings of hurt and rejection mount; anger and depression settle in. You may find reasons to stay away from home more, work longer hours, begin to fantasize about others; and as your eye begins to wander, your hopes for the current relationship may begin to fade.

While it is true that entropy is part of the natural order of things, it is equally true that we needn't succumb to its downward pull. We can and must develop skills to combat or oppose entropy if we genuinely care about having a lifelong loving and vital relationship. In this case, an ounce of prevention is worth a lot more than a pound of cure.

ENDLESS COURTSHIP: THE WELL-NURTURED RELATIONSHIP

A relationship is a complex living organism. As with all living things, if it is to thrive it must have what is basic to life itself: adequate protection and nourishment.

During courtship we seem to have little difficulty providing the relationship with ample amounts of these fundamental needs. In fact, if we hadn't attended to them adequately, the relationship probably would never have moved beyond its most superficial, opening phase. As we court one another we infuse the relationship with many forms of energy, and we protect it by giving it a privileged status among our personal priorities. These forms of care are *anti-entropic*.

It is unrealistic to expect that you can continue to dedicate the same amount of energy to your relationship that you did during courtship. In truth, however, keeping love alive doesn't really require enormous amounts of time and energy, it simply requires ongoing thoughtful attention to the things that nourish a relationship: laughter, sex, social activities, vacations, tenderness, good conversation, adventure, dreams, romance . . . All things considered, more input should be included in a relationship than the output demanded of it. Like a well-managed bank account, there should be a net positive balance; thoughtfulness and caring can be "stored" and drawn on in stressful and difficult times.

If you find yourself longing for the good feelings you had during courtship, you might reflect on what you can do to fuel those feelings. Don't complain about their absence. Create their presence.

There are healthy habits you can establish that will be of immeasurable help in keeping the positive, forward momentum of the early stages of a relationship from entropizing into a static dullness. These habits comprise what we call the "endless courtship."

Personal Conversation

Although both men and women require intimate verbal communication to strengthen their bond, men, in general, seem to be somewhat less inclined to use talking as a way of connecting. In this regard, one man told us, "When we were first married I didn't think that we needed much conversation. I used to think that we talked just to keep *her* satisfied. Real macho of me. But now *I* feel the need. Sometimes I'll even miss a meeting or something to be together and it isn't because she asks me to stay home or anything. A longing grows in me when we haven't sat down to talk together for a while."

One-on-one, face-to-face conversation undistracted by television, the telephone, the newspaper, children, or other domestic demands is absolutely essential in an intimate relationship. Our busy lives allow us less and less free time for such discussions. Without daily contact to work out the minor snags that occur in the lives of every couple, molehills can easily become mountains, eventually requiring much more work to reach a level of resolution than would have been necessary had the lines of communication been kept open from the start. Consequently, a good rule of thumb is to take fifteen to twenty minutes to talk *every day* in order to debrief, catch up, and say hello. That's all that's needed to keep most relationships healthy and on track. When problems occur, of course, more time will be required, and it is most important that you talk promptly, certainly within a day or two of the time a problem crops up. The longer you wait, the larger the problem will grow and the more alienated you are likely to become from one another.

Couples that do best, even those with exceedingly busy schedules, regularly create the time for such communication. Leo and Cheri are an impressive example. They have been married for fourteen years and have three children, ages nine, six, and a new baby a year and a half old. Leo has his own business and works over fifty hours each week, and Cheri, in addition to taking care of the children, works about twenty-five hours each week in her office at home. If any couple should have difficulty finding time to talk to each other, you would expect it to be them, but when they tallied it, Leo and Cheri discovered that they actually spent about seven hours a week talking together, more than most couples with half their responsibilities. Early in their relationship they became determined to maintain their connection, to keep each other abreast of what was happening in their lives, their thoughts, their feelings. By now their communication is a well-established healthy habit, part of the culture of their relationship.

Creating opportunities to talk often means cutting other concerns short and devoting that time to the relationship. It may require rearranging your schedule so that you can have a quiet adult dinner after the children have gone to bed, or, if you have teenagers, closing the bedroom or study door so that you can have some undistracted time for yourselves.

Telephone calls to your partner during the day or during evenings when your schedules don't mesh, and especially when one of you is out of town, can do a good deal to sustain intimacy. In fact, one woman said that when her partner was out of town on business they talked as much as three-quarters of an hour every day—more than they managed when he was at home.

It must be emphasized that conversations should *not* be limited to discussions of problems and grievances, otherwise you will begin to avoid making time to talk to each other. Or, if you only talk when you *do have* problems, you may unwittingly develop a tendency to generate them in order to have something to talk about.

As you discuss necessary matters of personal concern, be sure to include what you feel good about, your hopes, your future plans, your love for each other, as well as the events of the day, items in the news, even simple gossip.

Romance: In Words and Deeds

Romance is the art of embellishing the mundane or usual fare of life. It is the icing on the cake. Romantic attention transforms the ordinary into the extraordinary and prevents the humdrum routines of everyday living from casting their dull shadows over the color of the relationship.

The varieties of romance are virtually limitless, as limitless as the human imagination. If your desire is to have a loving relationship that will maintain its vigor and appeal throughout a long life together, it is essential to keep romance alive. It is one of the most effective antidotes to entropy, and a primary source of emotional and spiritual renewal. Romance resurrects enthusiasm for one another and spawns passion.

Words: tender words, sweet words, silly words, nicknames and terms of endearment, baby talk, poetic words, compliments . . . words are the currency of romance. Take the time on a daily basis to express loving thoughts and feelings, to tell your partner how good they look, how much you appreciate the errand they ran for you or the meal they cooked. Let them know how funny, or bright, or competent, or cute, or special you find them.

But when words are repetitive, perfunctory, disconnected from underlying feelings, they become empty and meaningless. Even well-meant words can seem insincere, however, without loving deeds to back them up, yet the deeds need not be elaborate. One man talked about how he would go out late at night to buy ice cream for his wife because she loved ice cream and he loved pleasing her.

In addition to flowers and other inexpensive personal gifts that say "I was thinking of you," don't forget the gift of touch: pats, foot massages, hugs, head and back rubs, caresses. All of these are common during the early days of a relationship and tend to fade in frequency as the years pass: another hallmark of creeping entropy.

Leaving a partner notes is another simple way to express your caring—a note on the pillow when you have to get up before your partner does, or in the suitcase or underwear drawer when one of you has to leave town for a few days, can stir loving feelings. "Irene went to a meeting downtown the other day and forgot her lunch," said Emil, who had been married to her for forty-four years, "so I put a little note in it along with some chocolate kisses and a rose from our garden and took it down to her. I gave it to her really quickly and disappeared. Sometimes it's more fun when it's not expected."

Arrange time on a weekly basis to go out together, or do something that is mutually enjoyable at home. Take turns planning activities that are a bit out of the ordinary on the evenings you've set aside. Listen to live music, go dancing, watch the sunset, make reservations at a restaurant that you haven't been to before. At home, embellish dinner with candlelight, buy a special bottle of wine or champagne, put on the cologne you got for a gift or an outfit that looks especially well on you . . . or wear almost nothing at all. Quality time spent together does not have to be in the evening. When was the last time you prepared breakfast in bed for your lover? And when did your lover last prepare it for you?

No healthy relationship can afford to ignore romance for very long, or to limit it to rare and special occasions. To do so is to stifle it with predictability and deprive it of the marvelous elements of surprise and originality.

Although predictability is unquestionably a comfort, and to a certain extent even a necessity for the development of a harmonious relationship, too much of it can settle over the relationship like a wet blanket, stifling its flame, diminishing the joy and life force. Repetitive routines have a tendency to become ruts, low-energy states leading to an easy slide into the entropic drift.

Diversity and the unexpected keep life from becoming stale or boring. From time to time any relationship will benefit from being "goosed" by some surprise—a new adventure or special

event that departs from the ordinary. These moments of renewal actually can be quite modest in scope: from an impromptu midweek luncheon date at a restaurant, park, or even
at home, to the staging of an unexpected sexual escapade or
surprise romantic weekend away.

Vitalizing Yourself

The ruts we must guard against are to be found not only
within the relationship with our partner, but in the relationship we have with ourselves. When we stop being interested in
our own personal development it only stands to reason that our
partner will lose interest in us as well. As the writer and Nobel
laureate Saul Bellow has said, "Not to fall asleep is distinguished. Everything else is mere popcorn." It really is easy to
"fall asleep" in life. Staying "awake" requires vigilance and
dedication.

Women who are at home caring for children all day may find
themselves feeling intellectually barren and hungry for the
company of adult conversation and new ideas. They may need
to hire a babysitter for a few hours a week, not only as a break
from their routine, but in order to visit a museum, take a class,
work on a project, reflect on their other interests, read a book,
or spend time with friends. Employment outside the home can,
of course, be equally draining, and as intellectually or spiritually confining.

A hybrid life, one that ranges broadly over a variety of ter-
rains—the physical and sensory, the intellectual, the emotional
and spiritual—is most likely to ensure our vitality and keep us
interesting to ourselves and to our mates.

Taking courses, expanding our hobbies and interests, going
off on adventures that do not necessarily include our partner,
all enable us to bring something new and refreshing back to the
relationship, and in this way we continue to open new horizons for each other.

In addition to self-development, every human being needs

time *alone*. Some need it more than others. This need is *not* to be taken as an indication of an unhealthy selfishness which should be conquered. Abandoning oneself too fully to the priorities and demands of the relationship is *no favor* to the relationship. In his first marriage Zane had great difficulty taking time off to be with himself. "If I wanted to do something in the afternoon and my ex-wife didn't, I always felt pressed to figure out what we could do together, and I would usually forfeit the experience that I really wanted to do on my own. I thought that if you loved somebody you *always* wanted to be together whenever possible, and the only legitimate reason not to be together was because you were at work. It took a divorce to make me realize how wrong I was. Now if I need time alone and my wife seems to be feeling a bit rejected, I just say, 'It's not you and it's not that I want to be with anyone else either. I just want to be with *me* right now.' When I get that time alone without guilt I come back so much happier, and she reaps the benefits as well."

Solitude stimulates the flow of reverie, and reverie provides a wellspring for ideas to form, time for problems to be solved, to allow one's imagination to soar freely without restrictions, a time to reflect on the present, past, and future, a time to daydream and a time to rest. Time spent alone, therefore, is a necessity for self-healing; it gives us respite from the crush of an ever more complex and demanding society and is a tonic to the psyche and the spirit. The better we maintain the health of our own individual selves the more resources we will have available with which to maintain a healthy relationship.

Absence, within limits, *does* make the heart grow fonder, as the adage says. Without adequate time alone, conflicts are more apt to break out, serving as unconscious excuses to be apart. The resulting tension, guilt, and anger then burden the solitude, rendering it useless as a restorative.

Some couples find that if one partner travels, even if only for a few days, the excitement of reuniting can enhance the relationship considerably. Having friendships other than those you share with your mate fulfills a similar function: the separate experience gives you something fresh to bring back into conversations with your partner.

In addition to personal growth, it is equally essential to enliven the entity of the couple through involvements in joint projects or cooperative ventures. Find activities that you can both enjoy together: sports, home projects, games, cultural events and outings. Community projects, charities and religious organizations or political activities can also provide excellent opportunities for strengthening your bond as you commit your efforts to something you both care about.

For couples experiencing problems in their relationship or those who just want a deeper understanding of their dynamics or greater intimacy, there are seminars, weekend retreats, church-sponsored courses such as marriage encounters, or couple's therapy with a therapist who specializes in marital counseling.

Symbolic Opportunities

Symbolic dates such as birthdays, anniversaries, Valentine's Day, Mother's and Father's Days provide opportunities to express caring. While it isn't always easy to ignore the coerciveness of crass commercialism associated with many of these occasions, it is possible to find original ways and times to communicate our affection. In fact, the best and most meaningful rituals are the ones we create for ourselves. On the anniversary of the day they first made love, one couple we know takes a bottle of champagne to their favorite hill, has a picnic, and watches the sun set. It is the very same hillside where they first made love. Another couple spends each anniversary at a different country inn, and yet another celebrates each New Year's Eve by staying at home alone, building a fire, having a lobster dinner, and looking back over the year that has passed while making plans for the year to come.

The Art of Gift Giving

Gift giving is an important way of expressing our love for one another, but there is a definite art to the giving of gifts. When done badly, it can leave your partner feeling unloved and unappreciated, just the opposite of what you intended.

There are three errors that are most frequently made when giving a loved one a gift, and the first two have to do with selection. We are most likely to err when we choose something that we ourselves would like to receive because *we* think it is beautiful or useful. Instead, when we are giving a gift, we should try to suspend our own prejudices and attempt to enter the world of the recipient: their feelings, values, pleasures, tastes.

Esther loved fountain pens. She loved the feel, the look, the process of writing with one, so she bought her husband a very expensive model for Father's Day. He didn't much care for fountain pens and soon after receiving it, lost it. Esther's feelings were deeply wounded and she vowed never again to give him such a special gift.

Calvin, a very practical, down-to-earth person, was married to Mariana, a romantic if ever there was one. He couldn't understand why Mariana got so upset when he bought her an expensive, labor-saving vacuum cleaner for their anniversary. He thought he was doing her a favor by lightening her work load. He was hurt and insulted when his gift was greeted with a half smile and faint enthusiasm. He had spent hours researching vacuum cleaners, and this was the *crème de la crème*. However, Barbara Ann gave Clinton a refrigerator for his birthday and, while most other people might consider such a gift to be ridiculous if not insulting, Clinton loved it. He very much enjoyed cooking and was always complaining about the crowded disarray of the old refrigerator. The new appliance was a great improvement and he appreciated it every time he used it.

The second common mistake people make is to choose a gift

that harbors an ulterior motive. The particular item somehow is intended to change their partner. The selected gift may have to do with something you might *wish* your partner would like: a style of clothing you wish he would wear; a book on a subject you wish she would be more knowledgeable about. But the hidden agenda is usually obvious to the recipient, who is left feeling criticized and confused instead of feeling loved and acknowledged.

To learn what your partner really likes and to help him or her discover what *you* like can take years. During your time together, if you listen attentively to casual remarks that express each other's enthusiasms, you will eventually become quite well informed about the kind of gifts that would be most welcomed. Another way of learning about one another's preferences is to go window shopping together. While strolling along, each of you can comment on the various items you see, indicating which ones you like or don't like. In this way you might learn more about your respective tastes, and even come upon something so special that you secretly double back later to purchase it for a future occasion.

When you get something you don't like, gently educate your partner by being honest but tactful. Rather than feigning delight and never wearing the article of clothing you were given, try something like this: "You know, this is really quite lovely and I appreciate your thoughtfulness, but it's just not a style [or color or whatever] that I'm comfortable with." Then suggest that you go together to pick something else out that would please you both.

Gift giving is not only about selection, but about presentation, and this is the third common oversight that can reduce the meaning and impact of a gift. The timing of a gift and the manner in which it is presented is inseparable from the gift itself, and can either diminish or enhance it. Gifts should be presented only when you have your partner's undivided attention, even if it means a small delay. An artful presentation can make all the difference. In one case, a woman gave her husband a tie, some socks, and an inexpensive wallet for his birthday, but she put each item in a separate box within a nest of other beautifully wrapped boxes. In each box there was a sweet, funny, or sexy note expressing her love for him. By the time the man got to the last box he was so pleased by the presentation that the comparative ordinariness of the objects was irrelevant. The obvious thought and effort that went into the gift made him feel deeply loved.

Creating a bit of fanfare or suspense can embellish the presentation. Taking the blouse you bought her out of a wrinkled brown paper bag is one thing; surprising her with a lovely brooch which is hidden in the recesses of a crumpled brown paper bag is quite another!

When we think of giving a gift we usually think of some material object that we either purchase or make for our loved one. Yet some of the most creative, personal gifts are not material, but experiential. One woman gave her boyfriend, a golfer, a three-month membership at a driving range. A man arranged for his wife to have a facial and a manicure at a downtown salon; another man took his lover on an exhilarating hot-air balloon ride; a woman gave her husband a book of five gift certificates for massages, to be redeemed over the course of the year. For the accomplished gift giver, thinking of an experiential gift opens up an extensive range of opportunities to be thoughtfully original, and for many people, being gifted with a pleasant experience provides a memory that will be savored far into the future.

LOVEMAKING

Many of the ways that we awaken romantic feelings in a relationship either begin with sex or eventually end there. Sexual lovemaking has a unique role to play in expressing love. During sexual intercourse the interpenetration of our bodies and the contact of skin upon skin can lead us to a mystical union, a state of egolessness, where our separateness dissolves and we become one for a time.

Making love is a genuinely important source of healing. When the stresses and distractions of our lives divert us from one another, sex can bring us back together. By making love we can help to heal the abrasions and minor rifts that may occasionally get in the way of our intimate relationship. Regardless of the problems that must be handled or the needs that must be attended to, when we can take leave of these mundane demands, even briefly, by making love we can replenish our spirits and strengthen our connection.

In many ways sexual lovemaking provides us with an experience which is the very antithesis of the alienation and estrangement that are the unfortunate by-products of living in contemporary society. Making love with someone we love and trust allows us to be rid of the keyed up, vigilant consciousness that we maintain during most of our waking day. The profound physiological release of orgasm is a cleansing act that refreshes and relaxes the body as well as the soul; in a way, it is an act of renewal.

Last, but no less important, sex is a way of having fun. It is a pleasure that requires nothing more than two willing partners. It is one of the ways we can most fully explore our bodies, our fantasies, and other aspects of our private selves that we might otherwise feel constrained from revealing.

Consequently, having a good sexual relationship is of no small importance. It allows us to express our tenderness, our passions, our vulnerability, our joy, and our interest in pleasing our partner, while pleasing ourselves. When two people can feel open and uninhibited with each other, when they can feel good about being lustful, they can enjoy tremendous satisfaction from making love, and in doing so, significantly enhance their relationship.

Fallow Periods

Regardless of how healthy and satisfying our relationship is, we are likely to go through times when sex is less exciting, less frequent, or even absent altogether. All living things go through fallow times; periods of growth are followed by periods of rest. Typically, when there is substantial stress from the pressures of work, ill health, or other things that consume our energy, the sexual relationship may recede to the background for a period of time while other, more pressing, needs are being addressed.

Fallow periods lasting weeks or even several months—following the birth of a child, for example—are not unusual during the course of a long-term relationship. Although such temporary fallow periods are not necessarily a sign of a serious problem between partners, they generally indicate that the relationship is in need of reprioritization and renewal.

Talking to your partner openly about your concerns without embellishing or belaboring them is the best first step to take when sex seems to have been placed on the back burner. A woman married twenty-eight years reported, "There was one year when we didn't have sex at all, it seems, and we weren't having a difficult time otherwise. Nothing was wrong as far as I could tell. It may have had something to do with Gabe traveling, but it was strange not to make love for all that time. Anyway, we did talk about it, but not much. We'd say humorous things to each other like, 'I guess we've transcended mere sex.' The humor helped us to let the other person know that we were each aware of what wasn't happening but that we weren't feeling resentful about it. And then we just started to make love again as if we had never stopped. I can't really account for it. It was like one day it wasn't there and the next day it was."

What *doesn't* work during periods of low sexual energy on the part of one partner is for the other to harp on the subject, or, as a form of punishment, to pull back themselves and intensify the emotional distance already created by the lack of sex. Although this may be a natural response to feeling rejected, it can significantly worsen the situation, because now two walls rather than one have to be scaled in order for the couple to reconnect. If, on the other hand, one person can remain nondemanding but physically affectionate and emotionally in touch while the other is sexually quiescent, the gap between them can be bridged more easily and more quickly.

Another response which is unfortunately rather common as a way of dealing with a lapse in sexual interest and activity, is to provoke a fight. The instigation of a fight with its accompanying tension and drama is used by some people to set the stage for reconciling in the bedroom. Too often, however, the fight itself leaves a bitter residue which is not completely resolved by the lovemaking that follows, and the toll levied by such fighting can accumulate and become quite destructive.

"I think that I create a certain amount of drama in order to keep sex exciting," offered Beatrice. "If we feel somewhat distant from one another and begin to have conflicts about that, then there's this kind of explosive situation created. It's during that explosion that we finally start communicating with each other, and then it's that communication that enables me to make love with Claude. I don't think I know how to maintain that sense of intimacy on a day-to-day basis. It can be so boring being with the same person every day; I think that I'm the one who creates the distance in order for us to come back together again and really enjoy sex. I'm just now beginning to acknowledge this pattern of mine. For years I've blamed it on Claude, but I wasn't getting anywhere with that one so I had to start taking a good look at what *I* was doing."

Yet another ill-advised tactic that is sometimes employed as a way to stimulate a de-energized sexual relationship is that of creating jealousy by openly flirting with others while deliberately ignoring one's mate. Such behavior usually provokes resentment, erodes trust, and leads to other problems—various forms of protective withdrawal or retaliations in kind—which in turn continue to wound the feelings of both partners and compromise their intimacy.

Inertia

While creating jealousy or provoking a fight are obviously harmful to a relationship, other, more benign, attempts to stimulate the relationship may not be immediately effective either. This is because of inertia, another principle of physics. Inertia refers to the fact that, unless acted on by some other force, things in motion tend to stay in motion and things at rest tend to stay at rest. In terms of sexuality, this means that once a couple has stopped making love for a period of time, more effort is required to get the lovemaking started again than would have been required to keep it going if it had not been allowed to wind down in the first place. One man noted, "If we don't spend regular time together, there's a period of awkwardness that we have to get through, a bit like going out on a first date, even though we've been together for eleven years. It's odd, but it's true. I prefer it when we spend more time with each other because I don't like having to overcome that awkwardness."

When a negative inertia has settled upon the sexual relationship, one partner must take the risk and initiate a move to reconnect. If intimacy is to be restored, these gestures of tenderness and reconciliation must be welcomed, not rejected by the other partner out of a desire to punish; nor must they await other agendas to be fulfilled before they are accepted.

Because it *does* take energy to overcome inertia, you may have to find ways of actively stirring your own sexual feelings in order to move forward. Since the quality of the sexual connection is dependent to an appreciable degree on the emotional connection, restoring and opening the *nonsexual* communication can be the most rewarding and effective first step to take. Intimate conversation, in which deeper feelings are explored, can help to reignite the spark of sexual desire. In addition, you can try reading something that turns you on, fantasizing, renting a sexy video, or imagining that you are at another time in your life when you felt more libidinous. Once you've succeeded in restoring forward momentum to the sexual relationship it is easier to keep it rolling, but the need for ongoing maintenance cannot be ignored.

Preventive Maintenance

Unequivocally, the best way to keep a sexual relationship healthy is to keep the rest of the relationship healthy. When you prioritize regular and open communication, particularly about feelings, ensure ample amounts of nonsexual affection, encourage an atmosphere of support and generosity, and have fun together, you will have done a great deal toward reducing the awkwardness that can accompany the initiation of sex. An easier flow between sexual and nonsexual lovemaking exists when there is sufficient physical affection so that kissing, hugging, and cuddling are not always seen as a prelude to sex.

Another crucial component of a good sexual relationship involves an understanding of one another's sexual preferences. This means communicating about what you enjoy sexually, even when this feels awkward or uncomfortable at first.

Everyone has their own idiosyncratic delights, and if you presume that your partner enjoys the same things sexually that you enjoy, you are likely to be making a mistake, at least in some measure. It is essential to discover the particulars of what turns your partner on, and you can do this by talking as well as by watching your partner's reactions during lovemaking. A couple gets to know each other well sexually only if they are willing to be open and honest with one another. Like accomplished musicians, they learn how to "play" their partner like a fine instrument by practicing their lovemaking until they are able to provide the most exquisite sensual pleasure: a lover's ensemble.

Once you have learned how to delight each other, avoid using sexual pleasure as an agent of barter, giving it only in return for other services or actions. For instance, a woman may need to have a certain kind of conversation that provides her with a sense of connectedness, which in turn leads her to be more open to making love. Her husband, on the other hand, may feel that making love first opens him up to the possibility of having deeper, more intimate conversation. If either person stands on ceremony, insisting on having their own needs met before they are willing to go forward and satisfy their loved one, the couple will soon find themselves in a standoff, with both of them feeling frustrated. When each person remains flexible, generously attending to the other's needs, the sexual relationship is likely to be most fulfilling.

Keeping yourself in good shape and caring about your appearance is essential to maintaining a good sexual relationship. This means, among other things, that rather than simply dressing for comfort alone, you might also consider wearing clothing your partner will find attractive. Change often stimulates interest and ardor: experiment with buying new clothes, changing your hairstyle or wearing a different cologne. Men can try growing a mustache or a beard for a time, or shaving them off if they already have one. Alterations such as these can be a boon to renewed excitement, though they may take a bit of getting used to at first. Changing something about your appearance may also increase your sense of personal attractiveness, which may lead to your feeling more sexually alive as well.

Flirting with your partner is another way to keep sexual energy stoked. In an ongoing way it lets your partner know that you continue to find them desirable. It can also make you feel good about yourself. Even flirting with someone else can help to keep the juices flowing, but you have to be absolutely scrupulous about your intentions. A saucy conversation that is fun for the moment is quite different from parlaying the conversation into a future meeting together. One couple told us about the way they used flirting to enhance their relationship: "We might be at a party and Daryl will be talking to another woman in this animated way, but it doesn't bother me. In fact, we both flirt but we never let it go beyond flirting. Neither of us hides the fact that we have a mate. Sometimes I pretend that I'm jealous, but I'm really not. I do it to encourage play. Actually, I think flirting gives both of us the opportunity to feel attractive to others, and a sense of freedom."

Planning

Too many of us fill our calendars with business and social obligations but not with time to spend with our spouse: by default, our intimate relationship often assumes the lowest priority. We easily become overextended and exhausted by all the other demands, and when we have an evening off we either use it to recover by relaxing at home and being somewhat lethargic, or we try to catch up with all the petty household tasks that have accumulated. If we do have a few moments to spend with our mates it may not be quality time, when we have the spirit and energy to bring to the relationship.

Planning ahead so that interesting and rewarding activities that enhance intimacy can occur is no less important in the later years of a relationship than it was during the first year. If you have young children, employ a babysitter on a routine basis if you can afford it, or make weekly arrangements with your babysitting co-op or with relatives so that you can count on being alone together regularly. Occasionally arrange to have your children stay at the home of a friend or favorite relative. Then you can party together, staying up as late as you like— and extend the pleasure by sleeping late the next morning— just as you did in the early stages of your relationship.

Overnight or weekend adventures away from home are of enormous help in rejuvenating a relationship. We have talked with couples who swear that what enabled them to remain enthusiastic about their sexual relationship, especially during the years they were raising young children, was their ability to plan a night away every two or three months.

The idea that planning takes the spontaneity out of sex is

actually quite erroneous. After all, no one would suggest that planning for a vacation robs it of spontaneity and fun. Planning sets the stage so that spontaneity can occur. Look carefully at your courtship period, a period during which most people would say they were quite spontaneous, and you will see that it was populated by *plans* to do things together. Dates were generally set up in advance—you would shower and dress with care before going out, making sure you looked your best. Then you might have an intimate dinner, just the two of you. The hot and heavy passion that came at the end of the evening was an outgrowth of all that came before. Actually, if we all put *that* kind of "spontaneity" into our ongoing relationships, we would probably be in a lot better shape, with the divorce rate a fraction of what it is now.

Seizing the Moment

The necessity for planning does not negate the equal importance of acting on the feelings of the moment. When the urge to make love hits, our partner may be about to make dinner, pay the bills, or watch a news broadcast. If we decide to delay lovemaking until later, "later" somehow never arrives—or if it does, much of the intensity has been lost.

During courtship, couples easily and regularly put other activities aside, and hop into bed, showing up a half hour late for the party or whatever. Too often, once a relationship has matured, this lively and refreshing spontaneity exists only in memory; routine and responsibility have driven it so far from consciousness that it is no longer even a consideration. This is a tragic and unnecessary loss.

Creative Lovemaking

The prescription for sustaining a rich sexual life requires some creative thinking and a mutual agreement to break the routine and invest the lovemaking with a measure of art, energy, and inventiveness, to prevent sex from becoming a bore or a burden. Ways to reawaken the romance and passion are virtually innumerable and are really rather simple to achieve.

You can surprise your partner by wearing sexy undergarments (men as well as women can wear silk or satin), make love by candlelight, view an erotic video, or share a bubble bath for two. These kinds of activities invite healthy sexual play, as do role playing and the acting out of your private sexual fantasies with one another. The spirit of play and the willingness to break the entrenched patterns of your lovemaking are ways to restore the ardor within your long-term relationship.

Language is a great stimulant to erotic feelings. Speak to each other as you make love, say things that are tender or risqué. Tell your partner what turns you on, what pleases you best. Allow your mounting sexual ecstasy to be vocally communicated to your partner through deep breathing, soft moans of pleasure, and the like. And finally, give your orgasm a voice. It is amazing how many people have suppressed and inhibited their natural orgasmic sounds. So put aside your concern for decorum and see what happens when you freely abandon yourself to the feelings of the moment.

Take some risks and do the unpredictable. When you have some privacy, make love in the garden or on the living room sofa or in a deserted spot outdoors, or experiment in your parked car as you might have done in your earlier years. Make love in the afternoon; try different sexual positions. Tease each other, make love very slowly, and keep each other on the brink of orgasm where ecstasy can be prolonged. Experiment with massage oils and sexual lubricants, or other sexual accoutrements that can be found in adult sensuality stores or catalogs. Board games like Evening Encounters or good old-fashioned strip poker can add spice to your sexual life. Break the tired routines that have slowly settled over your lovemaking and *innovate*. The innovation needn't be major; just something a little out of the ordinary can be surprisingly titillating, and the memory can be used as fantasy material for some time afterward.

Of course, this is not to say that there is anything wrong with continuing to push many of the same buttons when you make love. Specific kinds of sexual stimulation have probably become an integral part of your lovemaking *because* they are so pleasurable. Experimentation, however, even in rather minor ways can make your lovemaking more dramatic, playful, or intense, and in the process you may reawaken feelings you haven't experienced in a long while.

Passion and sexual enthusiasm within monogamous relationships are really quite fragile things, and they are vulnerable to the vicissitudes of stress, fatigue, preoccupation, repetition, and a myriad of other influences. Consequently even if you are attentive, you probably can expect your sexual relationship to flag a number of times during the course of your life together. However, you can also take solace in the fact that with the proper care it can be resurrected and reinvigorated. There is no reason why sexual intimacy should not be a fulfilling and pleasurable part of your lives even in advanced old age.

DIRE STRAITS

When there are lengthy periods of sexual abstinence, or perfunctory, unsatisfying sex, where tenderness is rarely expressed through the lovemaking, where resentment is brewing beneath the surface but not being directly expressed, when the couple is avoiding conversation about the sexual issues or other unresolved sources of dissatisfaction, there is every likelihood that these are symptoms of something considerably more complicated than a run-of-the-mill, circumscribed fallow period. When such a menu of symptoms exists, serious problems are threatening the viability of the relationship and one or both partners are more susceptible to having an affair.

Affairs

By an "affair" we mean a clandestine relationship of some duration that involves romance, sex, and an emotional connection. The existence of an affair must be considered to be strong evidence that the primary relationship has either undergone significant deterioration or has failed to develop in ways that would cause it to thrive. Quite often, an affair is the culmination of the search for something of importance that is missing in the relationship: excitement, acceptance, affection, sexual diversity, or companionship. But an affair can also represent an escape from a partner's demand for greater intimacy.

Many affairs are motivated by a desire to resurrect flagging self-esteem. Problems on the job, a partner who is overly critical, the shock of an aging appearance or an anxious concern with other changes that accompany midlife, are all things that can lead to an impaired self-concept. In a desperate attempt to compensate for these feelings, to feel more powerful, sexually attractive, valuable, vital, both men and women may seek partners outside their primary relationship, trying to add new polish to their tarnished egos.

Issues that arise around the time of pregnancy and childbirth can also increase the likelihood of an affair. Most typically the man rather than the new mother or mother-to-be is the one to seek out a lover. He turns to an extramarital relationship because he may be feeling deprived of attention as his wife's focus turns away from him and more toward the unborn child, her imminent motherhood, and her own bodily changes. He may be trying to escape from his own anxieties regarding fatherhood, or he may find his mate's radically changed body undesirable. After the birth of the child, the man may feel jealous of the attention his wife pays to the infant, and this, coupled with many women's temporary diminution in sexual interest, may provide the impetus for his seeking an outside relationship.

For example, Georgine and Stanford had just had their first

child when Stanford went into the hospital for an operation on his back. While he was temporarily incapacitated by the operation, Georgine's attention was divided between Stanford and their new son. "Since they didn't know how long my recuperation would take or whether the partial paralysis I had suffered would be permanent," said Stanford, "my sexuality was in question. As you can imagine, the anxiety was enormous. Georgine's interest in sex dropped off dramatically after Kyle's birth, so after my paralysis went away we began to have terrible fights about sex. After a time of hanging in there, I finally gave up. It wasn't a deliberate thing, but something started between Trudy and me at the office and before I knew it, it had developed into a very powerful affair."

Obviously, there are many ways in which affairs can poison the primary relationship, but one thing can be said for certain: an affair inevitably introduces enormous complications that make it far more difficult to resolve the problems that led to the affair in the first place, principally because it superimposes the grievous wound of betrayal upon the existing difficulties. In some cases, and over an extended period of time, the relationship can be resurrected, but a certain level of trust may have been destroyed, perhaps forever. In the words of Georgine, ten years after Stanford's affair: "I don't know if it's ever going to be totally healed over. It doesn't run me like it did for the first year or two after it happened, but I wouldn't be so naive as to think that it couldn't happen again. And when I think about it, I still shut down."

When feelings have been hurt by betrayal, it becomes difficult to resist the desire for retaliation and punishment. Revenge may be sweet for the moment but it is also provocative; no solution to what ails the relationship can come from it, nor from self-pitying martyrdom. What is needed instead is an open discussion between the partners in which *both* people explore how they contributed to the relationship problems that may have led to the transgression. This is a tall order, of course, and is best done in therapy with an experienced professional who can help guide the couple to a deeper understanding of their issues and to a place of forgiveness and healing. If the underlying problems truly can be resolved, a further affair is unlikely.

Deirdre and Clay had been married about seven years into their now twenty-four-year marriage when Deirdre had an affair. "She lied to me several times, supposedly going off to meetings and conferences," said Clay, "and at first I sort of just accepted it—I was a bit suspicious but I guess I didn't want to believe it could be happening. But then I couldn't stand it anymore, so I confronted her. I told her that I had a pretty good idea of what was going on but I didn't want to end the marriage. I told her that if she would stop the affair I wouldn't comment on it again except in therapy, which I insisted on. She agreed, and we worked things out eventually. My father had an affair and my mother never let him forget it. I decided that was not the way I wanted to handle it—it would just have driven Deirdre away and I knew I still loved her even though I was very hurt and angry."

When we talked to Deirdre she told us that she thought Clay had given her a tremendous gift. She felt indebted to him for not making her suffer for her actions and she respected him all the more for the way he handled the situation.

In contrast to a full-blown affair, some sexual transgressions are of a brief and limited nature; they are primarily physical and contain little emotional involvement. While such a dalliance is usually less complicated and less damaging than an affair, it is not to be dismissed as simply trivial and without significance, because, for one thing, the discovery of such a sexual liaison can play havoc with the trust and healthy vulnerability that are the bedrocks of intimacy. If the sexual transgression is not discovered, the guilty secret being kept by the adulterous partner is likely to alter his or her feelings, consciousness, or behavior in some way that will negatively influence the tenor of the relationship. In many cases the guilty secret is "telegraphed" to the other partner, who feels puzzled by certain barely perceptible changes. If the one who has strayed is questioned and then lies, the cover-up can create additional distrust and the damage may snowball. Although there is no doubt that many relationships continue to do reasonably well despite occasional dalliances on the part of one or both partners, habitual sexual escapades of this sort limit the depth of intimacy that is attainable. They create potentially explosive situations and their momentary pleasure is almost never worth their possible cost.

THE PULSE OF THE RELATIONSHIP

It is all too easy to take your relationship for granted as you live together day in and day out. To keep from falling into this easy trap, take the pulse of your relationship from time to time. Check in with each other and find out how you are feeling about the time you spend together. Make sure that the communication pathways are clear so that problems are not brewing beneath the surface. Ask yourself if you have been too preoccupied with your work, if you are bored with your lovemaking, if you feel appreciated by your partner and have shown your appreciation in return. Pay attention to whether or not you are talking about things that have been bothering you and whether your time together has been given the priority it deserves.

Renewal

Like any living thing, a relationship goes through many cycles of growth and rest during its course. If it is to continue to maintain its interest and its usefulness to the partners over the years, it will always benefit from being renewed.

Set aside time once a year to celebrate the relationship you have created together. Recommitting yourselves to each other can have a spiritual and symbolic importance that rejuvenates the relationship and reminds you both of the sanctity of your bond. This renewal celebration can take place on the anniversary of your marriage, of the day you first met, of the day you first made love to each other or declared your love for one another. As one woman married thirteen years remarked, "It helps me to remember all the good things about the relationship and about Dylan that I really love. I don't want marriage to become a habit, like wearing comfortable old shoes and forgetting they are on my feet. So each year we make a conscious recommitment on our anniversary to give some special thought to the ways that the relationship is important to us, and it isn't simply an empty gesture."

Some couples go so far as to renew their marriage vows regularly; every year or every several years they have a symbolic remarriage celebration—a ritual during which their relationship is reaffirmed and the meaning of their union clarified.

On the occasion you take to recommit, take time to talk about your hopes and dreams as individuals and as a couple. Talk about your dissatisfactions as well as those aspects of your life that are fulfilling, so that you can be consciously moving forward toward realizing the life you've hoped for.

A relationship is a long journey. All such journeys need their way-stations and oases, places that are restorative and revitalizing. Without its hopes and dreams a relationship is apt to travel too much in the world of the known and the predictable, deadening its spirit. Dream together, even if your dreams seem somewhat out of reach—the African safari, the country house you'd like to build on that special plot of land, the time you'd like to have available to do that joint project you've been thinking about over the years. There is more than momentary pleasure in these flights of fancy, there is the certain truth that keeping your dreams alive is the best way to encourage their eventual actualization.

Claudia and Quincy have always wanted to take a year off to live in a small town in Tuscany. Over the years together they have collected information about renting houses in Italy, language programs, and special travel arrangements. While the circumstances have not yet materialized to enable them to take off for such an extensive period, they continue to act as if it is just a matter of time before their dream will be fulfilled—and they firmly believe that it will be.

The Beatles said, "The love you take is equal to the love you make." The Bible says, "As ye sow, so shall ye reap." In the end it all boils down to the inescapable economic truth: *you can't take out what you didn't put in.*

Creating a healthy lifelong mateship, the journey to intimacy, can heal you, nurture you, provide you with life's ultimate companionship, and lend an incomparably rich meaning to your existence.

With vigilance and care you can go the distance and go it well.

Appendix

The Compatibility Questionnaire

Our intention in creating The Compatibility Questionnaire is to help you evaluate the overall quality of your relationship with a view to appraising its chances for success. While we make no claims for the scientific validity of this measure, the questions have been designed to help you to clarify your feelings and thoughts about elements which we believe are fundamental to a healthy and happy relationship.

You may complete this survey alone; however, it may be most useful if both you and your partner fill it out *separately*, comparing your answers and exploring the similarities, the differences, and their possible ramifications.

A word of caution, however. The purpose of this questionnaire is educational. It is to be understood as it was constructed: in the spirit of inquiry, not judgment. The natural disparities in your points of view will be reflected in your responses to the various questions. If you use these differences to criticize or blame each other you will have missed the point. The object of discussing differences is to generate understanding, not acrimony.

Answer these questions forthrightly and honestly, neither exaggerating nor minimizing your responses—as though no one else will ever know how you answered them.

Assign a number from one through five to each of the questions, according to the following scale:

RATING SCALE

5 Strongly agree. Virtually always true. Excellent.
4 Mostly agree. Generally true. Quite good.
3 Unsure. True at times. Fair.
2 Mostly disagree. Not true much of the time. Poor.
1 Strongly disagree. Rarely true, if ever. Awful.

QUESTIONS

Rating

——— 1. I believe my partner tells me the truth.

——— 2. My partner has a fine sense of humor.

——— 3. My partner understands my sexual needs and satisfies them.

——— 4. We feel the same way about how others should be treated.

——— 5. One-on-one talks occur frequently in our relationship.

——— 6. We are never abusive with one another, physically or emotionally.

_____ 7. I trust my partner to do what s/he says s/he will do.

_____ 8. My partner is easily able to laugh at himself/herself.

_____ 9. I like the way my partner looks, smells, tastes, and feels.

_____ 10. We would both choose to live in the same locale.

_____ 11. Our political views are nearly identical.

_____ 12. When we discuss our difficulties we always come to a reasonable resolution.

_____ 13. Deep inside I know that s/he is the right person for me.

_____ 14. I feel cared for by my partner.

_____ 15. Our senses of humor get us out of difficult moments.

_____ 16. I feel relaxed and sexually uninhibited with my partner.

_____ 17. We never have conflicts over money management.

_____ 18. My partner is very sensitive to my feelings.

_____ 19. My partner is my best friend.

_____ 20. I believe that my partner is honest with others.

_____ 21. I find my partner very interesting as a person.

_____ 22. We talk openly and forthrightly about our lovemaking.

_____ 23. Our spiritual convictions are very closely aligned.

——— 24. Our arguments get resolved within a short time.

——— 25. I'd rather spend time with my partner than anyone else.

——— 26. When I'm in need, I go first to my partner for help.

——— 27. We share many interests and activities.

——— 28. We frequently express our affection in non-sexual ways (cuddling, small gifts, kissing, "sweet talk," etc.).

——— 29. We are both comfortable with the same standard of living.

——— 30. I would trust my partner with my life.

——— 31. When something is bothering me about our relationship I always bring it up directly with my partner.

——— 32. We play well and have fun together often.

——— 33. My partner admits it when s/he makes a mistake.

——— 34. I would choose to spend as much free time as possible with my partner.

——— 35. Our sexual life is varied and interesting.

——— 36. I feel totally accepted by my partner as I am—shortcomings notwithstanding.

——— 37. I respect my partner's opinions and viewpoints.

——— 38. I never feel suspicious of my partner.

——— 39. We have an excellent time when we go on vacation together.

———— 40. I look forward to making love.

———— 41. When our viewpoints differ, we can agree to
disagree.

———— 42. We feel the same way about having children.

———— 43. I don't think my partner would make an
important decision that affected both of us
without consulting me first.

———— 44. I believe that my partner genuinely respects my
intelligence and competence.

———— 45. My partner is a thoroughly ethical person.

———— 46. We are well matched in the amount of time we
each need to spend alone.

———— 47. We see eye to eye on most social issues.

———— 48. I admire my partner for who s/he is.

———— 49. When we have a misunderstanding, my partner
forgives and forgets rapidly and easily.

———— 50. I like my partner's friends.

COMPATIBILITY INDEX

Total your answers to all the questions and divide this sum
by fifty. This average represents your Compatibility Index.
Compare this score to the descriptions below. Your score, of
course, will probably lie somewhere between the discrete categories described here. Since the reliability of your answers is
likely to increase with the length of your relationship, if you
are in a new relationship, you may want to wait six months and
take the test again for a more reliable score.

5 You and your partner are very well matched. You are likely
to go the distance and go it well.

4 Your relationship is quite good. You are satisfied most of the time and have a very good chance of going the distance as long as you keep the communication lines open.

3 Your relationship has important limitations. Work is needed in order to increase the likelihood that your relationship will be an enduringly satisfying one.

2 Your relationship has very serious difficulties and unless things change radically, you would be best off looking elsewhere for a life partner.

1 You and your partner are totally unsuited. You should definitely not be considering a future together.

Index